LET ONLY RED FLOWERS BLOOM

LET ONLY RED FLOWERS BLOOM

Identity and Belonging in Xi Jinping's China

EMILY FENG

CROWN

NEW YORK

CROWN
An imprint of the Crown Publishing Group
A division of Penguin Random House LLC
1745 Broadway
New York, NY 10019
crownpublishing.com
penguinrandomhouse.com

Flower image on title page by Shutterstock.com/kotoffei
Leaves on title page and ornaments throughout by Shutterstock.com/Max Filitov

Library of Congress Cataloging-in-Publication Data is on file with the publisher.

Hardcover ISBN 978-0-593-59422-3
Ebook ISBN 978-0-593-59423-0

Printed in the United States of America on acid-free paper

Editor: Madhulika Sikka
Assistant editor: Fariza Hawke
Production editor: Serena Wang
Text designer: Amani Shakrah
Production manager: Jessica Heim
Copy editor: Sarajane Herman
Proofreaders: Carla Benton, Sibylle Kazeroid, Karen Ninnis, and Tess Rossi
Publicist: Lindsay Cook
Marketer: Kimberly Lew

9 8 7 6 5 4 3 2 1

First Edition

The authorized representative in the EU for product safety and compliance is Penguin Random House Ireland, Morrison Chambers, 32 Nassau Street, Dublin D02 YH68, Ireland, https://eu-contact.penguin.ie.

To my parents

CONTENTS

PREFACE

An immigration holding room is not my usual place for finding creative inspiration, but that October night in 2019, in the Beijing Capital Airport, my mind was racing with ideas: ideas of how to spend the next few months if tonight I were to be barred from re-entering mainland China and prevented from going back to my apartment near the capital's Chaoyang Park. I was trying to come up with ideas for how to continue reporting about China from outside its boundaries, if need be.

For the last few months I had been shuttling from Beijing to Hong Kong to cover the anti-government protests there. Leaving the mainland, however, was getting more difficult. Each time I passed through immigration check at Beijing's main airport, I was stopped by officials for additional questioning. The way back was even more fraught, usually entailing two to three hours of interrogation about my work in Beijing, my activities in Hong Kong, and electronic searches of my phone and work laptop. Failure to submit to these electronic searches would result in deportation, the airport police officer told me that night. Because of my journalism, I was a "person of interest," he explained, and my American passport would be flagged every time I crossed a Chinese border.

Phoneless, and sitting on the cold metal seats of the holding room, I pondered my predicament. I felt battered by the last three months, by the rigors of the relentless news cycle, and also wearied by the increasingly personal attacks on me and my reporting. I was told by officials that I was inherently Chinese, despite being born and raised outside of China, and thus should "tell the China story well" in my reporting for international audiences. In the years to come, I was to be labeled by Chinese state media a race traitor, accused of being aligned with a "hostile foreign force," and derided as a "banana"—white on the inside, yellow in appearance only—who callously wore my Chinese-ness as a camouflage while gathering information for my malicious reporting. These attacks intensified in both the state-run press and on social media as China shut its borders in 2020 during the start of the global coronavirus pandemic. And yet, I felt an overwhelming desire to stay in China and keep working, even if it meant constant airport delays and state surveillance. Why did I find the country so compelling to report on? And despite its hardships, why did I love living in China?

The answers to these myriad questions returned to themes of identity—not just my own, but how Chinese people saw themselves and perceived what Chinese identity meant to their fellow countrymen. That night in the airport planted the seeds for this book. I was eventually let in to Beijing that night and continued reporting on the ground there. Three years later, my luck finally ran out when, in 2022, China refused to let me return to the country. And so I started writing.

This is a book about identity in China, how the state controls expressions of identity, and who gets to be considered Chinese. This preoccupation with identity is not mine alone. During his twelve years as head of China's ruling Communist Party, Xi Jinping has concerned himself with the project of Chinese rejuvenation, and in the process, redrawn the contours of Chinese identity. He has prescribed a much narrower definition of the ideal Chinese citizen: one who is ethnically Han (and not the other fifty-five officially recognized ethnic groups), speaks Mandarin Chinese (not one of China's hundreds of local dialects and minority languages), is heterosexual, and, ultimately, is loyal to the ruling Communist Party. Strengthening China requires participation from the country's citizens, and forging a uniform identity among them became a chief priority for authorities during my time reporting in the country.

For readers who are not Chinese, who have never lived in China, or who do not belong to the small circle of "China watchers," you may be wondering: Why should you care about identity in China? I argue that understanding how the Chinese state sees itself and who it wants its citizens to be are foundational to understanding China's policies, which, in turn, are increasingly influential in shaping foreign and economic policy around the world, especially in the United States. This is not a history book, however; it focuses on people living in the present day. When access to China for outsiders is becoming so limited and living there and understanding the texture of everyday life is becoming ever rarer, I wanted to focus on the ordinary people both creating identity and subject to identity-related policy in China.

All nation-states are naturally motivated to foster a joint

identity and promote national unity, and China is no exception. What struck me during my time reporting in China, however, was the overwhelming preoccupation with identity beyond broad political values, a preoccupation that drilled down into the minutiae of daily life. This preoccupation is driven by a base fear that the arc of the Communist project in China might ultimately mirror that of the Soviet Union: a long period of internal division, a societal splintering, and a final, sudden collapse. "A big Party was gone just like that," Xi said in an internal speech in 2012. "Proportionally, the Soviet Communist Party had more members than we do, but nobody was man enough to stand up and resist."[1]

Xi intends to resist. His response to this fear of collapse was distilled early on in his tenure as head of the Party in a communiqué later called Document Nine. I was still studying in university when Document Nine leaked. It was the first piece of China news I remember taking note of after reading the papers, and thinking: *Reporting on China could be interesting.* Document Nine heralded a new front for state control: a fight over culture, identity, and thought. The communiqué made it clear that this new front was a principal concern for Xi and for the Party apparatus he would marshal in an epic battle for the hearts and minds of his 1.3 billion citizens.

For decades, these citizens had been dangerously tempted by Western ideas about universal suffrage and government accountability, according to the communiqué. A robust corps of muckraking Chinese journalists and burgeoning internet platforms had infused the general public with radical ideas incompatible with Communist rule. Now, in Xi's eyes, his job was to allow "absolutely no opportunity or outlets for incorrect thinking or viewpoints to spread." As an ancillary, in negating the universality of ideas like a free press or human rights, Document Nine and its writers were making a bold claim: that there was a uniquely "Chinese" way of running a country, one administered by the Party alone.

The precepts of Document Nine did not accord with my first years in China, where I moved after graduating from university. These were the years when I was falling in love with the country, a place more massive and more diverse than I had ever imagined. China is not a monolith. Just one small example: in the capital of Beijing, I worked on my spoken Mandarin, a semi-artificial collection of organic dialects and accents that is taught as a standard language within China. However, the language my parents spoke with my relatives in the south, belonging to the Wu group of Chinese languages, remained incomprehensible to me and my northern neighbors in Beijing. A short, high-speed train ride farther south and variations of Cantonese dominate, unintelligible to Wu dialect speakers.

In university, I had read in a history class about Chairman Mao's exhortation to "let one hundred flowers bloom; let one hundred schools of thought contend." Mao would later persecute many of the independent thinkers who heeded his call for free expression. After I moved to Beijing, however, I got a small sense of what a Chinese society, intellectually unleashed, could be capable of. I met Chinese beatniks and writers, activists and models. Most of them had been born and raised outside of Beijing, and from them I learned about the rhythms of life and the local histories of different provinces. They brought me to events on queerness, on the rule of law, on labor organizing. For the first time in my life, I heard new ideas and read essays in the Chinese language that challenged my old patterns of thinking.

I also traveled all the time. On assignment, I crisscrossed the country, visiting everywhere, from mining communities and factory towns to religious sects and Communist pilgrimage sites. On weekends, I took short trips to see the ocean, the mountains, and the mighty rivers that bisect the country. I especially loved the landscapes of the northwest, in provinces like Gansu, Ningxia, and Qinghai, which looked more like the surface of Mars than the scenes of canals and willow trees I found in the Chinese watercolor paintings I had grown up with.

Begrudgingly, I realized Chinese authorities might be right: my identity was in part Chinese, despite my birth and upbringing in the United States. My love for living in China stemmed from discovering that a kernel of who I was was magnified across an entire country. I just was not Chinese in the way authorities narrowly prescribed. For, falling in love with a country also meant getting to know it better, and I was quickly learning that the diversity I cherished was seen as a liability under Xi Jinping. The online space for discussion became increasingly censored. Surveillance of dissidents was growing, and who could be considered a dissident was expanding. Suppression of religious and ethnic minority communities was magnifying. Riffing off the Mao-era slogan, one source told me the state now would "let only red flowers bloom."

I preferred the Chinese idiom *baihuiqianpa,* 百卉千葩, meaning a myriad of thousands of plants and flowers, meant to indicate a flourishing diversity. The idiom better reflected what drew me to reporting in China in the first place: the ability to briefly be allowed entry into the lives of people in one nation-state who ate, thought, spoke, and behaved entirely differently from one another, and, of course, a resilience that kept these people true to themselves even in the face of enormous intimidation and pressure to conform. These became the central themes in my reporting, and their stories are the ones that stayed with me in the years after I left China.

This book is a collection of those stories. I start with people living in China's mainland who encapsulate different political visions for China. The book then proceeds to the border regions once considered the fringes of the Chinese imperial empire, namely the Xinjiang region, and the provinces of Inner Mongolia, Ningxia, and Gansu, where language, ethnicity, and religion remain contentious within the state project of Chinese identity. We then depart the Chinese mainland for Hong Kong, the site of multiple rounds of protests revolving around themes of identity and how the city-state should develop within the broader Chinese project. Returning home to the United States, I discovered questions of how to be Chinese percolated the diaspora communities I had grown up with, and the book ends in the American context.

Much of the book was written and edited in Taiwan, the self-ruled, democratic island that China claims control over and has threatened to invade if necessary. I moved to Taiwan at the start of 2023, after Beijing canceled my residence permit and refused to reissue my journalist credentials. Emotionally adrift, wounded by the abrupt amputation of my life in China, I sought comfort in learning the stories of the one million or so residents of China who left their civil-war-torn home for Taiwan, more than seventy years before I retraced their steps. Almost all of these refugees believed their stay in Taiwan would be short, and they pined for their lost home in China. Most of them never returned. I did not want to be like this generation of exiles, lost in nostalgic reveries and blind to the beauty of Taiwan. Over the next two years, I found a new home, and in doing so I learned ways in which identities existed outside of a nation-state's borders, unmoored to any one political regime.

These thoughts were running through my mind in December 2023, when I sat down with Taiwanese politician Ma Ying-jeou. Our interview was just a handful of weeks before a pivotal presidential election in Taiwan. Like me, Ma had been born to Chinese parents. They fled the mainland after a civil war, bringing him to Taiwan, where he eventually was elected president after the island democratized, though his father taught him to never forget their roots in China. Earlier in 2023, Ma had visited China for the first time, and I asked him about the trip. Ma was ecstatic. Where I perceived political closing off under Xi Jinping, he had felt a burgeoning liberalization among the crowds who enthusiastically greeted him in China. "If you compare China today and China thirty years ago, there are a lot of differences. They understand the importance of democracy, although they don't know the term." He smiled slightly at my incredulous expression. We seemed to be talking past one another, about entirely different countries.

Now, looking back at that conversation, I am more sympathetic. I, too, wanted to be considered Chinese and missed China though I no longer lived there. But I realized—like many of the characters in this book—we were all yearning for different Chinas, and we were all chasing after visions of a China that no longer existed, or perhaps never had.

CHAPTER 1

THE LAWYER

Yang Bin was born wanting more. Her parents had wanted her to be like them: factory workers with a stable income, a guaranteed pension, and state-assigned housing. They both worked at a state-run auto parts factory that never closed even though it almost never turned a profit. But Yang was consumed by a gnawing sense that the purpose of her life could be bigger.

In person, she exudes energy: gregarious, with bright eyes and deep dimples that appear whenever she smiles or laughs (which is frequently), but her easy confidence was learned. As a young girl, she was shy and prone to blushing. She was born in the midst of the Cultural Revolution, a decade of political violence starting in the 1960s that killed at least an estimated half-million people, and she learned to value compliance. Growing up, her parents hinted darkly at previous purges under Chairman Mao Zedong, who ruled the Communist Party until his death in 1976. These tales taught her that standing out made one an easy target in the next political campaign that cropped up. At university, she chose what she thought would be the politically safest major: a now-nonexistent field of study called Building Chinese Socialism, an arcane discipline designed to study Deng Xiaoping's famous phrase of creating a socialism "with Chinese characteristics."

Yang had the good fortune to enter adulthood just after China was looking for a way to redefine itself post-Mao. Economic and political reforms begun in 1978 by Deng, a senior Party leader himself twice purged by Mao, meant people could choose their own jobs, if they dared, at the handful of new private businesses starting up. And so, after graduating in 1990, when Yang was offered a position to join her parents in the same factory *danwei*, or Communist work unit, she turned the offer down. Two decades ago, her actions would have been unimaginable, but she was of a new generation. "I did not want a life where I could already envision its ending," she told me. While she didn't exactly know what she wanted just yet, she did know with certainty that she was not going to find it in a Hunan provincial state company where "it is possible for a person to live and die in a ten-thousand-worker factory, from kindergarten to the mortuary home," as she described it—the "iron rice bowl" of the socialist safety net.

Her search for adventure landed her in coastal Guangdong province, where her brother had already moved. It was a fortuitous choice. Yang quickly secured a job at a new, private pesticides factory. In the 1990s, in the heady days of China's opening and reform policy, enormous financial opportunities were up for grabs after nearly four decades of strict ideological controls on the economy. Guangdong was in prime position to benefit given its proximity to the then-British colony of Hong Kong, where wealth and business acumen were plentiful. Guangdong's massive port also made it an attractive location to place one of the country's first economic pilot zones, where private businesses could set up and trade internationally, accelerating China's economic opening.

When she was fired from the factory, which had sponsored her Guangdong residence papers, Yang couldn't stomach the idea of returning home. One of the factory managers—a man she still calls her guardian angel—stepped in and arranged another job as a copywriter in a county-level prosecutor's office. The job did not pay well, but it was a position in the civil service, coveted for its benefits and stability.

The job allowed her to reinvent herself. At the prosecutor's office, it did not matter that she was the daughter of factory workers who had, just a few years earlier, been destined to be one herself; in Guangdong she could learn to be a servant of the law. She knew little then of the challenges ahead of her over the next four decades, and even if she had, she would not have changed her mind. Her career would put her on the front lines of a struggle to define a nascent Chinese system of law, to determine whose interests it fought for, and to decide what kind of country this system aspired to create. This was the purpose she had been looking for.

Yang started her career when much of China's economic and Party system was up for reinvention, including the legal system. China wanted to build a more cosmopolitan legal system that governed by the rule of law. Controls on private businesses were lifting, and economic growth was booming after three decades of repressed demand. China would need fair courts and transparent laws to guide and contain this economic experiment. It also wanted to project itself as a modern country that was a safe destination for foreign investment. To do that, it needed a body of law to adjudicate disputes and train legal officials like Yang to enforce its rules.

The Party brought in foreign experts and talents and absorbed as much know-how as it could. "A considerable part of our rule of law construction achievements in the past 40 years have been achieved on the basis of absorbing foreign advanced experience," Xiao Yang, a former president of China's supreme court, wrote.[1] In Hong Kong, a British-style common law system was already fairly developed, and Xiao sent more than two hundred Chinese judges to the former British colony to study international law. Several returned to China and became prominent judges. Far and away, however, it was admiration for the American system of constitutional law that dominated legal circles. Throughout the early 2000s, the Party sent dozens of mid-level cadres to Harvard University and Duke University each year, where they took classes with leading professors in political economy and constitutional law. Chinese scholars studied the U.S. system of checks and balances and the dynamics of the American Supreme Court. One member of China's top court, Judge He Fan, went so far as to write an emotional tribute to conservative American Supreme Court justice Antony Scalia when the justice died.[2]

China's legal overhaul was crucial to making the case that the country was ready to join the global economic order. In 2001, China was granted admission to the World Trade Organization—the result of a years-long campaign to prove it could and would abide by international trade rules of fair competition, at least for a time. Unfortunately, intellectual property theft and counterfeiting were rampant, particularly in Guangdong province, where thousands of Chinese factories continue to manufacture much of the world's consumer goods. Yang's procuratorate office barely made a dent prosecuting trademark cases.

Instead, her office focused on underworld crime. China's economic miracle had created an explosion in lawlessness.[3] Crime was growing exponentially in the 1990s as people moved from their villages to expanding cities. Yang encountered horrific incidents as a state prosecutor. Gang violence had shot up; in coastal Fujian province, twelve young pirates, flashing explosives and knives, terrorized fishing boats until they were caught and executed.[4] Authorities discovered a syndicate that smuggled in about $10 billion in oil and cars over a period of three years. A rising Communist cadre named Xi Jinping was then the province's deputy Party secretary. Thirteen years later, he would be anointed as Party secretary of the entire Communist Party as its top leader. In the midst of this uncertainty and chaos, Yang believed wholeheartedly in maintaining social order through a rigid application of the law, and she attacked her job with an activist's zeal other bureaucrats found abrasive.

She was eager to get started, yet the first tasks assigned to her in the prosecutor's office were deeply boring: filling out reams of court paperwork and writing transcripts. Her fellow officemates were generally unmotivated. They occasionally pulled out a mahjong table in the office during the afternoons and played the popular, tabletop game for the rest of the day. In a fit of pique in 1996, Yang quit and took a short break to pursue her dream of being a journalist, writing for a small, private newspaper before realizing the owner cared more about advertisement sales than reporting. Chastened, she went back to the procuratorate's office, where she proved herself to be an ambitious prosecutor.

She impressed the right people. In 1997, Yang was promoted to assistant prosecutor, then delegated to the provincial office soon after, responsible for serious felonies and violent crimes. Not a natural public speaker, she was so overcome by nerves during her first case, she couldn't hold her printed statement steady. But she loved the satisfaction of building a case, and she learned to embrace the exhilaration of addressing the court.

Her job gave her the power to change—or end—someone's life. She made it a point to attend every execution in the cases she worked on. Five years into the job, Yang sent her first person to death row. She had been assigned the case of a man who had stabbed another man to death with a fruit knife. She encouraged the defendant to repent for those crimes and seek redemption.

Yang is reticent about when she became a Christian, but religion was undoubtedly a motivation throughout her career. She found the religion's teaching about redemption and forgiveness useful for understanding the senseless violence of the crimes she prosecuted. Religion could also make her a remorseless prosecutor. The man refused to repent. During one meeting, the man knelt to the ground, pulling at Yang's shoes as he begged her to give him a lighter sentence. Her heart filled with hate, she told me, recalling that moment. His groveling disgusted her. "He only feared death. I look down on these sorts of people. His repentance was all a performance," she said. When a judge found him guilty of murder, she asked for the maximum punishment—the death sentence. At his execution, she was the only person as a witness. The condemned fixed her with a glare of pure fury and malice. "I will remember you in hell," he spat at her. "I shall remember you, too," she replied, without breaking eye contact.

Later, the court sent her a photograph of his corpse to include in the case file. Yang looked at the picture, his last words ringing in her ears. She slept badly for days afterward. While rereading the French novel *Les Misérables*, by Victor Hugo, she was struck by the character of Bishop Myriel, who forgives the book's main character for stealing silver candlesticks from his house. Like

Yang, the fictional bishop also accompanies a convict to his execution, but the bishop comes to feel compassion for him. Yang was floored. She regretted her callousness. The man she had condemned had been born unloved, but he deserved her compassion. She had been born bumbling and tongue-tied, but she had transformed herself through strength of will to be a better person. The people she prosecuted deserved the same chance, she thought.

The opening and reform policies that had changed Yang's life were also changing the rhythms of life for rural residents who were now permitted to live and work in places other than where their *hukou*, or household registration, was located. By the 1990s, some 90 million migrant workers were packing up each year and moving from the countryside and small cities to the much bigger urban hubs of Beijing, Shanghai, or Guangzhou, drifting in and out of cities whenever they could find work.[5] Many of them endured harsh working conditions and long stints away from family and friends. They also helped fuel China's boundless economic growth, but their sudden move to only a handful of cities put strains on the social welfare systems there.

One of these migrant workers, a woman named Zhou Moying, would test Yang's capacity for compassion and forgiveness. Zhou worked in Guangzhou, far from her hometown. Life was hard. Zhou and her husband earned barely enough to feed their family of five, including a sickly, eight-month-old daughter. Zhou struggled to cajole her often-absent husband into taking on family responsibilities. One muggy July in 2005, she got out of bed and fed her daughter rice porridge, but the baby would not stop fussing. Her husband barely stirred at his daughter's cries. Feeling abandoned, Zhou impulsively headed for the river that flowed past their house and placed her infant into the water. She planned to throw herself in, but the thought of her two older children gave her pause. She turned herself in for drowning her daughter.

Yang was assigned to prosecute Zhou. She steeled herself before meeting a mother so cruel as to kill her own child, but the defeated woman sitting in front of her in the Guangdong detention center was not the monster Yang had imagined. Zhou was so distraught, she could barely speak at their first meeting. Between sobs, she begged Yang to sentence her to death; she had failed as a mother, had failed to kill herself, and now she was asking Yang to finish the job. Yang remembered the man she had sentenced to death and how meaningless the hatred she felt then had been. She could never understand Zhou's crime, she later wrote, but she understood the broad systemic forces of poverty behind it. She resolved to handle this case differently. "We must not forget the people behind her who are struggling at the bottom of society," Yang said in an interview at the time. "This is the conscience that the law should have."[6]

The prosecutor's file that Yang eventually wrote up was succinct and unsparing in its diagnosis of Zhou's case: "Life's hardships, an indifferent husband, disease, economic pressure, coupled with being away from home and relatives, as well as loneliness and depression, which cannot be discounted, coupled with her own ignorance, prompted Zhou Moying to this impulsive and stupid action." Yang asked for a reduced sentence of five years.

Her colleagues strenuously disagreed. As public attention for Zhou's case built up, the Guangzhou court trying her came under political pressure to pronounce a guilty verdict and give Zhou a longer sentence. Yang's supervisor called her in multiple times to dress her down for her female sentimentality, and the court sentenced Zhou to eleven years in prison for homicide.

Instead of giving up, the sentence lit a fire of resistance in Yang. She filed an appeal, in which she argued that while Zhou had committed a morally heinous act, the mother had been spurred to do so by dire circumstances outside of her control. A system of law was not only required to treat people fairly but also humanely; a modernizing Chinese legal system should aspire to more than simply assigning punishment, she wrote.

Her arguments galvanized the nation. Taxi drivers and office workers alike were glued to the radio, debating the merits of Yang's arguments. She also had the sympathies of a robust cohort of like-minded lawyers. By the early 2000s, the country's *weiquan*, "rights defense movement," was flourishing, powered by bold lawyers and idealistic legal scholars who believed the law could be used to force government accountability and even instigate long-term democratic reform of the Communist system from within. Many such *weiquan* lawyers were trained in corporate law, but they took on smaller, pro bono cases defending those given short shrift in a fast-changing China, such as those dispossessed of land sucked up by sprawling new cities, mothers chafing against birth restrictions, and advancing the labor rights of migrant workers. There was a mutual recognition between her and these human rights lawyers that they both, albeit from different sides, were working toward the same goal: an impartial system of law that protected a person's rights. "The execution of the law is cold, but the law's essence is warm," she argued in a legal debate widely televised in China. "In order to move someone's soul, you need love."

Eventually, Zhou served a shortened, six-year sentence. Much to Yang's surprise, rather than tanking her career, the Zhou Moying case made Yang a national figurehead for the legal profession. On state television, a beaming Yang was awarded a medal for being a top justice official. "When I am old, what remains in my memory is not how many people I have prosecuted, but how many people I have saved," Yang told a Chinese newspaper.[7]

The case also set her free. She was no longer afraid of breaking the rules. From then on, she would see that justice was served, no matter the political cost. In 2010, shortly before Christmas, Zhou was released from prison. Yang was one of the first people Zhou went to visit. The cameras snapped away as the two women fell into each other's arms and wept.[8]

The Zhou case was supposed to be the beginning of a long and illustrious career for Yang as one of China's leading prosecutors. Instead, she was starting to feel the first pricks of disillusionment. Rule of law was still an aspirational concept for the legal system. Corruption was a given—this she had known from her first day at the procuratorate—but she had a way of sizing up the judges, getting a sense of their personalities, and then tailoring her arguments in the courtroom to them. Yet nearly two decades of such maneuvering were weighing on her. In the years following the Zhou case, the hopes of the reform era were dissipating among legal circles.

In late 2012, Xi Jinping became general secretary of the Communist Party, effectively also making him the new top leader of the country. Then just shy of sixty years of age, Xi was the son of a revered revolutionary leader and thus a "princeling" in elite Communist circles, but he was largely unknown outside of China. He had emerged as the front-runner for the Party's top spot a year earlier, then quickly overtook his main rival, former Politburo member and fellow princeling Bo Xilai, after the latter's wife was implicated in the murder of a British businessman. (Bo and his wife were both given a life sentence in prison for corruption in 2013.)

Despite his prestigious political pedigree, Xi and his family suffered greatly during the political purges of the Cultural Revolution. Xi was banished from Beijing and spent seven years in part living in a cave hewn out of the compact yellow loess hills of Shaanxi province. He knew well how the vicissitudes of absolute power could bring society to a standstill, destroying families and stymieing the future of its young citizens in the process. China watchers thus anticipated a liberal reformer in Xi. Yang expected him to at least continue the policies of his predecessor.

Instead, his rise heralded a re-evaluation of the country's last four decades of economic liberalization and political opening up. As China's new leader, he harbored a preoccupation with diagnosing the causes of the Soviet Union's demise, and specifically, how to avoid a similar collapse at all costs. The USSR had survived for sixty-nine years before imploding; the Chinese Communist Party was now approaching that precise time horizon. In 2009, while head of the central Party school, Xi commissioned a historical study to investigate why the USSR fell. He blamed it on a lack of Soviet backbone to suppress dissenting voices. As he put it in an internal speech several years later, "A big Party was gone just like that. Proportionally, the Soviet Communist Party had more members than we do, but nobody was man enough to stand up and resist."[9]

Before the close of the year, Xi announced an aggressive anticorruption campaign. Many of his predecessors had done the same, though his was to be especially ferocious, and while addressing pervasive corruption, the campaign also conveniently eliminated officials linked to his political rivals. Xi's appointment also had a direct impact on Yang and proponents of rule of law reform. For example, up until the early 2000s, she and her colleagues in what she loosely termed the "reform faction" enjoyed substantial freedom to entertain concepts of judicial independence that had filtered in from the justice sector's engagement with American and British legal traditions. They frequently swapped messages on the prosecutor office's internal messaging forum, or BBS, a blog meets chat forum platform that was popular in the early days of the internet. By 2015, these legal forums were shut down.

The sense of accomplishment her job gave her was also fading. She had tried to work inside the legal system, aspiring to incorporate a more humane jurisprudential approach. That earned her enemies. In 2011, the same year she was named as a top justice official in the nation, she was reassigned to a desk job that took her away from the courtroom. On paper, it was a promotion. In reality, she knew this was a warning to back off. People inside the justice system were envious of her public acclaim and wary she might leverage it to take on more sensitive work. In an act mirroring her youthful rebellion three decades before, she turned the job offer down and quit the civil service entirely. She was at the height of her career and public fame when she stepped away. "I cannot work on cases, so staying here [at the prosecutor's office] has no meaning anymore," she told a Chinese newspaper at the time.

Then, in 2015, she crossed over to the other side, so to speak. She announced she was stepping outside the system to become a human rights lawyer. Instead of prosecuting those convicted of crimes, she would be defending them. She was forty-five years old and ready to reinvent herself again. She knew that the *weiquan* community of activist lawyers and human rights defenders were also coming under more political scrutiny, but she believed they were at least unshackled from the bureaucratic politicking and political directives the procuratorate was saddled with.

Switching sides in the legal profession felt like rediscovering an old identity, a version of herself she had left behind. Human rights law more closely hewed to her original mission as a young prosecutor. She was in the pursuit of justice, staying true to her original mission of using the law to shape a better, kinder society. She started her own social welfare organization and took on pro bono cases defending the very cases—political dissidents and petitioners—that, at her former job, she had had to look the other way on. This work was liberating but dangerous. I could hear the thrill of it in her voice as she recounted some of the current cases she was working on.

She told me she was unafraid of political retribution. She had spent years inside the very public security system that now intimidated and surveilled her and her clients, and she was intimately familiar with the range of legal punishments she faced for her outspokenness. Her work was worth these risks. "Why does a fish swim? Does it only do it for survival?" Yang once asked me. "It is because it needs a larger space. Even if you give a caged bird plenty of food, it will still try to fly away whenever it can. Humans need a wider and freer world of their own, too." Her commitment to the rights defense movement was soon to be tested.

*

At first, the torrent of emails and WeChat messages did not alarm lawyer Ren Quanniu. "Leave the country immediately," one colleague advised him breathlessly. Ren was unfazed. Being a human rights lawyer meant the risk of detention was the norm, not the exception. It was June 9, 2015, and the civil defense community was buzzing with news that fellow lawyer Wang Yu had suddenly disappeared that morning. She had just dropped her husband and teenage son off at the airport and when she returned to her Beijing apartment, she discovered that the lights had stopped working; her power and internet had been severed. Soon after, some of her friends received urgent text messages from her, saying unidentified men were trying to break through her door. No one had been able to get in touch with her since.

Her supporters, including Ren, were worried, but they knew Wang—like themselves—was mentally prepared for such an eventuality. China's rights defense community was at the very forefront of what was politically feasible in China. They took on deliberately provocative cases that tried to hold local governments accountable for protecting the civil liberties of women, ethnic minorities, the religious, and other groups the Chinese government considers political irritants. Their work was inherently dangerous.

Plus, on the day of Wang's disappearance, Ren's mind was elsewhere. He was busy beginning work representing nine Falun Gong students. They had been detained by local authorities in Cangzhou, a city in northern Hebei province, and allegedly tortured in custody, because they practiced a quasi-religious school of meditation that China believes to be a malicious cult. The district court in the eastern city of Cangzhou had delayed the trial for more than a year by insisting on lengthy background checks on each of the ten attorneys, including Ren. That July, a court had finally accepted the case and announced a trial date, so Ren was gearing up for a busy season of commuting between his home city of Zhengzhou, in central China, and Hebei province.

He was never able to make the trip. The next day, at about

ten p.m., Ren was roused from a deep sleep by a phone call. It was the Zhengzhou city security department, and they wanted to meet him. Ren replied with a practiced nonchalance: Weren't they human? Didn't they need sleep as well? Couldn't it wait until the next morning instead? He reasoned that if he was about to be detained, he wanted to get a good night of sleep first. The security official on the line was insistent that Ren come into the station immediately. As he roused himself, Ren checked his other messages. He was surprised to find his WeChat, a ubiquitous chat app in China, was full of unread texts: across the country, hundreds of his fellow human rights lawyers were being disappeared in the night. Dozens of raids nabbed lawyers as they tried to board planes, pulled them from hotel rooms, and lured them to cafes, where they were hooded and taken away. This was a coordinated sweep.

In the police station, Ren was questioned overnight. Officers from the provincial branch of China's state security ministry took turns shouting at him and accusing him of betraying his country by spying for foreign powers. One police officer grew so agitated, he lunged at Ren and began hitting him with his fists, berating him for selling out China, until another officer managed to restrain him.

Ren stayed calm. He had fought his way into the profession with aggressive tenacity and risen in the *weiquan* community by cultivating mental composure. The son of farmers, he had expected to till crops his entire life, as his brother chose to do. But Ren's rebellious streak pushed him first into singing opera. His compact stature belies a booming voice, though he gave up on a musical career when he discovered that he suffered from stage fright. In his twenties, he literally stumbled into the legal profession, stepping on a newspaper advertisement for law school and, on a whim, he applied. He had to take the bar exam three times before passing, because he barely had time to study in between the odd jobs he worked to pay his tuition. "I seek freedom, not comfort," he told me. He also harbored no illusions about how much political change he personally could effect as a *weiquan* lawyer. "We are an idealistic bunch with principles," he said of the *weiquan* movement. "We will work hard towards rule of law and democracy, even if our contributions are very small."

When he was let go the next day, he realized the scope of what had happened. In total, more than three hundred lawyers, legal assistants, and family members of lawyers would be detained or arrested from July 9 onwards. With its best people removed, the rights defense movement was over. The *weiquan* community knew the law was a weapon; they wanted the most marginalized groups in Chinese society to wield that legal weapon effectively and demand the rights promised to them in China's constitution. Ultimately, the law was also their undoing; the state would turn the law back at these lawyers, arresting and sentencing them on serious charges, such as subversion of state power.

The arrests were the clearest sign yet that Xi Jinping was no reformist leader. The 709 Crackdown (as it came to be named, after the date on which it started) also meant the brief window in which a handful of strong-willed academics, journalists, lawyers, and civil rights advocates could advocate for a rule of law system that held China's socialist government accountable to its own regulations was over. The fragile tolerance for people like Ren, Wang Yu, and Yang Bin had run out. They supported a vision for an alternative future for China: one that did not negate Party rule but asked the Party to follow its own constitution and tolerate alternative viewpoints and identities.

Now Ren knew such hope was folly. "In this country, it is a

crime to draw outside the lines. That is very scary," he told me six years after the crackdown over a lunch of noodles and soup near his law office, in his home city of Zhengzhou. "Many people in China know this, but they bury it because they face other pressures in life and do not dare, or do not care, to pay attention to difficult issues." Even those who were deeply embedded in the state's legal institutions, like Yang Bin, had a hard time comprehending just how devastating the 709 Crackdown would be.

In this post-crackdown world, Yang Bin's second career as a human rights lawyer did not last long. China's justice ministry rapidly lost patience with her out-of-the-box litigating. In 2019, Yang took on a case defending villagers seeking compensation for land that had been seized in southwestern Yunnan province. Justice ministry authorities warned her not to speak publicly about the incident. Instead, she fired off an online essay defending the villagers' property rights. Her law firm terminated her contract and authorities suspended her law license until she could find a new employer.

A Beijing-based law firm offered her a new job, but the justice ministry refused to meet with her, stonewalling her license application. She never was reinstated to the bar, though that did not stop her. When I first got to know Yang, she had just returned home after a grueling trip to southwestern Guizhou province, where she had attempted to visit the three children of Wang Zang, a poet detained for publishing politically critical verses. She was still sore from being interrogated in a police station because they had cuffed her hands behind her back for seven hours.

What kept her going was the tenacity of the other human

rights lawyers around her. One of her inspirations was fellow law-yer Xu Zhiyong. The pair met years earlier at an event hosted by a foreign embassy in Beijing. Xu, a pugnaciously political activist, made global headlines in 2010 when he founded a loose coalition of activist organizations he later termed "the New Citizens Move-ment." Its founders were constitutional scholars and human rights lawyers, members ranged from rural grassroots environmental ac-tivists to graying academics who all shared a belief that individual citizens should have the power to demand transparency and ac-countability from the government.

Yang admired Xu's grit and perseverance—especially as key members of the New Citizens Movement were arrested one by one. She knew how grueling it was to keep up a spirit of resis-tance, year after year. And they had acquaintances in common. Sun Dawu, an idealistic farmer who had founded a billion-dollar agricultural conglomerate, had once hired Xu as a defense attor-ney.[10] Sun openly admired Plato's idea of a philosopher king and fancied himself a gentleman scholar, gardening by day and debat-ing ideas of political reform and rural land policy by night. Throughout the early 2000s, both Xu and Yang were among the guests Sun invited for occasional meeting-of-the-minds type gatherings he convened at his home in rural Hebei province, just outside Beijing.

In 2018, Xu finished a four-year prison sentence for "disturb-ing public order." He immediately began writing again, and he had a clear target in mind: Xi Jinping. The outbreak of the novel coronavirus two years later gave him even more material for his vociferous takedowns of China's political elite. In one post from February 4, 2020, Xu called for Xi to step down, criticizing his handling of the outbreak. "Politicians should be unflappable in a time of crisis, but you are helpless," Xu wrote. "Where are you leading China? Towards democracy or dictatorship? Modernization or the Cultural Revolution?"[11]

Xu was a firebrand liberal activist—impulsive, outspoken, and uncompromising. Yang was measured, strategic, and—after years working among bureaucrats—patient. In short, theirs was an unlikely friendship. Which was why, with police after Xu again, he chose to hide in the last place authorities would think to look for him: in Yang's home.

Xu's latest troubles began the day after Christmas in 2019. He and several of his old compatriots, survivors of the purge against the New Citizens' Movement, convened at the home of an old friend, as they often did, in the port city of Xiamen for dinner.[12] They toasted the new year and traded stories of the last year's hardships. They also held an informal discussion on the future of human rights work in China. Pretty dismal, they concluded. It was about to get worse, however. Within days, four of the dinner party guests had been arrested; police saw their meal as an activists' strategy meeting. Xu was on a train back to Beijing when he learned of his friends' arrests through a flurry of text messages. He got off at the next train stop and immediately went on the run.

He ended up at Yang's house. She lived off the coast of Guangdong province on an island shaped like a gull's wing. The island remained isolated despite its proximity to one of China's biggest cities, and it came with a yard where Yang could occasionally do some gardening. She and her husband fixed it up, turning it into a remote escape from the stress of her human rights work.

Its tranquility also made it a suitable place for a political fugitive to spend some time away from the prying eyes of law enforcement. Yang had bought a small retreat on the island to rest and to let others fight the good fight. She was tired of the continuous harassment that came with representing sensitive cases, but when Xu showed up on her doorstep, she found herself unable to say no. He lived out of her blue-walled guest bedroom on the third floor of her balmy home for most of the next month, until the day two dozen police officers showed up at Yang's house and took him away.

I woke up one February day in 2020 to text messages that Xu had been arrested. I was not surprised. Chinese police could martial a vast array of electronic surveillance measures to monitor his acquaintances, and nearly all transportation requires using a Chinese identification number. But Xu had managed to evade the digital dragnet for nearly eight weeks. A friend who knew Xu well boasted that he had been going out to eat at restaurants and doing daily jogs by a river in the weeks before police finally caught up with him. In April 2023, Xu and Ding Jiaxi, a fellow lawyer who had been at the same holiday dinner meeting, were sentenced to fourteen years and twelve years in prison, respectively, for subverting state power.

Despite the fallout from sheltering Xu, Yang Bin remained in China and plowed on with her work. She and her teenage son were briefly detained and interrogated. Yet Yang was more like Xu than she had realized; she wanted to fight on. Plus, her services were needed more than ever. Their old friend Sun Dawu had come calling. He was in trouble again, facing multiple criminal charges touched off by a minor property dispute. Yang took up the case and literally camped outside the county-level courthouse to petition for more information. When his trial began, she attended every hearing. She wrote long legal briefs, which she dutifully forwarded every evening in chunks over text message to me and others following the case. "To be continued tomorrow," her missives always concluded. I liked her little sign-off. It displayed a dogged optimism, a belief there was always another day to continue the fight.

On the day of the final hearing in Sun's case, the day of his sentencing, she stopped sending me her courtroom scribe's notes. Perhaps she knew what the outcome would be, long before the judgment was announced. She knew how the judicial system worked. After all, she had helped to build the system herself, faithfully serving its ends for decades. But it was no longer a system she recognized. The Party controlled the law, and the law primarily served the Party. Xi's anti-corruption campaign was broadening out, reaching beyond Party ranks into the worlds of private business and entrepreneurship. Public prosecutors—what Yang used to be—were ordered to use the law to stamp out perceived corruption. They were under pressure to deliver a precedent-setting legal win. They just needed the perfect case.

CHAPTER 2

THE BUSINESSMAN

Emma Wang was blissfully unaware of how the country of her birth was changing in her absence. It was 2016, and she was preparing to move from the United States back to China. To do so, she had quit a cushy finance job in Kentucky, a job that granted her a work permit that would eventually become a U.S. green card if she stayed long enough. However, after eight years of studying and working in the U.S., she longed to be close to her family in China's province of Inner Mongolia. She especially wanted to be near her father, who had chronic health issues, including diabetes. China's economic future also looked bright, especially in her hometown, the Inner Mongolian city of Baotou. There, in the span of just three decades, gleaming high-rises had replaced the dusty, squat brick tenements of Emma's youth.

Emma and her family played a role in this modernizing of China. Some of the very skyscrapers now dominating Baotou's skyline were financed by her father, Wang Yongming. The patri-arch of the family, Wang was a pioneer in what is now called "shadow banking": off-the-books fundraising and lending that often bypass China's official banks. The Wang family's lending business involved giving out peer-to-peer loans to clients who lacked the financial credit or political connections needed for a formal loan. At their worst, lenders like the Wangs were loan sharks, giving out short-term loans to individuals desperate enough to be willing to pay higher interest rates. At best, they were essential to China's entrepreneurial economy, making up for gaps in the financial sector and keeping liquidity flowing and GDP growing.

Places like Baotou were awash with shadow financing in the 2000s. Once a ramshackle mining town cut out of the Mongolian steppe, Baotou flourished on the extraction of rare earth minerals that are critical materials in our technological devices.[1] The new wealth that this generated and a low stock of existing infrastructure meant there was high demand for financial capital to meet the need for new construction—shiny office spaces, luxury condominiums to house the nouveau riche, mass apartment complexes—a need that outstripped state banks' capacity to lend. That was where Emma's father came in.

In 2008, in the depths of a global recession, Chinese policymakers hastily approved an economic stimulus that sent trillions of renminbi (the official currency of the PRC) in loosely monitored funds pulsing through China's financial institutions. The stimulus was needed to ward off a domestic economic contraction, but it also created a lot of bad investment decisions. There was so much money sloshing around that the central government lost track of some of it as it was parceled out to smaller institutions. By then, Wang Yongming had parlayed a decades-long career as a long-haul truck driver transporting fruits and vegetables into a large logistics business. When the demand for capital hit, he started lending and earning interest on small loans to real estate entrepreneurs, amounts that rapidly grew into millions of dollars as property moguls ripped up Baotou's brick slums to build high-end shopping malls.

Some shadow financiers formalized their operations and kept accounts tidy, becoming established businesses. As a child, Emma remembered her father taking her up and down the shopping street next to their apartment and pointing out the dozens of shadow lenders—some far shadier than others—whose offices populated the new office buildings. They enabled a property boom in Baotou and across China that still underpins up to a third of the country's economic growth today (and also a good chunk of corporate debt). Despite her father's wealth, he was frugal with Emma and her younger brother. Each week he gave them the equivalent of about sixty cents in pocket money. Respect the power of money, he told them, and money will come to you—but stay away from politics.

Emma's father intuited a tacit bargain with the state: people could not oppose the Party, but they could get rich within its limits, as he had. After becoming Party leader in 2012, Xi Jinping issued mixed signals about whether he would continue this compromise. "We can brook no delay" in pursuing fresh economic reforms, Xi declared in a speech during a southern tour of manufacturing zones in his first month as leader,[2] buoying optimism among China's private businessmen and international policymakers that China would further embrace global market-based standards. They hoped that business, as long as it also served the interests of the Party, would be protected by law. Instead, the equation was about to be turned on its head: the law was going to be used to squash entrepreneurs with enough influence to challenge Party rule.

By 2016, the Party was reining in shadow financing firms and other illegal financing schemes because it realized China's debt had ballooned, much of it in off-the-books lending and borrowing it didn't know existed nor had direct oversight over. Sensing the political winds shifting, Wang Yongming began transitioning to real estate development. His new dream was to build a modern China in Baotou. Some of his deals were risky, involving huge volumes of cash that he had no guarantee his debtors would repay in time. But the Wang family patriarch was not worried about running afoul of the law; one had to take risks to stay relevant in a country as large and ever-changing as theirs, and the Wangs were at the vanguard on the northern fringes of the Chinese project.

Emma fully bought into her father's ambitions for China. She was patriotic and wanted to serve her country. With her overseas experience working at American credit cooperatives and various pension funds, she and her father could professionalize rural lending cooperatives and regional banks, which still suffered from crises of confidence and bank runs. A plump, petite twenty-nine-year-old, she proudly called herself a *xiaofenhong*, or "little pink"—an internet slang term for nationalist, female millennials who could brook no foreign criticism of China. And so, in early 2019, she decided to move back home and help with the family business. She had also just gotten married and was expecting her first child.

One chilly April day that year, her mother was at Emma's apartment cooking for her daughter, something she did daily now that Emma was suffering from morning sickness. Just after dinner, they heard a knock at the door. Outside was a group of policemen, and to Emma's shock, they strode right into her home, pushed her mother to the wall, and handcuffed her. A policeman Emma had never seen before walked into the middle of the chaos.

"You may not know me, but I know you very well," he said, pointing his index finger at Emma. His said his name was Wang Gang, and he had a vendetta against Emma's family.

At the same time Emma's mother was being arrested, police officers were taking her frail father into police custody as well. Hours later, under harsh interrogation, the elder Wang collapsed and was taken by ambulance to the nearest hospital. His kidneys were failing due to complications with his diabetes, necessitating the amputation of his left leg. Emma feared for his life.

Emma suspected her parents' arrests were a shakedown: the Baotou property scene was fast and loose, operated in conjunction with local cronies embedded in the civil administration and municipal police force, and the elder Wang's influence in the city likely had made him enemies over the years. Her suspicions were bolstered when Wang Gang, the police officer overseeing her family's case, called Emma's father while he was recuperating in the hospital, demanding RMB430,000 (US$66,000) in cash. (Wang is one of the most common surnames in China, and there is no family relation between the policeman and Emma's family.) Emma immediately sold off several of the family's cars and valuables and sent Officer Wang the cash, waiting for her parents to be released back home.

They never were. And a year later, Baotou police announced her parents' official charges. Emma was floored. District prosecutors were forging ahead with a case against her parents despite the hefty bribe she had paid, and they were levying a charge against them that she had never heard of before: "gang-related crimes." The Wangs had become a test trial, part of a broader, national campaign against corruption and an alleged plague of organized crime. The campaign was dubbed *saohei chu'e*, or "sweep away the black and dispel the evil." Local Communist branches hung red banners of all sizes emblazoned with this slogan on telephone poles, bus stops, billboards across the country, and even printed the slogan on free calendars that year.

The *saohei* "sweep away the black" campaign was the second phase of a sweeping anti-corruption initiative that Xi Jinping had made one of his signature policies, starting in 2012 during his first term as Party chairman. The first phase of Xi's purge had involved rooting out corrupt officials within the Communist Party. Within three years, the Party's disciplinary watchdog said it had investigated more than 4.7 million "tigers and flies" at all ranks of the Party apparatus for, among other things, embezzling public funds, taking on mistresses, profiting off backroom deals, and leaking state secrets. Using this success as a springboard, the anti-corruption campaign went into its second phase. It was to be turned on the rest of Chinese society, especially private business. Private scions from technology to heavy industry had grown immensely wealthy—and thus powerful. It was time to rein them in.

In 2020, the *saohei* campaign was hailed as a smashing success: nearly forty thousand supposed criminal cells and corrupt companies were busted, and more than fifty thousand Communist Party and government officials were punished for abetting them, according to official statistics. The campaign also gave cover to local officials to remove people they deemed political irritants. For example, in China's Shaanxi province, authorities arrested an environmental activist in 2018 for "being an evil force."[3] Her apparent crime was repeatedly reporting two local quarries for damaging village roads, illegal mining, and for pollution. (Fortunately, her verdict was ultimately overturned.)[4]

The anti-corruption campaign marched on. Its third phase turned on China's justice and law enforcement apparatus, the very people who had enforced the first two phases of the rectification purge in a three-pronged campaign. "Drive the blade in" and "scrape the poison off the bones," the Party ordered its law-and-order ministries.[5]

Old grudges were given new power with the anti-corruption campaign. Emma learned that Officer Wang had been quietly pestering her father for the last three years, after a debtor unable to pay off his loan had been court-mandated to sign over his assets as collateral, per the original loan agreement. Officer Wang had informally lent the debtor some money, and he demanded Emma's father give him a cut of the debtor's collateral. Emma's father brushed him off, but the officer was persistent. He phoned in periodically, leaving threatening voicemails that Emma's mother recorded.

In 2018, Officer Wang saw his chance to retaliate. The Party had announced it was now targeting "umbrellas of influence," criminal networks that had to be rolled up and prosecuted harshly. Officer Wang phoned in a complaint: he claimed Wang Yongming and his family were running a "black society" (the Chinese term for a criminal organization) because they used fear and violence to extort people for money. (I tried repeatedly to get in contact with Officer Wang. After several unanswered texts, I called him; he hung up the phone.) His accusations set in motion the chain of events leading to the arrest of Emma's parents.

When a demand for a second bribe was passed to her from one of the case's prosecutors, a career justice bureaucrat with a receding hairline named Li Shuyao, Emma capitulated. She hurriedly pieced together another RMB300,000 (US$46,000) in cash and sent it off to prosecutor Li via an intermediary. At the very least, she hoped the sum would lessen her father's sentence. Then she began looking for a lawyer.

Unfortunately for Emma, there were very few willing and able lawyers left to take her case. The 709 Crackdown that nabbed Ren Quanniu and sidelined Yang Bin had done serious damage to the *weiquan* community. Of the more than three hundred lawyers arrested or detained, more than a dozen were still languishing behind bars. Most lawyers, like Ren, were questioned and eventually let go, but they were marked men; many of them would be systematically disbarred like Yang in the coming years, their law licenses suspended or permanently revoked for their work on politically sensitive cases.

Ren resolved to keep working for as long as China's Ministry of Justice recognized his license. A swarthy, stocky man with silky eyes and a mustache, he exudes intensity and rebelliousness. He and his remaining human rights lawyers were growing more and more preoccupied with the new category of untouchable legal cases that emerged: those prosecuted under "gang-related crimes." By the last year of the *saohei* campaign, it was clear a broader shake-up of China's private sector was underway, in sectors ranging from real estate to e-commerce, and from smaller local businesses to the nation's largest and most recognized names. At the very top, the colorful Jack Ma, China's most famous entrepreneur, was dethroned after regulators blocked the public offering of his financial technology spin-off, Ant Financial.[6] He stepped down from his corporate responsibilities in 2024. Property tycoon Ren Zhiqiang—nicknamed "Big Cannon Ren" for his outspoken tirades on social media—had his internet accounts shut down by censors. Financial giant Anbang Group's chairman Wu Xiaohui was arrested in his office.[7]

This was the cycle of creation and disruption under Party rule; a hundred flowers could bloom, the choice ones picked—but even that was no guarantee that a few of the most beautiful buds were to be trampled on later when tastes changed. None of the entrepreneurs were perfect, but they had been pioneers in their own way. They had dared to dream of a dynamic private sector and a more globally connected China. It was also a side of China that had grown too powerful for the Party's liking. "Political power ultimately controls the economy," says Cai Xia, a former professor at the country's top Communist Party academy, now living in the United States. "If Chinese entrepreneurs want to succeed, they have to depend on the system built by the [Chinese Communist Party]." Wu, once the cocky billionaire owner of New York's storied Waldorf Astoria Hotel, was sent to languish in isolation for eighteen years in a Shanghai prison, reduced to handwriting petitions collected in a thick volume by his lawyers.

Sun Dawu's fall was especially precipitous. Despite Yang Bin's help on his case, agricultural billionaire Sun had his corporate fiefdom dismantled after he, too, was sentenced to eighteen years in prison for gathering crowds to attack state agencies, illegal fundraising, and "provoking trouble." Sun, a gentleman farmer with a lifelong commitment to social justice, made his fortune selling animal feed and fertilizers, then used his fortune to bankroll experiments in rural development. "It is hard to uniformly redistribute the wealth of the society / But it is possible to make equal commoners and aristocrats," Sun wrote in a poem engraved on a stone slab near his company headquarters. He also used his company's profits to build a self-contained company town for his nine thousand employees, complete with free hospitals, schools, and a sports stadium—all named after himself, naturally. His current employees spoke glowingly about him when I visited Dawu Group's offices in Hebei province, just outside Beijing.

However, at trial, his largesse was construed as buying influence. Over the years, he often rallied employees during his efforts to push back against burdensome state regulators—actions that prosecutors interpreted as organizing political dissent. Furthermore, the sixty-seven-year-old farmer turned tycoon had defiantly befriended and supported Chinese political dissidents, some of the very same activists who later mentored lawyer Ren Qianniu. Now Sun was seen as a dissident himself. He, like Anbang's Wu and tycoon Ren Zhiqiang, was sentenced to eighteen years of prison time for financial misdeeds. In 2021, Sun's agricultural empire was auctioned off to the highest bidder, with the proceeds going to the local government.

Small and medium entrepreneurs took the real brunt of the *saohei* campaign's force, and being branded "black society" meant entire extended families were being arrested for their alleged mob connections. "Sweep away the black is a political campaign, so the cases are not decided according to the evidence," says Li Jinxing, a defense attorney who had taken on about two dozen "sweep away black" cases. "Cases like these are [decided] so they fulfill the campaign's quotas."

For the entrepreneurs like the Wangs who were targeted in *saohei* cases, the turn in their fortunes was disorienting. One day you were part of the core of elite Chinese society, keenly attuned to deciphering the Party's policies signaling which sectors were hot and where to invest money, racing against the competitors who also sensed blood. The next moment, you could be cast out, deemed an undesirable element, and purged. In the end, the Party trumped all. It gave you opportunities to create fabulous wealth, and it could also take everything away in an instant.

Because the *saohei* cases unraveled entire families and often arrested their patriarchs, frequently only the women were left to petition on their behalf. Petitioning is hard, risky work, and it tended to alienate most people, who instinctively knew that guilt by association might endanger themselves as well. That was why about four dozen women formed a chat group, in which they could share tips and updates, and give each other emotional support on each of their legal cases. They were the daughters, nieces, and sisters of business clans who had been prosecuted or jailed. It was an online support group for an unlikely gathering of women, former daughters of privilege, and I wanted in.

Eventually, I met one woman in this group. Zhang Xiaohui was the sister of a bauxite ore mining scion in China's central Shaanxi province. Decades ago, the family had secured the lucrative rights to dig under the parched hills near her home village. The bauxite ore they found there, used to make aluminum, enriched the family, until her brother was accused in the *saohei* campaign of being "an evil leader disguised in red clothes"—a tyrant pretending to be a good socialist. Zhang invited me out to their home so she could show me how the case had destroyed not just her family but an entire village that depended on them for employment. She couldn't guarantee I wouldn't get beaten up—local officials could be thuggish, and they wouldn't take kindly to foreign reporters coming out to report on their case—but she would do what she could to quietly set up interviews with some of the case's defendants. My then-producer Amy Cheng and I booked flights out to the city of Luliang the next day.

The tiny city of Luliang had only one major commercial road, but in a nod to catering to the extravagantly wealthy mining barons and their families who had made their fortunes there, it bizarrely had its own airport. The city reminded me a bit of how I imagined the American Wild West had been: extreme emptiness contrasted with extreme wealth. Its barren hills were sandy and bare, riddled with mine shafts to extract the valuable ores within, while Land Rovers drove on narrow streets.

Zhang was a loud woman with broad cheekbones and an open, expressive face, and she was used to speaking her mind. She hadn't been that close to her brother and his family; she preferred to live by herself. But now that he was in trouble, she rallied the remaining clan. After her brother, his wife, their business partners, and many of their employees were arrested, Zhang sold the family's luxury cars and the apartments without any hesitation. Instinctively, she understood that the family's future generations now depended on her, and she was especially concerned that the legacy of a *saohei* charge would affect her nieces and their future children.

She brought me to their old mining offices, the walls buckling inward because tunneling from other mining companies nearby had collapsed the ground underneath us. Across the street, abandoned apartment towers were already overgrown with ivy, part of a land dispute that was related to her brother's *saohei* charges. Zhang told me they were throwing the little money they had left unseized into an appeal, but they could not find a legal team to represent them. One lawyer reviewed their case but declined to take it on and returned the printed court judgment with only one word written on it: *yuan*, the Chinese character for injustice. As their appeal preparations dragged on, Zhang and her niece began posting less and less in the online chat group. The other women weren't engaging as much either. No one had good news to share.

Emma had hit a wall in her father and mother's legal case as well. Several well-known corporate lawyers in Inner Mongolia had agreed to take her parents' case, despite the political sensitivities: it was the province's biggest gang-related case, and her legal team knew prosecutors were under pressure to deliver a high-profile win. From the very first day, they ran into successive legal hurdles designed to wear down their resolve. The first team quit after provincial justice ministry officials contacted them privately, threatening to suspend their legal license if they continued with the case. Undeterred, Emma cast about for lawyers who had their licenses registered outside of Inner Mongolia, figuring that it would be harder for provincial officials to bully out-of-state lawyers.

During the pretrial hearings in July 2020, Emma wasn't even sure if her father was still alive. She was repeatedly blocked from visiting him in the hospital where she believed he was being kept, but she knew his health was worsening. During hearings, Emma's legal team and the witnesses they called up were kept behind a phalanx of police, their plastic shields sometimes muffling spoken testimony to such an extent the judge had a hard time hearing the lawyers.

The night after the last pretrial hearing, Emma's team of lawyers were decompressing in a shared Baotou hotel room, not only to save money but also for their shared safety. Their caution was prescient, because police stormed their room late that night, accusing them of taking money for legal work they had never done.

Eventually, nearly all the weary lawyers agreed to give up all lawyer's fees they had received for the case and work pro bono for the Wang family going forward—all except for the lead lawyer, Xu Xin. He had given an impassioned plea earlier that day, but it was less a rousing call for justice and more of an admission of defeat. "This case cannot be decided through legal means . . . the obstacles to justice have just been too great," he said. After that night, he announced he was quitting the case.

Emma's case could have been just like any of the other forty thousand *saohei* cases authorities said they opened from 2018 onwards. Those cases raked in a total of 544 billion RMB (US$76 billion) in confiscated assets. Then came a bombshell twist: Li Shuyao, the Baotou prosecutor heading their case, was detained for taking bribes. The graying functionary who had politely asked for the second bribe that Emma duly paid, was now being kept under *shuanggui*, or "double designation," a special form of detention only used on Party members.

It turned out Li had actually only taken part of the RMB300,000 (US$46,000) bribe Emma had ferried to him; the intermediary had pocketed a RMB100,000 cut for his services. When Li learned that Emma's parents would be charged with "gang-related crimes," he had actually tried to return his portion of the bribe; the earnest prosecutor admitted he had no sway in a political case like this one. His honesty did not save him from being officially expelled from the Party days later. It did, however, necessitate a retrial of Wang Yongming and Wang Hongyan, Emma's parents. Suddenly, her case had legs again.

The retrial was an immense source of hope in the group support

chat where Emma and other daughters shared updates; there
hadn't been any good news in a while. Privately, Emma was more
cautious. Every few days, she called me from her Baotou apartment, where she was under de facto house arrest. The signal was
horribly patchy; she suspected the police monitoring her had installed signal blockers on the apartment towers nearby, meaning
she could not receive reliable cell service or internet. During the
first few months of her legal ordeal, Emma adopted a defiant,
confrontational approach, including screaming matches with doctors and police. Now, on the phone with me, she sounded exhausted. Every so often, I could hear her young daughter fussing;
she was teething, a reminder of how much time had already passed
since her grandparents' arrest. "I don't think we have any choice
anymore in the matter," Emma told me heavily. She was prepared
to take whatever verdict this second court handed down.

Shortly before China was to go on break for the Lunar New
Year, I spotted a short news item online saying the retrial of Wang
Yongming was about to wrap up; I did not have time to get to
Baotou to attend the proceedings, which had been closed to the
public anyway. Emma's father had been given a reduced sentence
of ten years, rather than the quarter of a century he originally
faced, and her mother was sentenced to a year and a half for time
served. I tried calling Emma, but none of her accounts and numbers worked anymore.

CHAPTER 3

THE SCOOTER THIEF

There is no shortage of Chinese-language content online. Open up Douyin, the Chinese version of TikTok, and skim an endless waterfall of videos by creators from all corners of China. On WeChat, the chat app, thousands of bloggers pump out daily essays on music, history, and international affairs. Sign up for alerts from China's state media channels or their news aggregator sites, and you will receive dozens of notifications a day for breaking news and commentary. This content is why, upon first look, the Chinese internet appears diverse and vibrant, thrumming with a constant flow of gossip and data. This is a mirage. In reality, this diversity is highly managed, and human censors and algorithms on China's biggest internet platforms can erase politically subversive content in minutes. Step outside China and go online, and that world of censored information lives on, in a kind of shadow existence, on the open web. Inside China, however, it cannot be seen.

These two parallel worlds of information exist side by side. I inhabited both while living in and reporting on China. To access both from within China, I used several VPNs—short for virtual private networks—to toggle between the two. VPNs are a type of software that serve as a portal between China's cybersphere and the rest of the world. The software virtually tunnels through China's slew of cyber censorship mechanisms dubbed the Great Firewall. The difference between the two sides of the Firewall was once not so great: in the early 2000s, sites like YouTube, Gmail, and Facebook remained accessible. Today, China walls off virtually all major international social media sites, and errant content in all formats is erased in real time.

This world inside the Great Firewall has become more restricted under Xi Jinping. Obsessed with national security, he has boosted defense spending and invested heavily in domestic research and development hubs for cutting-edge semiconductor manufacturing and military technologies. In the same vein, the internet must also be tamed for the sake of national security. Driving this are understandable concerns over online scams and hackers and the spread of disinformation. It is also motivated by more subjective worries about the proliferation of salacious or critical content that must be "rectified" through routine clean-ups, closing tens of thousands of accounts at a time.[1, 2]

Xi has coined the phrase "cyber sovereignty," referring to the right of every country to define how free or closed its internet should be depending on the path of development its leaders desire.[3, 4] In this worldview, the internet does not exist to serve the pursuit of knowledge, but rather to support state objectives. Uncontrolled, the internet is seen as dangerously powerful, even destructive. "Like in the real world, freedom and order are both necessary in cyberspace. Freedom is what order is meant for, and order is the guarantee for freedom," Xi told foreign dignitaries in

2015.[5] As a result, censors are increasingly asked to make not just political judgments about what is appropriate, but also to enforce moral dictates to remove lewd, vulgar, or materialistic stories. Entire events and people can be erased in these postproduction purges, and the absence they leave is immediately filled with mass-generated *zhengnengliang,* "positive energy," stories: feel-good content, much of it designed to support state interests or to distract from more pressing problems.

As always, this system of erasure and replacement is not perfect. Some things fall through the cracks, and the online and the offline start to mirror each other. For brief moments, the worlds intermingle, but never for long. A scooter thief named Zhou Liqi would find out the hard way that it was impossible to live in both worlds.

Zhou Liqi grew up without internet, or much of anything at all. His family was the poorest in a poor village. Their fortunes were tied to their crops, and when the weather brought rains or long, arid stretches, as it did frequently, their crops failed. Zhou was known as Ah San, or Number Three, because he had been born third in a string of brothers. Together, they all lived in a crumbling brick home with a dirt courtyard and a leaking roof in China's southern Guangxi province. His family could not regularly afford groceries or clothes, and Zhou dropped out of school in the third grade to work.

Most children in his village went to work at the semi-legal brick kilns that dotted the periphery of the village. Zhou knew from his brothers, who had done stints there, that the work digging up clay and retrieving bricks from rudimentary ovens was exhausting and dangerous, and it paid very little. He decided to work construction in the next province over, but he dreamed constantly of living in the cities he was a migrant in, of having his own home instead of building them for other people, and of simple luxuries, like getting to wear clean clothes each day. To fulfill those dreams, he needed to be daring. He ran away to the nearby city of Nanning, where he picked up temp jobs outside the train station. There, he met a girl he intended to marry, whom he called Ah Zhen. But his family could not afford to pay the dowry price her family wanted, and Zhou did not own his own apartment or car, which are usually social prerequisites for marriage in China. That was when he tried for the first time to steal a scooter. He was caught.

The 2012 video of his second attempt and subsequent arrest was shot by a local television station in Guangxi. In the video, Zhou is tanned and unshaven. He is slurring his words. Both his hands are handcuffed to the bars on a police station window, the sweat under his prominent widow's peak shining under the fluorescent lighting. The local reporter dispatched to interview Zhou asks him why he keeps stealing for a living. Zhou seems baffled by the question: "It is impossible to work part-time; it is impossible to work in this life!" he says. "It is very nice to come to the detention center. It feels like coming home. I love it here." After the interview concluded, Zhou served a year and a half of prison time, then promptly went back to stealing scooters, sometimes successfully.

The video did not immediately go viral, but in 2016, it suddenly blew up. China, it turns out, has a lot of wannabe slackers. "I had this secret, depraved desire, too," the journalist Chu Zijing wrote of Zhou's defiant laziness. Chu, a thoughtful writer in his late twenties when I met him, had tested his way into one of China's top universities, Tsinghua University, in Beijing. His entire life had been geared toward academic success. However, as an adult, Chu questioned what that hard, repetitive work had been for, and he marveled at Zhou's honesty and audacity. He saw in the scooter thief's laid-back persona a sophisticated approach to rebellion and wrote a nuanced magazine profile of him. "It is not the dissatisfaction of working itself, but rather the dissatisfaction of not being able to have a decent life, despite that work," he told me over coffee in NPR's Beijing bureau some years after the video had gone viral. Though he had no formal education, Zhou had intuited that no matter how hard he worked, the real profit from his labor was being captured by other people.

Zhou touched a nerve in Chinese society, which had become more economically unequal even as its economy grew rapidly. The country still suffers from a culture of overtime and underpaid work. I found people in China remarkably ambitious and hard-working, but that also meant stiff competition in the domestic labor market. Add to that a glut of college graduates and a slowing economy and that meant people's prospects were no longer as bright as they had been before 2020. Internet slang terms like *neijuan*—meaning "involution"—and *tangping*—Chinese for "lying flat"—were peppering everyday vernacular. Tired of working hard but getting nowhere (involution), China's youth just wanted to lie down and lie flat.

In a country where organized social dissent, both online and offline, can be a criminal offense, Zhou's rejection of work offered an alternative, more passive mode of protest. Unable to change the institutions in which they worked, people simply withdrew from them. His jailhouse interview inspired an entire internet subculture. One magazine profile designated him "the spiritual leader of slackers." With his wispy goatee and long black hair, Zhou looked more than a little bit like an Asian Che Guevara, the guerrilla Communist fighter celebrated in Cuba, and memes of Zhou photoshopped to appear in Che's signature beret proliferated across the Chinese internet. Several large online forums populated by his fans outright encouraged practicing delinquency and time theft on the job. One of these forums, named Quit Gambling, grew to 4 million participants who posted screenshots of themselves goofing off at work. The group also attracted scammers who used Zhou's trademark "I can't work" motto to sell online loans and dubious financial products. By one estimate, articles about him in The Paper, a well-known news outlet, had been read at least 160 million times, and videos of him had been watched some 300 million times.

Zhou himself was oblivious to the media storm because he was back in prison. This time he was serving out his fourth prison sentence for, once again, stealing scooters. He had never seen a short video or heard of TikTok before, but suddenly, on the outside, he was a video star. His brothers were forced to slaughter all their chickens and ducks to feed the well-wishers who began coming to their family home.

When Zhou was released from prison in April 2020, dozens of cars were waiting for him at the prison entrance and at his parents' home. "This is like a dream," he told a reporter as he was escorted home by police.[6] Some of the cars waiting for him were full of superfans. Most of the people there, however, were talent scouts. They tried to stuff stacks of cash into Zhou's hands, proffering contracts offering to compensate him up to 2 million Chinese yuan (about US$300,000) in exchange for signing him on as their newest live-streaming star.

But Zhou turned them all down, an audacious move that endeared him even more to his legions of fans. "I have said it before: I will not work for anyone. Signing a contract means I would become their employee. That would be eating my own words," Zhou said.[7] Instead, he said he was going back to farming. "You have to follow orders for everything . . . There is no freedom at all," he said of his decision to turn down the contracts. "Farmers have freedom. It is up to you how much you want to plant."

Zhou's rejection cemented his cult status as an incorruptible iconoclast. However, soon after getting back home, he had a change of heart. His father was suffering from arthritis, and his mother was exhibiting early signs of dementia. He needed to find some way to pay for their care. Plus, Zhou's agriculture plans to grow snow peas had gone miserably; years of migrant work in cities meant he was unfamiliar with farming.

He could see China was changing around him, but his family remained as poor as ever. The consumer technology sector had blown up in China during his last stint in prison. Even in his small farming village, people could pay for food and farming equipment with their cellphones. For entertainment, his friends sat around watching TikTok videos. Zhou learned that top live streamers selling goods like lipstick or popular snacks like snail noodles, a smelly local specialty from his home province of Guangxi, could earn hundreds of thousands of dollars a year. He decided to capitalize on his newfound fame, but on his own terms. He would make his own way on the Chinese internet, even if he didn't totally understand how it worked just yet. Perhaps the internet would finally give him the freedom he craved: the opportunity to be his own boss and own his own labor.

Zhou could not imagine himself putting out anything that could be considered controversial. There were plenty of other people already doing that. China's internet sectors had taken off, and even though censorship and political controls picked up in kind, dissent still rippled under the surface. Dissenters hid their samizdat content like easter eggs all over Chinese cyberspace. Some critical blogs hid their writers' identities through disguised IP addresses and anonymized posts. Others taught internet users how to set up their own VPNs. Cybersecurity enthusiasts passed around manuals about which mobile chat and video conferencing apps remained available for download in the Chinese app store but offered end-to-end encryption or did not require real-name registration. That way, people in China could talk to one another anonymously and avoid using WeChat, which is intensely surveilled. On GitHub, the open-source coding repository, users archived manifestos and videos banned from Chinese sites, making them impossible to erase completely.

Much of the Chinese internet is pure entertainment, however. Overworked yet overwhelmingly connected online, China's some one billion internet users spend inordinate time on their smartphones watching online stars—including live streamers—hawking the latest "it" bag or beauty products. Among the top live streamers was male makeup influencer Li Jiaqi, whose pucker once sold fifteen thousand lipsticks in five minutes, earning him the nickname the "Lipstick King." Other live streamers specialized in comedy: one of the most popular was Teacher Guo, a thickset auntie known for her brash humor, profanity, and desire to find a younger boyfriend.[8] These were the elite live-streaming ranks that Zhou wanted to join. He started an account on Weibo, a Twitter-like social media site, and he quickly racked up 3 million followers.

His populist appeal did not mean he was safe from censorship. The Party wanted productive citizens, ones who could contribute to the country's technological race with the United States, keep building its skyscrapers, and birth multiple children who would become the country's future workers. Zhou's online ethos was the antithesis of the kind of citizen China wished to cultivate, for he represented a camp of people who celebrated unproductivity. "To build, market, and consume Zhou is to propagate a twisted social value that honors vulgarity and praises what is ugly," wrote one cultural critic in Beijing, slamming the live-streaming companies that had tried to recruit Zhou out of prison. "These companies and platforms that hope to sign Zhou are endorsing the acts of stealing and reaping without sowing."[9] Zhou let the criticism wash over him. He had served his sentence and was ready to turn over a new leaf; a few editorials were not going to tank his live-streaming career. However, a new world was about to dawn, one that would bring with it new rules whose influence would reach even Zhou.

The fever hit people like the fishmonger Mr. Wen first. He made a living selling fresh seafood to hotels and restaurants in the Chinese city of Wuhan. It was hard work, demanding long days in the damp Huanan wholesale market around burbling fish tanks while standing ankle-deep in warm water, and he frequently came home with a throbbing back and feet. This feverish ache was different, however; it seemed to emanate from within his joints, a pain exacerbated by violent chills he could not sleep off. The next morning, he had trouble breathing. Wen's son drove him into Wuhan's Jinyintan Hospital. It was December 2019.

The hospital's vice director, a respiratory specialist named Dr. Huang Chaolin, watched Wen being wheeled in that afternoon. Based on Wen's lung scan, Huang guessed the illness was a virus related to severe acute respiratory syndrome (SARS), a rare but very deadly coronavirus that had terrorized mainland China and Hong Kong from 2002 to 2004 before being contained. However, three days later, Huang had forty other patients under his care with symptoms identical to those of Wen: a dry cough, a high fever, and chest CT scans that showed pockmarked lungs. Twenty-seven of the patients worked or had met people who worked in the Huanan market.[10] This suggested the new virus could pass easily from person to person, unlike SARS.

Within a month, China announced that all 12 million Wuhan residents and anyone unlucky enough to be in the city at the time were banned from leaving the city. The entire city was going under lockdown, indefinitely. Panicked residents tried driving their way out that night. One such driver later told me she abandoned the skewers and beers she had just laid out for a pre–Lunar New Year's dinner, joining a flood of vehicles headed toward the highway, only to find all the exits blocked. Others managed to leave in the hours before the lockdown was enforced, only to find no city would accept travelers from Wuhan. One man survived by living in his car under a bridge for a month.

The writer Fang Fang, who lives in Wuhan, channeled the city's uncertainty and fear into near-daily musings on life under lockdown. Reposts of her blog garnered 380 million views on Chinese social media even when the original posts were censored within hours. She told me later she was compelled to write her blog as a form of self-therapy and to offer a collective archive of memory independent of the official record.

Chinese state media was filled with heroic stories of white-hazard-suit-clad volunteers, but far more volunteers went un-acknowledged and were even critical of the local government response. Mr. Zhang, one such resident, managed to secure a city pass exempting him from home isolation so he could ferry food and medicine to other Wuhanese trapped in their homes. That was how he met Fang Bin, a local clothing salesman with sunken cheeks and a stubborn spirit. Fang was looking for a driver to ferry him around Wuhan so he could see for himself whether the new disease—soon to be dubbed COVID-19 by the World Health Organization (WHO)—was being effectively contained, as the state promised. Face masks, medication, and hospital beds were running low, and Fang's meandering videos, uploaded to YouTube, gave outside viewers a glimpse into the desperate conditions in Wuhan. In one of his most-viewed videos, he counts six, seven, eight body bags being quickly loaded into a funeral home van. "So many dead," he groans. Weeks later, four police visited him. He disappeared soon after, and his whereabouts are still unknown.

Amateur video bloggers like Fang Bin were going against government exhortations to exude only *zhengnengliang*, "positive energy."[11] Censors were working overtime taking down hundreds of posts from desperate Wuhan residents on social media, begging good Samaritans to help them find medical care for loved ones dying of COVID-19 at home or from other ailments left unattended to during the lockdown. I hastily copied such posts into a Word document whenever I saw them, because invariably, half an hour later, they would be deleted. I didn't always manage to find the writers in time. When I reached one man, he said volunteers had managed to find his stricken mother a hospital bed, but it was too late. "I came to the hospital with my mother. I left with a box of her ashes," he told me.

China, already fenced off in cyberspace by the Great Firewall, became quite literally fenced off during the pandemic. Its borders closed and would not open for nearly three years. The country's energy turned inward in this time of emergency, intent on purging itself of dissonance and disorder. In 2021, the Chinese Writers

Association cast out the Wuhan writer Fang Fang for penning her "biased diary."[12]

Another backlash against her erupted after an American publisher announced it had issued an English translation of her blogs. After her home address and email address were leaked online, Fang Fang received hundreds of mailed and emailed death threats, plus tens of thousands more on social media. Critics accused her of treason and profiting off China-bashing. But Wuhan residents I met who became regular readers of Fang Fang's blog told me they felt energized after reading her updates, because they made them feel less alone. Zhang, the volunteer, told me he was anxious about driving Fang Bin around; being at home felt safer. But he felt empowered doing the work because he knew the videos Fang Bin made were reaching millions of people a day. These voices wanted to spread positive energy: not the kind that boosted the state but rather the kind that lifted ordinary citizens up.

On January 12, Mr. Wen, the fishmonger, woke up in Wuhan's Jinyintan Hospital, in a changed world. Unlike many of his colleagues in the Huanan market, he had made a full recovery. I met him outside a new seafood store he had opened in another market, but his heart wasn't in the business anymore. "Having a healthy life is all that matters. Before, we would go out of our way to make a buck. Now we no longer wish for much," he said. I sensed he wanted to say more, but he was nervous about straying too far off script. He and I both knew criticizing the country's pandemic policy was off-limits for ordinary citizens like him. In the years that followed, China would tolerate no dissent against what authorities called "zero-tolerance" policies to contain the spread of ever-more contagious variants of the coronavirus. Glowing profiles of the country's frontline health workers continued to fill state media channels. They had become untouchable heroes and martyrs in the battle against the virus.

In 2018, China's legislature had created a new criminal charge: insulting, slandering, or otherwise infringing upon the reputation and honor of heroes and martyrs.[13] After the COVID pandemic began, that charge was amended to carry jail time. Now, those who questioned the veracity of the Party's mascots and long-dead figureheads could be imprisoned for up to three years.[14] A few months later, China's increasingly powerful cyberspace regulator launched a hotline on the cusp of the Party's one hundredth anniversary, which hawk-eyed citizens could call to report their fellow compatriots who "distort" Party history and "deny the excellence of advanced socialist culture."[15]

Among those arrested as a result was a blogger, writing under the moniker "Little Spicy Pen Ball," who questioned the number of Chinese soldiers killed in a brawl on the Himalayan border with India. Qiu Ziming, the thirty-eight-year-old former newspaper journalist behind the blog, was detained and criminally charged along with six other people who had made skeptical comments online. "Little Spicy Pen Ball maliciously slandered and degraded the heroes defending our country and the border," the notice for his arrest read. Weeks later, a chastened Qiu gave a filmed confession behind bars, calling his actions "an obliteration of conscience." Another court found beverage company JDB Group and Sun Jie, a blogger, guilty of "unraveling core socialist values" after Sun referred to a Korean War hero who burned to death as "barbecued meat," and JDB jokingly offered to provide free drinks should Mr. Sun start a barbecue joint. Television anchor Bi Fujian was fired from the state broadcaster for taking digs at Chairman Mao at a private party.

People perceived to be critical, even merely impolite, around serious topics ran the risk of being reported. Leaked files from a Chinese hacker group contracted by local government security bureaus showed they were concerned not just with dissident speech within China's cyberspace, but also with speech on international social media platforms censored within China, such as X, formerly known as Twitter. "We must not provide fertile soil or space for internet rumors to spread, to jointly create a clean and fresh online world where rumors are not believed or spread," one of the group's memos said.

This scrutiny also extended to foreign journalists, including myself. In 2021, nearly half a year after I filed a dispatch from mountainous Guizhou province on poverty alleviation efforts, I made the unpleasant Sunday-morning discovery that my face was all over Guancha, a vitriolically nationalist website. A local official I had interviewed about his successful efforts at reducing poverty levels by boosting incomes through industrial mushroom farming had reported me for "sneaking" into the town and conducting "illegal coverage."[16] The local propaganda department said he was financially rewarded for tattling on me. Soon, dozens of state media outlets picked up the story and every few months, a state media outlet would rehash a new criticism of me and other (usually female) reporters.

Zhou, the scooter thief, didn't see how China's shrinking space for expression would affect him. He was putting out personal videos that had nothing to do with politics. He was also dabbling with entrepreneurship. He co-founded a local electric scooter company in Guangxi province and sat on its board. Their scooters' selling points involved an anti-theft security system designed and tested by Zhou himself to ensure thieves (like he had been) could not make off with them. He also opened a late-night barbecue joint, which became a hit with young men because the restaurant let them drink and smoke until dawn, shirts and shoes optional. Zhou kept an office on the restaurant's second floor, and he wandered out frequently to partake in the revelries himself.

While his business ventures were tongue-in-cheek references to his past life, he was eager to prove that he was the kind of "positive energy" cybersecurity regulators wanted more of from the Chinese internet. He was fully aware of the mainstream criticisms of his persona, and contrary to his public reputation, he yearned to be a good person. His family's poverty, his lack of a formal education, and his criminal record all shamed him. They made him feel he had not earned his fame. Moreover, fame itself was not the windfall he had thought it would be; he still felt like a rural outsider, parodied by the urban elite.

After being released from prison, he had been taken first to undergo "psychological counseling" with the local police. "Have you really changed?" he was asked. "I have earned my freedom, and I will certainly cherish it. I will not be stealing scooters anymore," he promised. He also agreed to film a video with the police. "Please do not repeat this behavior again. I believe you will not return to that. You must always respect the law," the officer is recorded saying. Zhou's response is edited out, but he sits chastened across from them. His desire for self-reform was genuine.

That desire was great enough that he was now willing to risk alienating his core fan base. After he decided to embrace his internet fame, his first short video on the Chinese streaming platform Kuaishou was an apology. "I have to apologize. I did some bad things. I see online some people criticizing me. Some young people are copying me, learning from me. Do not copy me," he tells

viewers. "Just mind your own business. Live well."[17] In follow-up
Kuaishou videos, Zhou performed charitable acts, delivering food
and supplies to remote villages near his and offering his support to
the country's national poverty alleviation campaign. He acts stiffly
in these videos, as if he is wary of saying too much. "All the leaves
have fallen," he observed during a photoshoot one cold, Beijing
autumn, then caught himself, worried the comment was too negative and could be interpreted as criticism of the country's capital.

His reputational makeover pleased no one. His fans decried
him for selling out. His critics accused him of trying to white-
wash his former crimes.[18] Life, Zhou mused, had been easier
when he had just been an anonymous construction worker. Sometimes, he thought of Ah Zhen, the woman he wanted to marry
before he had been arrested, before he had become a household
name. "When we were together, I was really happy. That period of
time was like living in a different world," he reminisced in one of
his videos. After getting out of prison, he had gone down to the
local convenience store where Ah Zhen once worked, but she had
quit, and no one knew where to find her.

The end to Zhou's budding internet career came quickly. Soon
after getting out of prison, he was listed by a state-run professional association as one of the influencers explicitly deemed to be
a negative influence on society. "A former prisoner's comments
about contempt for the law, disdain for workers, and mockery of
social rules in interviews with the media have become popular on
the internet, leading many internet celebrity brokerage companies
to ignore public order, good customs, and moral bottom lines," the
China Association of Performing Arts said.[19] This critique was

tantamount to a banned list. Social media sites immediately shut down Zhou's accounts. Talent agencies refused to work with him. Zhou had been canceled—by the state. "Companies that ignore the [live-streaming] industry's moral bottom line and disrupt its healthy ecosystem will be added to a negative list," the performance association threatened.

Chinese regulators were concerned about disinformation, scams, excessive clickbait, and hate speech being proliferated on the internet—issues other countries, including the United States, are worried about as well. The difference is that Chinese regulators are increasingly focused on setting guardrails for content along moral and political lines, to better shape online content to fit state directives from month to month. Some stars who were politically canceled were even blurred out of videos and movies in post-production.

In the fall of 2021, China's broadcasting regulators announced a ban on portraying "sissy men and other abnormal aesthetics."[20] As a result, live-streaming stars who had previously entertained millions of people with their fifteen-second clips found themselves canceled. Teacher Guo, the trash-talking auntie, had her accounts erased for "vulgarity."[21] Li Jiaqi, the Lipstick King, was temporarily pulled after eating a cake in front of cameras on June 4, the anniversary of the Tiananmen Massacre, because the cake looked a lot like a military tank. Over the next three months, a total of twenty thousand live streamers were "cleaned away" for "polluting" China's internet, per internet regulators.[22] The Party wanted feel-good clickbait, but nothing deeper. "Be a model of social morality and a builder of positive energy," the National Radio and Television Administration advised.

Zhou quickly registered new social media accounts. He tried bringing more "positive energy" to the table. He posted videos encouraging students to apply for colleges and filming charity work he kept up in villages around his hometown. Invariably, a few weeks later, his accounts would be mysteriously shut down.

After watching his videos online for months, I wanted to meet Zhou, this leader of the lazy, a Robin Hood of the social media age, but who had been punished for trying to be good. Finding him turned out to be surprisingly easy. I called ahead to his late-night barbecue restaurant, whose manager confirmed Zhou still worked there and came in a few nights a week. Excited, my producer Aowen Cao and I flew from Beijing down to Guangxi province immediately and went from the airport straight to his barbecue joint. We continued our stakeout until midnight, when, exhausted, I made an executive decision to head to the hotel, though my producer left a handwritten note for the night manager to give to Zhou. We giggled as we handed it over, feeling silly and, suddenly, a little unprepared.

We found him on our second night in Guangxi. He was holed up in his upstairs office. To our surprise, he seemed to be in the middle of entertaining about a dozen police officers. His trademark long hair and T-shirt stood out among the dark uniforms and crew cuts surrounding him. Zhou ushered us out into the hallway, looking harried. Aowen and I were both a little starstruck. He was a little thinner and sallower than the Zhou from his original 2012 viral video, but here was the spiritual leader of the slackers, in the flesh.

He was also looking much less relaxed tonight. Shutting his office door behind him, he explained to us that a group of police had surprised him with a health inspection. Additional security officers had called him earlier that morning warning him that two journalists from Beijing would try to interview him—and he was to refuse at all costs. Embarrassed he could not be a more hospitable host, he offered to treat us to dinner downstairs, where his intoxicated older brother—the spitting image of Zhou, but shorter—tried to lighten the mood with a drinking game. Soon, three pairs of men filed into the restaurant, conspicuously ordering fruit juice rather than the crates of beer the bare-chested clientele around us were throwing back. They acted more like plainclothes police, I realized. Flustered, I accidentally ordered rooster testicles for the hotpot. (So that was what "male chicken eggs" were!) We hastily left after seeing one of the men filming us with a handheld camera disguised as a phone charger. Back in Beijing, I wrote up our trip for a news piece on NPR, filed away my notes, and moved on to other stories.

Half a year later, Zhou threatened to sue me. He hired a lawyer to send a letter to NPR's Beijing office, accusing me of slandering Zhou by falsely insinuating that he was under police watch. "Since Mr. Zhou Liqi was released from prison, he has been living with a grateful and positive attitude and has worked hard to establish his upright social image. His personal freedom has not been supervised and controlled by any department, within the scope permitted by law. Inside China, he can live as freely as an ordinary citizen and run his own businesses freely," the letter read. The threat of the lawsuit took me by surprise. I had recorded a sympathetic portrayal of Zhou, and I largely empathized with his efforts to exude more positive energy. I had the feeling, however, as my trip had shown, that the idea for the lawsuit was not his but rather that of the security system that still looked after him. Soon after, I learned that I would not be allowed to re-enter China. Zhou's restaurant eventually went bankrupt and shut down. Both Zhou and I, it seemed, were not positive enough.

CHAPTER 4

THE CHAINED WOMAN

One of the most common questions I received when I arrived in China in 2015 as a twenty-two-year-old reporter was whether I had *chengjia*—gotten married and "become a family" by having children. The first few times, I spluttered a red-faced and emphatic *no*, before realizing such questions were considered within the realm of polite chitchat in Beijing. That was because reproduction and marriage remain influential in shaping how the country understands female identity and the role women should play in Chinese society.

Reproduction also remains heavily legislated. The year I moved to Beijing, policymakers announced the end of the One Child Policy, an assortment of regulations that limited married women for nearly four decades to having just one child, a cap sometimes enforced through methods like forced sterilization. After 2015, couples could have up to two children, and in 2021, the national cap was further lifted to three children. This change was less to grant couples freedom over their family planning choices and more to do with reversing a demographic decline that could see the country's population halved in the following eighty years.[1] Such a decline would mean a deficit of young workers to replace China's aging workforce and disproportionate demand for senior care and pension payouts—serious challenges to domestic development.

"General Secretary Xi Jinping attaches great importance to the population issue," read an explainer in the Communist Party's main newspaper, *People's Daily*. As far back as 2017, Xi told Party functionaries, "we must promote the linking of childbearing policies and related economic and social policies and strengthen research on population development strategies." His proclamations set in motion a complete retooling of a state apparatus once built up to eliminate excess births. Now it was tasked with encouraging more births, even though social preferences in China meant women were less willing to raise larger families. The public reckoning with this tension, created by decades of state reproductive and natalist policies, would come soon after.

The reckoning started with a TikTok video. The video is casually shot, focusing on a woman who huddles in the corner of an earthen shed, shivering in the January chill of 2022. In Beijing, it was cold enough for ski resorts to start pumping out artificial snow to coat the arid hills around the capital. Thousands of international athletes had already gathered in Beijing for the Winter Olympic Games that month. Yet the woman in the video wears nothing more than a thin pink sweater and cotton pants. Her uncut hair is matted, her face dark with grime. A metal chain is fitted around her neck, tethering her to a wall behind. A man—

her husband?—fusses over the woman. He calls her "Mom," fitting her with a jacket picked out of a pile of castoffs while she stutters incoherently. A child—her son?—enters the video frame, saying he brings his mom lunch each day. The remains of that day's meal sit untouched, congealing on the chained woman's wood plank bed.

The video blew up, and "the chained woman," as she quickly came to be known across the country, racked up 1.92 billion clicks, eclipsing public attention for the Winter Olympics. The video appeared to expose one of the tragedies of China's decades of reproductive control: the trafficking of women and girls, exacerbated by gender imbalances caused by female infanticide under the One Child Policy.

Xuzhou, a city in southern Jiangsu province, near where the video was filmed, tried to calm the public by issuing a flurry of statements. They said the woman was named Yang Qingxia, aged fifty-two, and that she suffered from schizophrenia. She was tied up because she was frequently violent. Her marriage license showed she was married to a Mr. Dong, and together they had eight children, the oldest of whom was now twenty-three years of age and the youngest child less than two years old. More digging from online sleuths revealed Mr. Dong liked making home videos, which he posted on his TikTok channel specializing in "positive energy" propaganda videos showing how state poverty alleviation programs supported his unusually large family.

Internet users pointed out that tying a person up was no way to treat someone mentally ill, and they questioned how the chained woman had given birth to eight children, given reproductive controls. Under pressure, the Xuzhou municipal government issued a perfunctory second statement two days later. Yang Qingxia had been discovered begging on the streets in 1998 by an elderly man, who decided to adopt her, then marry her to his son—Mr. Dong—two months later. The public was not convinced. "How old was she when she was married?" one person commented online. And how had she ended up homeless in the first place? Ms. Yang could not answer for herself, because after the video of her went viral, she was hospitalized for psychiatric treatment for her schizophrenia. Feminist advocates cried foul. "Trying to cover up everything by claiming the woman is insane is absurd," wrote Peng Ruiping, a well-known civil rights lawyer. The video was becoming a public relations disaster.

The chained woman and the official obfuscation around what happened to her tapped into a groundswell of uncertainty and angst among Chinese women, buffeted for decades by state policies to either have fewer or more children. Now under pressure to have larger families, they felt a profound sense of insecurity about their hard-won gains seeking fair employment, fair pay, and equal rights in society. "We cannot accept any glossing over of this incident, because every woman could easily be her," wrote one woman online.

The state's evasive answers set off a hunt both online and in the real world to find out more about the chained woman. As the public furor about her swept across the country, a handful of ordinary citizens emerged as the most effective agents for discovering new information about the chained woman. China's professional journalism circles were hollowed out by political controls, and many of the country's top investigative journalists had already left the profession. Demanding answers but stonewalled by authorities, internet users dug into the story on their own. Together, these "citizen journalists" would try to answer what hundreds of millions of video viewers in China were wondering: Who was the chained woman, and how many other women like her were there in China?

One of the searchers was a soft-spoken former magazine editor named Zhao Lanjian. Zhao had retired from journalism in 2014, and for the next five years he traveled the world and indulged in his hobby of horseback riding. However, he was feeling rudderless after returning to Beijing. While an editor, Zhao helped report and produce several stories on trafficked women, and the mystery of the chained woman reeled him in. "Her story touched a nerve in me. I knew I needed to do something," he told me.

Also searching for information were two women named Wuyi and Quanmei. They decided to go down to Xuzhou and try to visit the chained woman to show their support. They packed up their car, using lipstick to scrawl messages on their car window about the patriarchal exploitation of women. "The world has not abandoned you [Ms. Yang]. Your sisters are coming!" they posted on social media. Their mission was short-lived. They told me that hotels in Xuzhou refused to take them. Police even confiscated the reception computer at the one hotel they managed to make a reservation at, so they slept in their car. Even a bouquet of sun-flowers they tried to mail to the chained woman's hospital room was returned.

Officially, there was nothing out of the ordinary happening in Xuzhou. Chinese media outlets had received orders from the country's propaganda ministry not to publish anything about the chained woman and her whereabouts. Beyond a short, monitored interview aired by the state broadcaster, the chained woman van-ished from public view. "You have not heard of her? The entire country is paying attention to this right now," Wuyi incredulously asks Xuzhou residents in one of the video updates she shared online. "No, not at all," the residents mutter.

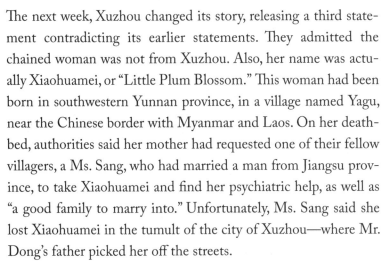

The next week, Xuzhou changed its story, releasing a third statement contradicting its earlier statements. They admitted the chained woman was not from Xuzhou. Also, her name was actually Xiaohuamei, or "Little Plum Blossom." This woman had been born in southwestern Yunnan province, in a village named Yagu, near the Chinese border with Myanmar and Laos. On her deathbed, authorities said her mother had requested one of their fellow villagers, a Ms. Sang, who had married a man from Jiangsu province, to take Xiaohuamei and find her psychiatric help, as well as "a good family to marry into." Unfortunately, Ms. Sang said she lost Xiaohuamei in the tumult of the city of Xuzhou—where Mr. Dong's father picked her off the streets.

An army of online volunteers picked this new explanation apart as well. Why had Ms. Sang never lodged a police report after losing the child entrusted to her? Was Xiaohuamei—a cute nickname that in Mandarin Chinese is better suited for a dog than a person—really the chained woman's legal name? The mention of Yagu village in Yunnan province, a land of wild, natural beauty, raised another possibility: given its long land border with several Southeast Asian countries, the province was historically a throughfare for smuggled timber, narcotics, and people. Yunnan's mountain villages had seen many of their young women disappear in the decades following the One Child Policy, kidnapped by traffickers and sold to bachelors farther inland who wanted wives.

A legion of online detectives—dubbed within China as the "human flesh search machine"—came up with yet another theory: they had uncovered a missing person report for a woman named Li Ying, whose age and looks they thought more closely matched those of the chained woman. On average, about one million people are reported missing in China every year[2]—but which one of these women was *the* chained woman? Perhaps authorities had unwittingly cracked a different case. In the absence of real answers, the chained woman was a stand-in for every family still searching for a kidnapped sister or child. Every one of them could be her.

The authorities doubled down on their current theory, however. On February 7, Xuzhou city said cadres showed photos of the chained woman and recordings of her voice to Yagu villagers, verifying she indeed was the Xiaohuamei who had gone missing years ago. A few days later, Xuzhou said it had arrested the chained woman's husband, as well as the couple who had allegedly trafficked her to Jiangsu province.

The mention of Yagu village caught the attention of a man named Tiemu. A former investigative journalist, he had found solace in early retirement brewing beer in his native Yunnan province. He was also familiar with the area around Yagu village, in the Nujiang valley. When a friend proposed they dust off their journalistic chops and find Xiaohuamei's family, Tiemu immediately agreed. "The motivation for the search for truth is the highest priority for me," he told *StoryFM*, a podcast in China. "It is in my DNA."

The chained woman—for that was how she was to be called now—had become a potent symbol of how reproductive controls had created the circumstances of her abuse. These controls stemmed from the belief that fertility could be regulated just as steel output and grain prices could be centrally planned. In the 1970s, engineers applied their algorithms for projecting missile trajectories to reproduction rates and predicted an impending population crisis.[3] Their mathematics appeared to show women would soon give birth to more children than the nascent people's republic could support. Over the next few years, policymakers devised a patchwork of provincial and national regulation, enforced by the National Population and Family Planning Commission, that gradually coalesced into the One Child Policy. Formally in effect from 1979 until its abolition in 2016, the policy restricted each married couple to having one child. Women who had given birth to two or more children were sterilized, and families who exceeded their quota could be fined, fired from their jobs, or demoted from public office.

All this has left scars on the psyche of communities that endure long after the One Child Policy ended. Some of the most vicious enforcement of birth restrictions centered in northeastern Shandong province where, in 2005, family planning officials were given strict quotas to reduce births. "Officials would kidnap you if you tried to have two children. If you were hiding and they could not find you, they would kidnap your elder relatives and make them stand in cold water, in the winter," Lu Bilun, a resident of the Shandong city of Linyi, told me. He himself paid a RMB4,000 fine to have his second son in 2006 (about US$500 at the time).

Noncompliance was punished with harsh methods. Women in Linyi bearing their second or third child could be essentially abducted for crude abortions. "The doctors would inject poison directly into the baby's skull to kill it," the activist lawyer Chen Guangcheng remembered, based on recordings he made of interviews with hundreds of women and their families in Linyi city. "Other doctors would artificially induce labor. But some babies were alive when they were born and began crying. The doctors strangled or drowned those babies."

Even after birth caps were lifted across China, wealthier women still went overseas, especially to the United States, to have their children, where there were no birth caps. Traveling around California's Orange County in the summer of 2022, I found a dense cluster of birth tourism houses within a handful of gated communities. For about $50,000, Chinese couples traveled to the U.S. on tourist visas, rented a house, hired a Chinese nanny, and finished their last trimester in the United States, where they could give birth to a new American citizen. For twice that amount, they could stay in luxurious group homes with food catered from local Chinese restaurants and Chinese-speaking medical staff on-site to assist new mothers during their first postnatal month.

One of the mothers I met who had chosen the do-it-yourself option by renting her own house was Lily, a lawyer in China who was having her second child in California. She joked that she came to the U.S. because she wanted a pain-free birth. "It is difficult to get full epidurals in China!" She laughed. She confided she also wanted to give her children American citizenship. "There are all-around advantages in the U.S.: freedom of speech, a sense of security. My child is definitely better off if they have these options," she said. Reproduction was, in some ways, an opportunity for her rather than a constraint. "Since my grandfather's generation, my family has always longed for democracy and freedom, and then this trait was passed on to my mother, who then subtly passed it on to me," she said.

Surrogacy is also popular among nonconventional parents with means. Even though birth controls have relaxed for heterosexual couples, single women and LGBTQ couples are still stymied from accessing reproductive services. China does not recognize gay marriage, yet marriage is an unofficial prerequisite for everything from obtaining fertility treatment, to adopting, to even registering a newborn for identity documents. There are no formal laws for additional birth controls on LGBTQ couples and single women, but in practice, medical institutions still deny such care. In 2018, a then-thirty-year-old, unmarried activist named Teresa Xu tried to test these controls by walking into a Beijing hospital and asking to have her ovarian eggs frozen. "The doctor dismissively asked me, 'Why not get a marriage license first?'" she told me. Xu sued them instead. The case is still pending.

However, the majority of women and their families do not have the resources to seek alternatives. In 2021, after the Three Child Policy went into effect, I paid a visit to Dongshigu village, where activist Chen Guangcheng grew up. It is now a shell of itself. Its residents were notified a few years ago that the village could be demolished entirely to make way for a dam. The stone houses are silent these days; most of the younger residents have moved to Linyi city for employment options beyond the local canning factory. Teams of black-shirted security guards no longer patrol the perimeter to keep out curious journalists and the actor Christian Bale, who unsuccessfully tried to visit Chen when he was under house arrest there.

Only one of Chen's neighbors remained when I visited one rainy afternoon. She lived just across a narrow, dirt alley from his old house. Her own battle for control over her body began in August 2008, when she realized she was pregnant with her third child. "I had already had two children but my heart just did not feel right" having an abortion, she told me. Carrying her child required going into hiding in a nearby town so family planning officials would not find her. When officials found her husband, he used a pickax to drive them off and was imprisoned for half a year. She had the child—a son, now a young teenager who diligently finished his homework next to me while I talked to his mother.

Ironically, after decades of controlling births, China's reproductive rates are now falling naturally. Having children is too expensive and too time-consuming for overworked millennials. In 2021, the year I visited the mother in Dongshigu, the national birth rate had dropped for a fifth consecutive year to a record low. The country's fertility rate of 1.16—the average number of children each woman has in her lifetime—meant it could no longer sustain current population numbers. In January 2023, state statisticians announced more people had died the previous year than were born. China was shrinking. Before I left Dongshigu, I mentioned to the mother that most of my Chinese friends did not want to have any children. "Women have it all figured out now—now they won't have more kids even when they are told to have more!" the mother chuckled joylessly. "People act in funny ways. There is no point in controlling them."

Reproductive control had another unforeseen consequence: instead of promoting gender parity, by encouraging families to devote resources to their one and only child, the One Child Policy sometimes exacerbated traditional biases for a male heir. Under the revolutionary ethos of Chairman Mao's proclamation that "women hold up half the sky," gender parity was central to the Party's socialist mission to do away with "feudal" practices, including gender discrimination and outdated customs like the footbinding of pubescent girls.

In practice, gender equality is still elusive. In the workplace, job advertisements that explicitly prefer male candidates are still common. Many companies, including the state agency from which foreign journalists like myself must contract our local staff, still ask some of their young female employees to sign letters committing to not having children for a certain period. While some women did attain high-level political positions, as of writing this book not one woman sits on the Party's twenty-five-member Politburo. Women have also never broken past a tenth of the seats on the Party's lower-ranking Central Committee.

The preference of males also meant that, when parents were limited to just one child, female babies were aborted, killed after birth, or abandoned for adoption at much higher rates. As a result, China suffers from a skewed gender ratio; there are nearly 35 million more men than women. In Feng county, where Xuzhou city is and where the chained woman was discovered, about three men were born for every two women on average. This skewed ratio incentivized the trafficking of women, because poorer, rural men who were unable to compete on the marriage market felt forced to procure brides elsewhere. They turned to brokers who trafficked women from Vietnam, North Korea, Myanmar, and among China's ethnic minorities; their lack of Mandarin-language ability made it harder for them to run away from their new owners.

Online sleuths hypothesized that the chained woman had perhaps been trafficked in just this manner, and her video sparked renewed public debate about human trafficking. China has been working on prohibiting human trafficking for years, but the practice remains endemic, in part because while trafficking itself can be punished by life in prison, people found guilty of buying a trafficked person face a maximum sentence of just three years.

The debate on trafficking unearthed a book of photos printed a few years earlier by a journalist from the southern city of Shenzhen. Publishers commissioned a second printing of his photographs as the chained woman propelled his volume back into the limelight. He had taken his pictures in a handful of villages outside the southern metropolis of Guangzhou, where the practice of buying and chaining women was still common. The women in the photographs all had been forced to bear multiple children. Afterward, some were sold again. There were chained women all over China.

Naturally, I wanted a copy of the photographs. But just as quickly as his pictures became famous, the photographer went underground. He had spearheaded the project in his off-hours from a job working at the local state paper, which was now putting pressure on him to retract his photographs.

My ace producer was able to track down a hip Beijing gallery that had recently exhibited this photographer's work, and she inquired as to whether they might still have copies of his prints lying around. They did, the gallery responded, but given the heightened sensitivity, they were not selling them anymore, and the photographer requested all remaining copies be sent back to him. My producer persuaded the gallery to let us simply view the one remaining set of prints in the gallery itself. We promised not to take pictures of the prints, nor to disclose the gallery's or photographer's name, and off we went to Beijing's 798 Art District, a former factory and warehouse complex.

The pictures we were covertly shown depicted a world of horror and torment. In many of the photos, the women are chained by their necks just as the Xuzhou woman was chained. In one photo, a naked woman cradles herself, the flesh on one of her arms deeply grooved by scars left after being slashed with a knife by one of the men who bought her. In another, children smile broadly up into the photographer's lens; behind them is the face of a chained woman imprisoned in a small cavity built behind their living room. All of these pictures had been taken just miles outside one of the largest and wealthiest cities in China.

While my producer and I were looking for the book of photographs, the search for who Xiaohuamei was continued. Police contacted a woman living in the central province of Henan whose older half sister, nicknamed Xiaohuamei, had gone missing in 1998. Officers came by her home to show her videos of the chained woman. She could barely remember what her older sister looked like, and she saw no traces of her in the lined face of the chained woman in the TikTok video. Her Xiaohuamei had chubby cheeks, and she was bubbly and kind. Before leaving, the police took a blood sample for a DNA test. Soon after, authorities announced Yang Qingxia, the woman they originally said the chained woman was, was also Xiaohuamei. There were reasons, however, to doubt the city's latest story. Tiemu, the Yunnan beer brewer and investigative reporter, had visited Yagu village in the Nujiang valley, where Xiaohuamei had been born. No one there believed she and Yang Qingxia were the same person.

He had pursued his investigation into the case of the chained woman with dogged determination even when authorities ordered people to back off the topic. Driving through the river valley, he had met an old woman washing ginger roots by the side of the road who was once Xiaohuamei's neighbor. The woman began talking excitedly when she saw the video of the chained woman, explaining that she had once lived in a hut by the village school, where Xiaohuamei used to come and play. She introduced Tiemu to another woman who, with halting Mandarin Chinese and sign language, led him up a twisting dirt road. She pointed to a pile of bricks; that was where Xiaohuamei used to live, she said. There was nothing, and no one, left. A former village Party secretary confirmed to Tiemu that Xiaohuamei's father, a steel factory worker, drowned in a river one summer afternoon soon after her birth. Her mother remarried but was widowed twice more. She became an alcoholic, eventually selling off the last of the family land and, finally, the timber beams in her own house for liquor, before dying of esophageal cancer.

From there, he found Xiaohuamei's cousin and her uncle, fifty-eight-year-old Li Yongyuan, in a village only six miles away from Yagu. Mr. Li remembered Xiaohuamei—how adorable she had been, how her family had fallen apart when she disappeared. "We don't care how she's been abused, if she is broken, if she is crippled. We want her back," Li said. He also remembered she had a half sister who was still alive. Her phone number was scrawled on the wall of his earthen hut. Tiemu called her; on the other end of the line was the woman who police had DNA tested and declared a match with Xiaohuamei's. She told him she'd never received a copy of the test results herself.

Zhao Lanjian, the retired journalist, met Mr. Li, too, and he filmed the encounter. His video shows the two of them sitting together on the floor, Mr. Li in rough khaki clothes and worn cloth shoes, smoking a cigarette. He is reviewing photos of the chained woman when three strangers burst into his house, shouting that his memory must be faulty because so many decades have passed. Rattled, Mr. Li backtracks and starts to echo them: he could not be sure this was *not* Xiaohuamei.

And so, the identity of the chained woman remains a mystery. Despite the private outpouring of grief over Xiaohuamei, public discussion for the most part was muted. Much of it was censored for the sake of keeping up "positive energy." Wuyi and Quanmei, the two women who tried to send flowers to the chained woman in vain, were detained before being sent home. Zhao Lanjian felt so threatened by repeated visits from security officials that he eventually sought asylum in the U.S., where he remains today. Tiemu has not spoken much publicly about the case.

Despite her absence, the chained woman may have helped save other women; public anger and updates published by citizen journalists like Tiemu and Zhao pushed authorities to arrest seventeen officials connected to her trafficking case in Xuzhou city. Public security officials also announced they were devoting more resources to clear a backlog of trafficked persons cases.

There are still people searching for her. By searching for her, they are also, in a way, searching for their missing loved ones. In her anonymity, the chained woman has become a poster child for the thousands of women trafficked over the decades. Several families came forward in the search for her, all believing that she might be the person they had lost years ago, and they complained bitterly when authorities decided she was a different woman. For families seeking closure, she was a tangible person to grieve, after years of trying to make sense of prolonged absence.

For women her age, some of them new parents, the chained woman was also a symbol of resistance, a call to actively live for themselves and to raise a new generation of women who would do the same. I texted Lily, the mother who decided to give birth to her daughter in California, four months after the TikTok video came out. She was nearing her due date, and she told me she had decided to call her daughter Xiaohuamei—the same name as the chained woman. She was determined her daughter would have a very different life.

CHAPTER 5

THE DETAINED

The knock at the door came in the slow, quiet evening hours. Meryem had bathed the children and put them to bed, and now, in the solitude of night, she could finally let herself feel the heartache of her husband's absence. During the day, the apartment was a whirlwind of chaos. Meryem juggled solo-parenting their two young children, and a constant stream of "relatives"—local Communist Party cadres sent to monitor the family—came by to eat meals with her. Sometimes they even slept over in her apartment, and she knew refusing them was not an option. Tonight, however, she was blessedly alone.

But here was the knocking again. Whoever was outside was insistent Meryem let them in. She checked the time; it was ten in the evening. A cold bolt of fear shot through her stomach. Few people came calling at this hour in the western region of Xinjiang. It had to be the police, and the police did not arrest people during the day. They only made arrests at night. She quickly called her husband, Abdullatif, and kept him on speakerphone. Then she took a deep breath and opened the door.

In Turkey, on the other end of the phone line, her husband, Abdullatif, was in a panic. He grasped to make sense of the sounds he was hearing over the phone: scuffling sounds, a sudden crash as something brittle hit the floor and shattered. Then the line went dead. He immediately dispatched a pair of cousins who lived near Meryem's apartment in Xinjiang's capital city of Urumqi to check on her.

The cousins arrived early the next morning to a tableau of disarray: chairs flipped over, books knocked askew. Meryem was gone—arrested. In the middle of the mess sat her and Abdullatif's son, Lotfullah, who was just four years old at the time, and daughter, Aysu, who was six years old and mute with shock. For the next few months, Meryem's cousins took care of the two children until they, too, were arrested, and the children went to live with Meryem's sister. Three months later, she was arrested, and the two children under her care disappeared. Abdullatif sat helpless in Turkey throughout the successive calamities, watching remotely as one by one his family in Xinjiang disappeared into a fast-moving detention campaign. To save them, he would have to return to Xinjiang himself.

For much of his first three decades of life, Abdullatif Kucar had done his best to get as far away from Xinjiang as possible. A tall brawny man, he immersed himself in sports from childhood, especially kickboxing. He found in the sport a sense of freedom he lacked growing up in Kuqa, a northern city in Xinjiang. Athletics were a way to escape from the tension at home, where his father and mother constantly quarreled and left him and his older brother, Abdureqip, on their own while they were growing up as young Uyghur boys.

The Communist Party has tried to placate the Uyghurs—an ethnic Turkic group who mostly live in Xinjiang—for more than seven decades, ever since the People's Liberation Army troops marched into the Xinjiang region in 1950 and declared it officially part of new China. They named it the Xinjiang Uyghur Autonomous Region, implying it was to have some sense of autonomy. The Uyghurs were among several prominent ethnic groups that hoped the Communists would grant them political autonomy under Party rule, and Uyghur nationalists even briefly realized their long-held dream of establishing their own nation in the 1940s. Their dreams did not last long; instead of granting statehood, the Communist Party annexed the Xinjiang region in 1950.

Abdullatif was born amid these dashed expectations. His grandparents were active as intellectuals and soldiers, members of stymied attempts to establish an independent Uyghur nation-state. This association politically stained subsequent generations of Kucars in the eyes of the Chinese state. Abdullatif's father coped by striving to make himself as Chinese as possible. He learned Mandarin Chinese fluently and announced to his devout Muslim in-laws that he was an atheist.

Despite these adaptations, Communist authorities still barred his father from attending university because of his family's political past. Depressed, he drank heavily. Abdullatif's mother did the opposite, burying herself in Islamic ritual and religion. Eventually, his father sued her for a divorce. A teenage Abdullatif and his brother took their mother's side, and when she announced she was moving to Turkey, the two boys went with her, soon acquiring Turkish passports. Yet Xinjiang kept pulling him back. Economic reforms in the 1980s were giving space to entrepreneurial Uyghurs to make their fortune, and the Kucar brothers decided to return to China—this time as foreign citizens—to open a series of export-import businesses in textiles and leathers.

Xinjiang was where Abdullatif first spotted Meryem. They met at the restaurant he was then operating with his brother in the capital city of Urumqi, a place where he finally felt he had found a measure of home. The brothers had started the restaurant so fellow Uyghurs from their hometown of Kuqa could gather after work and trade stories of exile and heartache in the Uyghur language Abdullatif had missed so much during his years in Turkey. These were the years when, for the first time in his life, he considered China where he belonged. Yet he never took on Chinese citizenship again, and after he and Meryem married, he constantly wheedled her to naturalize as a Turkish citizen, especially after their two youngest children—Aysu and Lotfullah—were born. She refused. China, she said, was where her family was and her home. It was one of the few things they argued about.

I first visited Xinjiang in 2016, and it captured my heart. For two weeks, in a post-college euphoria, I camped underneath the stars of a brilliant Milky Way with Kyrgyz nomads, explored frosty peaks on the backs of nimble horses in northern Xinjiang's Tianshan mountains, drank crates of beer with Mongolian herders on the grasslands, and sampled fragrant tea made of dried rosebuds.

But by the next summer, I could sense something was terribly wrong. Xinjiang contacts told me chilling stories about "the black gates" into which Uyghur men entered but did not come back out of, but they could not say much more than that. I immediately planned a reporting trip back to the region.

Traveling from Urumqi, Xinjiang's capital in the north, to the border town of Tashkurgan, in the far west of the region on the edge of Pakistan, I found a region still bubbling with ethnic resentment and fear. In July 2009, those ethnic tensions had exploded into deadly violence when a peaceful Uyghur protest in Urumqi against the killing of several Uyghur workers at a factory in southern China devolved into riots. The state said hundreds of both Han Chinese and Uyghur people died.

In the aftermath, the state arrested and disappeared hundreds of young Uyghur men they said had participated in the street violence, and the region's security and legal institutions started to formalize more aggressive controls on the Uyghurs. Xinjiang's borders effectively closed for Uyghurs. In 2016, I learned that no Uyghurs were allowed to keep their passports or apply for new ones anymore, effectively trapping them in the country. The next year, Uyghur students studying abroad in Egypt were summoned back to China; fearful of arrest, some stayed put. In an early display of China's long-arm policing, Xinjiang security agents traveled to Egypt, where they interrogated and in some cases forcibly repatriated Uyghur students back to Xinjiang.

The intensification of restrictions on Uyghur culture extended even to babies. In 2017, authorities made certain Islamic baby names off-limits, by ordering local clerks to simply refuse birth registration to newborns with monikers like "Muhammad" and "Fatima." Residents had to present government identification to buy everyday items like a kitchen knife or gas for their cars, because both could ostensibly be used as weapons. Many of these checks were only applied to Uyghurs and not ethnic Han Chinese residents.

These controls also made me feel complicit. I am ethnically Han Chinese, so I easily "passed" in this system. I felt guilty each time bored security guards let me through at the many checkpoints when fellow Uyghur travelers were stopped and hassled. "Why do we have to be checked when you can just 'swipe your face'?" a young Uyghur man named Yasinjiang complained to me, using slang for how police would make car passengers roll down their windows to look at their features, waving past Han Chinese–looking people but forcing Uyghurs out of their vehicles for extra security checks. Later that winter, while reporting in the southern, jade-trading city of Hotan, I regularly saw Uyghur men pulled out of their cars and strip searched at checkpoints, steam rising from their skin as they were forced to stand in their underwear in the cold.

Around this time, I met a bright young Han Chinese graduate student whom I will call Sasha doing her fieldwork in Urumqi, the capital city of Xinjiang. We became fast friends. We were about the same age, and both had family roots in southern China. We were also both fascinated by the rich cultural legacy Uyghur Sufis had left across the Xinjiang region in the form of pilgrimage routes and ancient shrines that dotted empty expanses of the Taklamakan desert. Unlike most of the Han Chinese majority in Urumqi, Sasha was very aware of the discrimination against Uyghurs and was appalled by it. She took great pains to learn Uyghur, and I watched with admiration as she fluently switched between English, Mandarin, and Uyghur when meeting friends and ordering coffee in the city's hip cafes.

Sasha was distracted from her research, however. Everywhere around her, people were buzzing about "going to study." It was

2017, and the detention campaign was so new, people had not yet learned that they should not openly discuss the security clampdown. In taxicabs, outside halal restaurants, and among the informal money-changing markets across Urumqi, I met Uyghurs who openly mused about the nature of the new "schools," as they were called in the official parlance—many of them hastily set up in repurposed office buildings or elementary schools—where young Uyghur men were sent. One of Sasha's classmates at Xinjiang University had been briefly detained to be bundled off to a "school" because police found Islamic scriptural texts on his mobile phone. His research advisor had to be summoned to the police station late at night to hurriedly explain the student was not a religious extremist but was in possession of the texts for his studies. Other Uyghur students returning home from their spring semesters found parents and relatives missing, sent to mandatory "re-education" classes.

The same returning students would also have noticed the new police stations being built on every city block, a technique called "grid policing," borrowed policies first tested in the Tibet region and imported to Xinjiang by its new Party secretary, an ideological hardliner named Chen Quanguo. The idea was to divide up larger neighborhoods into smaller, more manageable squares within which informants and security officers could keep an eye on the population at all times. Grid policing demanded mass participation, so during weekdays, a klaxon alarm would sound across entire neighborhoods, and I watched as civilians rushed out of their offices and shops for their noon drills, halfheartedly waving state-issued truncheons and riot shields as part of "anti-terrorism" exercises. In more remote towns and villages, Uyghurs and ethnic Kazakhs told me they were summoned each morning to Chinese flag-raising ceremonies to show their fealty.

This securitization of Xinjiang cost the region a fortune. A good deal of the costs was passed on to ordinary residents. One local Han Chinese store owner complained to me that he had to shell out $12,000 of his own funds to buy the X-ray baggage scanner and metal detector now required of all businesses his size. Some of the cost was also passed on to taxpayers and debt-laden municipalities; between 2012 and 2017, as officials engineered the groundwork for the coming clampdown, Xinjiang's public security budget grew by a factor of six, twice the region's spending on healthcare.

This security spending really ramped up in the wake of two deadly terror attacks, both in 2014. In March of that year, militants mounted a horrific attack, stabbing to death thirty-one people in a bustling train station in southwest China. Weeks later, Xi Jinping spent four days in Xinjiang; on the last day of his trip, suicide bombers set themselves off in Urumqi, injuring eighty people. Within weeks, Xi ordered the construction of the surveillance state and mass detention camp network in Xinjiang that would ensnare hundreds of thousands of people. "We must be as harsh as them and show absolutely no mercy," Xi said in a series of internal speeches. The root of the unrest among Uyghurs, Xi declared, was not systemic racism or decades of economic discrimination. Rather, the common denominator was Islam, exposure to which is "like taking a drug, and you lose your sense, go crazy, and will do anything," he wrote. The detention camps were designed "to eradicate from the mind thoughts about religious extremism and violent terrorism, and to cure ideological diseases," according to the region's Communist Youth League.

Xi himself laid out the detention campaign's designs against Uyghur identity in a work report after the attacks. "We need to use the socialist core value system to lead the construction of a shared cultural and spiritual home for all ethnic groups in Xinjiang and constantly strengthen the identification of all ethnic groups with the great motherland, with the Chinese nation, with Chinese culture, and to the socialist pathway with Chinese characteristics," he told Party officials. "One cannot bite the hand that feeds you mutton and still insult the Chinese Communist Party and the Han Chinese." Local ethnic policy officials were even more direct in their intentions to assimilate Uyghur people in line with Party dogma. "Break their lineage, break their roots, break their connections, and break their origins," wrote Maisumujiang Maimuer, a Chinese religious affairs official in 2017. "Completely shovel up the roots of 'two-faced people,' dig them out, and vow to fight them until the end."

After the 2014 attacks, authorities in Urumqi started implementing a residence registration program centering around something called "people's convenience cards," or *bianminka* in Mandarin Chinese. All Uyghurs who did not have household registration or *hukou* tied to an urban area had to return to the countryside and obtain a *bianminka* to return to and live in Urumqi. In practice, only a minority of Uyghurs were able to obtain this card. (The scholar Darren Byler, who did fieldwork in Xinjiang on this topic, estimates the success rate was as low as one in ten applicants.) By the time I started reporting on Xinjiang, the *bianminka* system had become even stricter, requiring even card-carrying Uyghur residents to obtain official permission to travel outside their rural home counties and to cross the security checks between towns.

Wandering around Urumqi in 2018, I found entire rows of houses in historically Uyghur neighborhoods in Urumqi abandoned, their doors taped over with white strips of paper declaring the date of when their inhabitants had been banished from the city. Those who were forced to leave were then ghettoized into southern Xinjiang cities. Later, large parts of emptied Uyghur neighborhoods in the north, such as the Hejiashan area in Urumqi, were demolished to make way for new real estate development. The terracotta-hued mosques that once dotted street corners in these Uyghur neighborhoods were torn down or used for storage. Authorities, however, were sensitive to accusations that they were destroying Islamic heritage and that spared some of Xinjiang's most distinguished religious sites from disappearing entirely. When I visited the central mosque in the southern city of Kargilik, or Yecheng as it is called in Mandarin, I found authorities had miniaturized it, razing the original and constructing a Disneyfied version about one-tenth the mosque's former size.

Even though they were shut out of the most high-ranking civil servant postings and state firm positions, Uyghurs could find stable and well-paying employment among the rapidly expanding security apparatus. Uyghurs were being enlisted to police other Uyghurs. Regional job boards I monitored shared jobs as security guards and police officers, offering starting salaries that were sometimes twice what local businesses were offering. "I knew in my heart that the government's policy was wrong," a former Uyghur policeman told me. He worked until 2019 in a police department in Korla, in Xinjiang's center, justifying the job as one he had to do to feed his family. He told himself he could work within the system to help his fellow Uyghurs: "If I don't work, someone else will take my place. If someone worse than me or less educated than me were hired, they might enforce police work more harshly, leading to further oppression of Uyghur people."

English-fluent Uyghurs were in demand to monitor the rising

numbers of visiting foreign journalists. During my first few reporting trips to Kashgar, a Uyghur city in the south, I was twice met at my hotel by two men who went by the names Mike and Max. Mike was a hip young police officer with bright eyes, slick hair, and a penchant for streetwear. Despite having never studied abroad, he spoke fluent American-accented English, which he told me he'd learned from watching movies. Max was a middle-aged, dour man who'd learned his English while studying English literature at Xinjiang University. When the region launched a campaign against "two-faced" officials—people who acted in support of state policies but secretly harbored anti-Party ideas—Max disappeared. On subsequent reporting trips, only Mike came out to check up on me. He wore a navy police outfit now. The streetwear was gone.

In their effort to re-engineer the human soul, Chinese authorities were reconfiguring the very landscape of Xinjiang. Though much of the detention campaign in its initial phases in 2016 and 2017 was off-limits to journalists, satellites orbiting overhead captured the frenzy of construction in the region's mountains and deserts, as a network of hundreds of austere buildings and fences went up. These were the black gates I had heard about. The Australian Strategic Policy Institute, an Australian military-linked think tank, has discovered at least 380 detention camps, capable of locking up to one million Muslims.

At first, many Uyghurs were sent to low-level, minimum-security detention camps, often in schools or office buildings requisitioned into temporary detention facilities. As the campaign picked up momentum, regional authorities invested in hundreds of purpose-built detention facilities and expanded existing prisons to hold growing numbers of inmates. Some satellite images of these detention camps were clear enough to make out the shadow of concrete guard towers and rows of barbed wire ringing them. Throughout these changes, the Kucar family remained in Xinjiang. Abdullatif was effectively banned from crossing in and out of China; he had been intensely questioned by immigration police after his last trip from Turkey. In 2016, the family's passports, including Abdullatif's Turkish passport, were all confiscated. Unlike his wife, Abdullatif did not have a Chinese ID card, and his lack of formal identification soon became a huge problem, because identification was required everywhere. "If you wanted to go outside, you had to pass through a security check. And without an ID card, you couldn't even go into your own home. We were a bit lucky because we had a special letter from the local government. Sometimes you had to explain what the letter was to officials or wait two or three hours to get through security checks since it was not an official ID card. Sometimes we got angry, and sometimes we could only laugh at our situation," he told me later.

Unable to leave China, Abdullatif decided to take his family on a road trip back to Korla, a central Xinjiang city famed for its pears and the rich oil fields in the Tarim basin nearby. On the drive through the hazy desert separating Urumqi and this energy boomtown, Abdullatif glimpsed something that shocked him: rows of dozens of military tanks driving past them. The Kucar family watched them rumble by in silence; no one dared ask what the tanks were for.

Soon after that trip, Abdullatif was given his Turkish passport back but deported from China and told never to return. He bid a tearful goodbye to Meryem and their two children, who still had not gotten their Turkish passports back yet, consoling them that he would get them out of China soon. It was the last time he saw Meryem before her arrest.

Leaving his family behind forced Abdullatif to acknowledge the Party system that had created the camps. It was something he and his older brother Abdureqip had been trying to ignore, especially as their leather and textile businesses flourished, enriching them despite the political controls on Uyghurs. For decades, the brothers believed their wealth and their foreign passports set them apart from other Uyghurs. Now, they could pretend no longer. "The oppression of Uyghurs was going on for many years, but the Chinese authorities did not target everyone in one day. Maybe I was too young or ignorant, but at the time I did not notice," Abdureqip told me later, from Turkey.

In reality, their ethnic identity alone implicated them as troublemakers, or worse, as terrorists, in China. "In real life, people who have been captured by religious extremism, regardless of age or gender, have their consciences destroyed, lose their humanity, and murder without blinking an eye!" Xi Jinping claimed, in a speech to Xinjiang officials in 2014. He admitted there would be a long and "painful" period in which such people would have to be forcibly indoctrinated. "Re-education" through mass detention was justified to break people down and build them back up as good, Communist citizens: "There must be effective educational remolding and transformation of criminals . . . And even after these people are released, their education and transformation must continue."

The Xinjiang issue was, to Xi, an existential one. "Without this premise, to talk of other tasks will be futile," he told officials in a series of speeches leaked to the *New York Times*. The speeches laid out the rationale behind the detention campaign in broad sweeps. Xi was explicit that many people had to be detained or arrested for such a "transformation" to take hold. He envisioned extremism working like a virus; the solution was indiscriminate inoculation against what he termed "cross-infection" of innocent bystanders. "Inoculation" was a brutal, dehumanizing experience. Former detainees described living in squalid, crowded detention camps where they were subject to hours of mind-numbing Mandarin language classes, punctuated by physical punishment and deprivation. The officials at these camps were frequently Uyghur themselves but seemed to approach their work with an evangelical zeal. "People here have been infected by extremist thoughts," one camp official told my NPR colleague Rob Schmitz during a rare visit to a detention camp. "They broke the relevant laws, but their crimes are so minor that they are exempted from criminal punishment. The government wants to save and educate them, converting them here at this center."

Among the first to be arrested in this crackdown against the Uyghurs were some of the very people who had loyally served the state by promoting Uyghur language and culture until such behavior suddenly became associated with extremism. In 2016, Xinjiang officials claimed to have uncovered a cabal of education officials who had allegedly conspired to radicalize Uyghur youth by inserting seditious stories into children's textbooks. One of them, a celebrated historian and editor named Yalqun Rozi, had been invited by authorities fifteen years earlier to draft the new textbooks because of his expertise in Uyghur folklore and identity. Now, authorities said his tales "undermined national identity." It was an about-face that demonstrated how one's fate in Xinjiang was tied up with the whims of state policy. In 2021, Sattar Sawut and Shirzat Bawudun, two Uyghurs who once headed the region's education ministry that greenlighted the textbooks, were sentenced to death. Five other editors were given long jail terms; Rozi was sentenced to fifteen years in prison.

Public intellectuals, as well as doctors, language teachers, computer scientists, and poets were among the first to be sent to prison, according to a list compiled by Abduweli Ayup, a writer and language-rights activist now based in Norway.[1] He knew from personal experience that the Chinese Communist Party feared not just Islam, but also the very essence of Uyghur identity—their language and distinct Turkic culture. When Ayup tried to set up mother-tongue kindergartens around Urumqi, authorities sentenced him to eighteen months in prison.

Later, as detentions and imprisonments ballooned to encompass the entire Uyghur homeland, enough people were being arrested that their children were effectively orphaned. A 2018 state-compiled list from Xinjiang's Karakax (also called Moyu in Mandarin) county lists the names and identification numbers of more than seventeen hundred Uyghur children receiving welfare payments because both parents were in detention or prison. "No ability to work, mother detained under Strike Hard Campaign, father being trained [in a re-education camp]," county officials wrote next to the entry for an eight-year-old girl. The girl received 151 yuan (US$24) a month as a subsidy.

In 2018, I was on a reporting trip to Kashgar, the famed Silk Road city whose rammed-earth buildings once captivated Russian spies and British explorers. I wandered down a residential street in the old town, where the last old buildings had yet to be torn down, and I was struggling to find people to talk to: nearly all the adults were in some form of "re-education" or in detention. A housewife spotted me and pulled me into her house. She pointed to a house a few doors down from her, padlocked from the outside. The family who lived there are gone, she told me, the father was detained in February and the mother, too, three months later for allegedly forwarding extremist Islamist content from their smartphones. That meant the couple's two youngest children, then seven and nine years old, had to be sent to a state welfare center. "The grandfather even wept, but the authorities would not let him keep his grandchildren," she remembered. She sounded defeated. What could the family have done? Her own husband had been sent to a re-education camp, she told me, but at least it was close enough to home that she could visit him once a month. She accepted her fate. It was a way to survive when she had no choices left.

Stories like these pushed me to continue digging for confirmation of what had been rumored for months: that at these state welfare centers Uyghur children were being forced to abandon their mother tongue. Sitting in his apartment in Istanbul, Abdullatif had heard the same rumors that Uyghur children could be sent to state boarding schools and forced to learn Mandarin Chinese. He feared he would lose his family twice: once, to the detention camps, and a second time, if his children forgot their mother tongue, were taught to speak the language of their oppressors, and became people he no longer recognized.

Abdullatif called every Turkish minister and parliamentarian he could think of, begging them for help with his case. His elderly mother helped, too. She had fled China forty years ago to give her two sons a chance to live their lives as devout Uyghur men. Now she petitioned outside the China embassy in Ankara every day, holding a sign aloft demanding the freedom of her grandchildren. In talks with Beijing, Turkish officials seized on one detail that set the Kucar children apart from the thousands of other Uyghur children wrenched away from their parents and relatives: the children were not Chinese citizens, but rather Turkish nationals.

Their strategy worked. Dozens of ethnic Uyghur and Kazakh family members outside China were petitioning for news of their disappeared children, but to this day, Abdullatif is one of the few people to receive an answer. After months of negotiation between Turkish diplomats in Beijing and Xinjiang authorities, he received a call from the Turkish foreign ministry. He could get his children back, they told him, but to do that, he needed to travel back to China himself, one last time.

Abdullatif gazed out the plane porthole at the snowy tips of the Tianshan mountain range passing underneath. The Turkish passport tucked into his pants pocket contained a new Chinese visa giving him up to 180 days in the country to find his children and bring them back to Turkey—if authorities let him leave the country at all. He steeled himself for the November cold as the airplane bumped down in the Xinjiang winter wind. He knew it was another thirty-minute ride in a drafty taxi to get from the airport to his and Meryem's long-empty Urumqi apartment, which he wanted to check to make sure the pipes had not frozen over.

To his surprise, a squad of police officers were waiting for him at the airport gate. They hustled him along, packing him and his baggage into a waiting car too quickly for him to talk to any of the other travelers, who studiously avoided looking at him and his security coterie. The police brought him to a hotel in downtown Urumqi where Abdullatif and his escorts seemed to be the only guests. The police reserved three adjacent rooms, with Abdullatif staying in the room sandwiched between the officers. Doors had to be kept open at all times. Whenever he went out for a walk, six of the officers would follow him in two separate patrol cars. Abdullatif silently seethed. He heard them everywhere he went, their boots crunching on the thin layer of dirty ice behind him. On his second day back, he spotted a friend walking toward him on the street, but when he recognized Abdullatif, he put his head down and crossed the street.

Abdullatif spent the first ten days frustrated. Police brought him to the community office each morning, where they spent hours running through the same questions: What did he do for money? Why was he living in Turkey? Who were his family members? He dutifully repeated the same answers he had given them the day before, but his own questions went unanswered. Where were his children? He feared he had been tricked into returning to China. If he were imprisoned, he thought, he at least might be able to see Meryem.

On the eleventh day, Abdullatif noticed a change. The usual female official asking him the same questions was not there. In fact, nothing seemed to be on the schedule. Even the police officers seemed to be waiting for something. Mid-morning, he heard a car pull into the parking lot outside. With a lurching shock, he glimpsed Aysu and Lotfullah's faces pressed up in excitement to the car windows. Then they were tumbling out of the vehicle and running—"like a bullet from a gun," he remembered—into his arms, taller than he remembered them, their baby fat gone. They were babbling excitedly and pulling at his face and clothes, but the sounds coming out of their mouths were unintelligible to him. He realized after a few seconds that they were speaking Mandarin Chinese.

Abdullatif tried to get them to speak Uyghur to him, but they seemed to have forgotten the language entirely. He could barely

hear their chattering now; blood was pounding in his ears, and
his breath grew tight as his vision narrowed to a black pinprick.
When he came to, he was lying on his back in the snow, as a
state-assigned photographer snapped away at their reunion, taking pictures.

The authorities told Abdullatif he could fly out before the end of
the year with his Turkish children, but Meryem was in a bit of a
special situation. After her arrest the year before, she had been
formally charged and then found guilty of separatism, and she was
now serving out her twenty-year sentence in a women's prison in
Kuqa. At the insistence of Turkish diplomats, Xinjiang officials
would bring her to a nearby hospital and permit a brief family
visit there. Tickets and accommodation for Abdullatif and the
children had already been booked. Once again, he found himself
in a near-empty hotel in Kuqa, guarded by a garrison of unsmiling
police officers. They searched his luggage at every stop—for what,
he could only guess. Any questions he had were met with a terse
order to shut up. The Kucar family was ushered into the hospital
and thoroughly searched: their pockets had to be emptied, their
shoes inspected, even Abdureqip's hair patted down, lest they
smuggle Meryem any scraps of information or a weapon. Abdullatif didn't know how he would react after so long apart. The reality of her prison sentence had not sunk in; he couldn't imagine
leaving the hospital without her.

The Kucars were given clear instructions: no hugging Meryem,
and no crying. They were forbidden to take pictures or exceed the
thirty minutes allotted for the visit. All these rules were promptly
disobeyed when Aysu and Lotfullah saw their mother. With a

shout, they beelined toward her. Meryem's eyes welled, but she remained lying on a hospital bed because, as Abdullatif soon realized, she did not have the strength to stand on her own. He grabbed her withered hand. He could see the chafing left by handcuffs on her wrists. "God help us," he begged. Meryem gently took her husband's hand and told him not to mention God ever again in front of her.

On impulse, he wrapped her up in a big bear hug. She had lost so much weight, he managed to lift her clear out of the bed when he stood up. The long-forgotten hospital staff were shouting at him to stop touching Meryem, but he ignored them all for a few precious seconds more. Seeing the physical state his wife was in, he knew her predicament was serious, and it would be a long time before he could see her again. Sensing his distress, Aysu and Lotfullah grabbed both his hands as he let go of their mother. "I looked at them, and I thought, I have to raise these two children for Meryem. I have to live for the children," he later recounted to me. Abdullatif hardened his heart and walked out of the room, leaving his wife behind.

Meryem had been sentenced for separatism on the flimsiest of evidence: a picture she had snapped with Turkish president Recep Erdoğan nearly a decade before, during a state visit to China. There are about fifty thousand ethnic Uyghurs living in Turkey, and to the Xinjiang government, the picture was photographic evidence Meryem had links to diaspora dissident groups—guilty by association.

She was not the only Uyghur to be given a long prison sentence. In 2018, the United Nations Committee on the Elimination

of Racial Discrimination as well as Adrian Zenz, a German re-
searcher, estimated up to over one million Uyghurs had been detained at some point in "re-education" centers and higher-security
facilities. Some of those detained were eventually released after
authorities deemed them satisfactorily remolded into pliant Chinese citizens. Others were reassigned to factories and workshops
often next to or within detention facilities themselves, sewing fast
fashion garments or packaging agricultural products, becoming a
cheap source of forced labor intended to recharge the region's ail-
ing economy.

Xinjiang authorities also kicked the detention campaign into
its next, more permanent phase. They doled out lengthy prison
sentences to the most religious, the elderly, and the most politically intractable detainees, moving them into expanding prisons
and clearing out, or even closing down, the detention centers. The
persecuted were usually sentenced in trials that lasted no longer
than a few minutes in makeshift courtrooms located within Xinjiang detention camps. "They did tell me I could hire a lawyer, but
based on cases of other people in the detention camp, those who
hired lawyers were given longer sentences because it was seen as a
sign of opposition to the state," says Ergali Ermekuly, a Chinese-
born ethnic Kazakh; he had been handed a three-year sentence in
2018 in a camp in Xinjiang's Huocheng county for allegedly sav-
ing pictures on his phone of a mosque being torn down. Like most
prisoners, he never saw the evidence presented against him and
was never allowed to read the court verdict.

Casual behavior that appeared too culturally Uyghur or too
religious was enough for a court to convict. In one leaked verdict,
a Uyghur construction worker building a new highway warned his
colleague not to use impolite language or watch pornography, or

risk becoming an "infidel." He was sentenced to a decade in prison for religious extremism. Ismail Sidiq, described as a middle-aged, illiterate Uyghur farmer, was sentenced to ten years in prison for "inciting ethnic hatred" after other inmates discovered him secretly praying in detention. "Are you Uyghurs? Do Uyghurs enjoy reporting other Uyghurs?" his leaked court verdict says he shouted at his fellow prisoners—proof, prosecutors claimed, that he placed his Uyghur identity over his Chinese identity.

I also finally heard about my friend Sasha. She had gone missing shortly after sending me a cryptic email in 2018. She had been detained that summer, though as an ethnically Han Chinese person, she was treated well, given sufficient food, and allowed some reading material, including the written works of Xi Jinping. In December, she was officially tried on charges of separatism by a Uyghur-language court in Urumqi. The evidence mustered against her by state prosecutors included her meetings with me, a foreign journalist. She was swiftly found guilty and given a fifteen-year prison sentence. Sasha had the tenacity to appeal, though she lost. I spent years trying to find out more about her imprisonment conditions. The politically well-connected friends I approached in China for help would not touch her case. Xinjiang's public security bureau operated in a league of its own, they told me. Sasha was twenty-three when she was arrested; she will be thirty-eight years old when her prison sentence ends.

Even the ones that do get away will bear their scars forever, thought Abdullatif. Back in Turkey, he sat by his children's bedsides every night for the first four months, watching them writhe in their sleep, twisting the sheets around their thin limbs as they shouted at imaginary tormentors. Lotfullah, by now eight years old, cried for hours and was easily startled by sudden sounds. When Abdullatif had picked up Aysu, his now-ten-year-old daughter, from Xinjiang, her head was shaved, and her shorn scalp remained patchy for months. He had taken the children to the doctor the first week to check for any signs of sexual or physical abuse. Other than malnutrition, the doctor said the pair had no visible injuries. The trauma, Abdullatif would find, ran deeper and was harder to treat.

Despite their language barrier, Abdullatif began to piece together what his children had gone through in the year they had been separated. At first, they communicated through an improvised pidgin; the few Mandarin phrases Abdullatif had learned from his years of doing business mixed with sign language. His two children sang Chinese songs to themselves when the quiet grew too oppressive. "My two children spoke Chinese as well as birds sing," Abdullatif remembered with a grimace.

He learned that Aysu and Lotfullah had become wards of the state after Meryem's detention and the arrests of their relatives, then sent to two different state schools organized by gender. Though run separately, both schools functioned much the same. Each day began with roll call, the children roused from sleep in their bunk beds. Teachers passed by for a mandatory bed inspection before the children could line up for breakfast, usually a corn or rice porridge. The food was nutritious, but Aysu did not get enough of it. Each dormitory was overseen by an older "sister" or "brother": an older Uyghur student tasked with keeping the other children in line. They also had first dibs on the best food at each meal. Eventually, Aysu simply stopped eating. She lost her appetite for the bland rice and soup the children were fed, and she missed the lamb and noodles she was used to at home. After breakfast came a Chinese flag-raising ceremony, for which the children were taught to chant Chinese political slogans and sing patriotic songs about "Grandfather" Xi Jinping and "Father" Wang Junzheng—the former security chief of Xinjiang, who has been sanctioned by numerous governments, including the U.S. government, for human rights abuses.

Above all, the emphasis at both schools was on teaching Mandarin Chinese and ensuring it replaced Uyghur as the children's main language. Chinese class was held six days a week. When the young children's attention wavered or they slipped and spoke a word in the Uyghur language, the teachers hit them with rulers. At first, Aysu and Lotfullah were resistant. They clammed up when teachers called on them and tried to talk to other students in Uyghur, but they quickly realized the other children could not be trusted. The older "brothers" and "sisters" reported anyone who spoke in Uyghur. Getting caught meant more corporal punishment. A common method was to force the kids into a "moto" position, where they bent their knees and held their arms out in front of them for up to an hour at a time. For Lotfullah, the worst punishment was being locked in the school's basement, which his dormitory monitors told the impressionable six-year-old was haunted by malevolent ghosts. Months after returning to Turkey, he was still terrified of the dark. Aysu said she spent much of her waking time alone or watching Chinese television, too scared to speak to other children. "I would just stare at the ceiling in a daze if I could not sleep," she remembered.

Even after leaving Xinjiang, the children remained distrustful and timid. Aysu enrolled in art therapy, where she drew dark scribbles of gore and demons. Loftullah was paralyzed in institutional settings. At school, Lotfullah's Turkish teacher noticed the young boy wet himself nearly every day, because he was too shy to ask to go to the bathroom. He barely spoke during his first semester. After-school tutoring in Turkish and Uyghur helped, but then he began asking adults for permission to leave and enter every room. Abdullatif learned to always keep the lights on at home, because darkness reminded Lotfullah of the basement where the ghosts had haunted him.

Abdullatif doted on his children. When I last saw the family in the fall of 2023, Abdullatif had just had major abdominal surgery to treat a serious case of cancer. He was losing hope he would see Meryem again in this lifetime. During long afternoons convalescing on the couch, he imagined what he would say to her if they had one more chance. "There is too much to say," he told me. Instead, he had placed his hopes on his children's happiness.

They often played chess together. Lotfullah was growing into a quiet, measured boy who, by thinking through the game's strategy, was able to calm himself down. Father and son could spend hours at a time like this: Lotfullah curled up on the floor next to the chessboard, Abdullatif's sharp eyebrows stuck in a permanent furrow, his hair whitened by grief, and his mouth pursed in concentration. On the board, the pieces moved according to clear rules, reassuring in moments of stress. The game took their minds off Meryem, still in her women's prison, serving out a two-decade sentence in Xinjiang, Abdullatif's birthplace, once his home and now his nightmare.

CHAPTER 6

THE BELIEVER

When Yusuf saw the big green sedan chair parked outside his family home, he knew his grandfather Laoye had finally died.

Inside the house, relatives were already washing the body. Later, it would be shrouded with long strips of white cotton, as Islamic tradition required. A lacquered sedan chair waited outside to carry the body first to the mosque and later, to the Muslim cemetery. Arabic scriptures engraved on the panels plating each side of the elaborate chair wished the recently departed a smooth trip to the afterlife.

Yusuf's father led a string of white-capped mourners behind the sedan as it was carried slowly and steadily to the Shanyitang mosque, the family's historical place of worship in China's central Shaanxi province. As a child, Yusuf had loved hiding in the mosque's cool basement during the summer and scampering on top of the mosque's tiled roofs in the autumn—but quietly. There was sure to be trouble if he disturbed the Communist Party *danwei*, the work unit that had been assigned to strip the mosque and use the place of worship as government office space—a bureaucratic decision that, though undignified, had at least saved the hundred-year-old building from being demolished after the Communist Party took control of China in 1949.

By the time Yusuf's grandfather died in 1993, the mosque had only been returned to its original religious purpose for about a decade. Political constraints over religion have remained ever since the Communist Party won control of China, but these controls ebbed and flowed over the decades. The mosque's reopening in the early 1990s was a sign of the most recent ebb: China was temporarily throwing off the atheistic, ideological restraints that had defined life under Chairman Mao Zedong and the terrible political purges of the Cultural Revolution in the 1960s. Yusuf's neighbors in the city of Kaifeng, once a major Silk Road trading depot, breathed a sigh of relief as economic and political reforms allowed private business to flourish once more. Buildings that were once Christian churches, Buddhist temples, and Muslim mosques were returned to their original congregations. The problem was, by the 1990s, few people still remembered what it meant to be a believer. Laoye, as Yusuf called his grandfather, was the only person he knew who still could do the five daily prayers of Islam.

And now the family was burying Laoye. Yusuf had never encountered death so immediately before in his previous nineteen years of life. That night after the funeral, when he closed his eyes, the white shroud against the blackness of the coffin kept flickering across his eyelids. Mourners had sealed the shrouded body inside the dirt tomb with clay bricks. The finality of that ritual terrified Yusuf. He could not stop imagining what it would be like for his own body to slowly rot, alone, in the confines of a dark tomb. He had been taught in public school that life ended at death, but the thought made his own life and that of Laoye's seem meaningless.

Sensing the young man's grief, Yusuf's uncle urged him to come back to the Shanyitang mosque the next morning after the funeral. As dawn rose over Kaifeng, Yusuf heard the call to prayer, a melodious chanting from the imam inside. He was suddenly overcome with a feeling of awe. He dropped to his knees in the prayer hall. *Oh God! Can you hear me? This is me praying to you. I salute you. I bow to you,* he would later write about that moment.

Four days later, Yusuf decided to embrace Islam.

His religious epiphany came at an opportune moment. China was reforming politically and economically, creating more room for religious activity. Such abject interest in Islam would have been impossible for Yusuf's parents, the generation before him. Soon after they established their new republic from Beijing in October 1949, the Chinese Communist Party began policing anything they deemed feudal or imperialist, as well as organizations—such as religious institutions—influential enough to challenge Party rule. Mosques, churches, and temples were shuttered or left to rot. Some mosques, like Laoye's, were turned into office space or factories.

During the Cultural Revolution in the late 1960s, teenage Red Guards goaded on by Mao went after the politically wayward. Religious communities, already battered by previous political campaigns, were targeted once again. Their religious leaders were publicly humiliated or beaten by Communist cadres. The unluckiest ones were shipped to labor camps. This was the period in which Yusuf's parents came of age. For Muslims like them, the decade of the Cultural Revolution was so traumatic they refused to teach their children anything about religion, even in the decades afterward. Yusuf's father was an atheist, and although he vociferously opposed Yusuf's religious devotion, he himself never gave in to eating pork.

In 1976, just two years after Yusuf was born, the Communist leader Mao Zedong died. However, the cult of personality that Mao created around himself persisted throughout Yusuf's childhood. The same year Mao died, Yusuf and his family moved to Zhengzhou, the capital of Henan province in central China. He and his mother spent their first night in the new city in a memorial hall set up to mourn Mao, next to a large portrait of the dead leader and accompanied by Mao's spirit, his mother claimed. For years after Mao's death, his parents continued to wear Mao badges pinned to their plain gray and blue shirts, and they considered Beijing, the capital of the new republic, to be their Mecca. Once, while taking a car back to Kaifeng, Yusuf's father grabbed the back of his son's neck and turned his face in the direction of the Communist capital, more than four hundred miles to the east. The Party was the savior of China, his father taught him, and Beijing its sacred city.

His father had only been to Beijing once, as a Red Guard, one of millions of teenage cadres mobilized in their devotion to Chairman Mao to attack their teachers, their parents, and finally each other, sometimes fatally. As an adult, his father was tyrannical at home, prone to mood swings, and easily instigated into beating his children. He wholeheartedly embraced the Communist revolution and shucked off religion. During Yusuf's childhood, his teachers sometimes surreptitiously mentioned Allah in folk stories they told the children. Their descriptions of Allah reminded Yusuf of his father; like his father, Allah was wise, but he could be fickle and mean.

Kaifeng, the Silk Road depot where Yusuf grew up, is one of the cities in which Muslims have historically made their home in China. But Yusuf's early childhood bore few traces of the historic Hui Islamic community into which he had been born. During his first few years in school, every lesson usually began with a slogan like "Long live the Communist Party," or "Chairman Mao will always live in our hearts." Yusuf memorized the political dogma, and he sincerely believed China was on its way to achieving the Four Modernizations, a socialist theory that China could make rapid gains in science and technology championed by the Communist leader Deng Xiaoping, who assumed de facto power after Mao's death.

However, outside of Kaifeng, Yusuf stood out from the rest of the Chinese population, despite his socialist credentials, because his Chinese national identity card categorized him as "Hui," an officially recognized ethnic minority. Yusuf wasn't actually quite sure how being Hui made him different from China's ethnic majority, the Han. Most Hui are visually indistinguishable from Han Chinese, and they usually speak Mandarin Chinese as their first language. The Hui are known chiefly for being adherents of Islam, but Yusuf did not explicitly identify with being Muslim as a child, especially given his parents' political beliefs. All he knew was he was forbidden from eating pork. Much of Chinese cuisine revolves around pork, but he and his Hui relatives found the idea of consuming the flesh of a pig sacrilegious. He even held his breath whenever he saw the creatures, so as not to breathe in their imagined contaminants. A few non-Hui children went to his elementary school, and Yusuf liked to gang up on them after school, shouting insults at them because they ate pork and occasionally hitting them until they cried.

Toward the end of his life, his Laoye, his grandfather, had dusted off his bicycle one day and headed toward Shanyitang mosque for morning prayers. It became a daily ritual, one he kept up until he died. After his death, Yusuf began going to the mosque each day as well. There, he soon met Yuhe, a precocious Muslim scholar. It was a productive friendship; Yuhe would later become Yusuf's primary book publisher. They instinctively understood each other. Yuhe came from a long line of Islamic scholars, and he embraced the same vocation for himself, though he had the bad fortune of being born right in the middle of the Cultural Revolution. His father, a local imam in the arid province of Gansu, had died from poor health sustained after years of daily beatings and public criticism sessions. Yuhe was just four years old. Much of his early childhood was marred by sudden visits from local Communist officials, who would search Muslim homes one by one. Before his death, his father dug a hole under the family's earthen stove and buried their most valuable prayer books inside to protect them. The books that Communist cadres did manage to find were burned or defaced with black ink. The penalty for possessing other religious items was heavier. Being found with a prayer mat or the Qur'an meant a brief detention. Some families owned multiple copies of the Qur'an, and in a panic, they tried to shred them or incinerate the pages and flush the ashes down the toilet if they thought a raid was coming. The paper clogged the toilets for days.

But China in the 1990s was changing and opening up. Yusuf

and Yuhe would get to experience Islam as their forebears had once been able to. The two young friends swapped history books, voracious to learn more. From them they learned that Islam had a long history in China, and that Chinese Muslims had endured numerous ups and downs in treatment. Historians believe Islamic envoys from the Middle East likely traveled to China starting in the seventh century, only a few dozen years after the prophet Muhammad received his divine missives from Allah while sequestered, fasting, in a cave. The descendants of these envoys settled in Chinese cities, intermarrying with the local population, and replaced their mother tongues of Arabic and Persian with Chinese. They adapted to living in China, incorporating many Buddhist customs and elements of regional folklore into their unique practice of Islam. Throughout the ensuing centuries, despite periodic discrimination against Muslims, China remained home to large populations of Chinese and foreign-born Muslims.

Yusuf read every Chinese text on Islamic theology he could find. His new job at a diesel engine factory was quite relaxed, giving him ample time to squirrel himself away behind a large piece of machinery with a thick book. Before, Yusuf had tried his best to blend in with the Han Chinese population, but after his conversion, he began wearing the small white cap Hui men often sport and taught himself the Arabic alphabet.

China's on-and-off-again open-mindedness was essential to building Chinese identity, Yusuf wrote later in books published by Yuhe. By opening itself to new ideas, China had allowed Buddhism and Christianity to enter its borders. Over time, these religions had become more and more Chinese, just like Islam had. In fact, throughout the Qing dynasty, prolific Chinese-born scholars equally fluent in Arabic, Persian, and Chinese labored to explain Islamic precepts to a Chinese-speaking audience by using language and concepts steeped in Confucianism and Daoism. The canon came to be called the Han Kitab. Its bilingual name reflected the spirit of fusion at the heart of the project: to explain how Islam's fundamental principles could actually be derived from a mix of Chinese philosophy. Cloaking themselves in the language and culture of traditional Han Chinese culture was also a way for Muslim minority communities to protect themselves.

When China's Communist Party won control of China in 1949, it realized it would need to work together with ethnically diverse communities to win enough popular support to maintain control over the country. It promised minority groups they could remain on their ancestral land, enjoy cultural freedom, and even have some limited political autonomy within territories or "nations" that existed in confederation with the Chinese Communist state. Such promises were attempts to assuage the concerns of distinct ethnic groups like the Mongolian tribes and powerful Uyghur community, who each wanted a state of their own after the communist victory.

Chinese Muslims were more divided over whether they should call themselves an ethnic group that needed its own homeland or a more dispersed religious community that could co-exist within a broader Chinese state. The Communists eventually opted for the Soviet system of ethnic policy, identifying the Hui as one of China's fifty-six officially recognized ethnic groups. To do so, they used religion to thread together disparate factions within the Hui and constructed an entire ethnic category where one did not exist before. Many Chinese Muslims welcomed the official designation because it bestowed formal recognition.

But a small subset of people, which later included Yusuf, were opposed. They believed that linking religion to ethnicity simplified the former into something biologically intrinsic to a person, passed down as a hereditary trait rather than the voluntary leap of faith of a believer. An ethnic distinction also created a buffer against proselytization and the further spread of Islam in China: to be Muslim now meant being born ethnically Hui or into one of China's nine other Muslim ethnicities. Many Han Chinese today still find it inconceivable that they can convert to Islam. Muslims, they believe, have to be born Muslim.

Ethnic designations caused Yusuf his first heartbreak. In high school, he became enamored with a female classmate who was not Hui. He wondered what he would do if she tried to kiss him with her pork-tainted mouth. Would his disgust be too obvious? The flush of young love and adolescent hormones quickly made him forget such questions. In the end, his mother found out about the budding romance and immediately voiced her disapproval. Even though she wasn't religious, she still abided by the ethnic divisions that separated the communities for centuries. We are Hui, and you are not, she told the girl's parents, and our children can never be together. Yusuf's girlfriend sobbed as she heard these words, but when Yusuf tried to comfort her, she pushed him away. He went home cursing his identity as a Hui. His ethnicity was the one thing he had no control over, yet it had cost him his first love. It was the first time he felt a gulf open up between him and non-Hui people.

The link drawn between ethnicity and religion drove Yusuf crazy. He had come to believe anyone could become Muslim if they wanted to, not because of what their identity card said. His Hui designation also seemed to insinuate he was less Chinese, an othering that he suspected was behind the waves of persecution

Muslims in China endured over the centuries. His ancestors had long been committed to the project of building China. They had even fought alongside Han soldiers against the Japanese during World War Two, and his relatives had supported the Communist revolution in 1949. Was he not ethnically Chinese, with a Chinese name on his identity papers and Chinese blood flowing through his veins? The construct of *minzu*—the vague Chinese concept of ethnicity—was one he would spend his entire adult life trying to dismantle.

As his commitment to Islam grew, so did his curiosity for other religions. One August night, he noticed a pile of bicycles parked outside the local Christian church. Christianity is a cult, his imam had warned him. But the loud music and laughter drew Yusuf inside, to the second floor, where a beautiful girl in a white dress smiled at him as she sang. After the service, he found an excuse to wait for her outside the church entrance and introduce himself. I want to learn more about your God, he said, blushing. She gave him her phone number.

She later became his girlfriend. Yusuf quickly grew to love the church hymnals and the open warmth Christians had when they greeted him. He had always been good at singing. Perhaps, he thought, he was more suited to Christianity than to Islam! Every time he went to church, people greeted him as if they had known him for years and said they would pray for him. It struck Yusuf that he had never prayed for a non-Muslim before. Love thy neighbor, his girlfriend would often admonish him. She was right, he eventually conceded; everyone deserved the chance to discover their faith. Again, Yusuf puzzled over why only the Hui were allowed to be Muslim. Maybe he could study to be an imam and change that.

In 1995, Yusuf was admitted to the Beijing Islamic Institute of

Economics to study the history of Muslim thought in China. He hoped to become an academic one day, and the study was a dream come true. He spent several blissful days wandering Beijing's historic Muslim quarter, Niu Street, devouring mutton skewers and heaps of sesame-paste desserts. But his enthusiasm quickly dampened. On the first day of classes, Yusuf declared his ambition to become an Islamic missionary. To his surprise, his teacher reprimanded him: "We are a socialist country, and we Muslims must never openly discuss Islam!" Yusuf was confused: Why else were they at the Islamic Institute if not to study theology?

Yusuf did not know it yet, but just a few years before his enrollment, about two hundred ethnic Uyghurs in Baren county, in the western Xinjiang region, had overrun a police station and killed several officers after organizing quietly through mosques. Around 7,900 Uyghurs were later arrested in connection with the attack. The incident would later be called the Baren Riots in Chinese. The riots were not meant to overturn Chinese rule but erupted from Uyghurs angry as thousands of Chinese migrated into Xinjiang, edged out Uyghurs as the region's ethnic majority, and dominated the best-paying jobs. Accounts of the riots are sketchy and vary widely as authorities tried to suppress all independent reporting on the event. But the Baren incident precipitated months of strict policing in Xinjiang, and it left Islamic schools across the country on edge.

The next time his teacher called on him to explain his study of Islam, Yusuf had his answer ready. He wanted to learn how to adhere to the leadership of the Party, he recited woodenly, and he aspired to live in a socialist society so he could maintain the stability and unity of the motherland. His teacher smiled in approval. Yusuf was learning that to survive, he would need to hide certain parts of himself.

For the better part of the next decade, Yusuf was a university student, rediscovering the Islamic culture of China that his parents and grandparents had never been able to experience. To seek out new imams who would improve his written Arabic and give him new insight into the Islamic mantras he was absorbing, he took up a semi-nomadic existence wandering China's northwest; trekking across Ningxia, Gansu, and Qinghai provinces; and even Yunnan province, on the border with Myanmar and Vietnam. Each of these regions now boasted dozens of Islamic schools for both men and women as the political atmosphere liberalized, within limits. Such schools were still controlled by the state. Imams had to be registered with the State Administration for Religious Affairs (SARA), a ministry set up to regulate the business of spirituality. In addition to licensing imams and priests, SARA also verified all "living Buddhas," the people believed to carry the reincarnated soul of illustrious Tibetan Buddhists. On paper, such mechanisms were meant to maintain the sacrosanct nature of religion within China, but in practice they also allowed the state to track and control all religious activity.

During his last year in school, Yusuf spent a week hiking the misty Qinling mountains in southern Shaanxi province, celebrated as a holy site in Taoism. At night, before his final prayers, he washed his feet in the clear mountain springs that trickled down from the peaks. During the day, he organized lectures among the Muslim villagers he encountered, but they often fell asleep halfway through. Many of them had forgotten their religious practice during the Mao era.

Yusuf refined his pitch. He traveled to a county in Henan province, where many Muslim families had moved back after fleeing during the Second World War. There, he painted the crumbling local mosque and touched up the Arabic inscriptions in gold. Only about ten people left in the village were still practicing Muslims, though the occasional Uyghur traveler stopped by. Yusuf decided to reopen the mosque school, with the idea of teaching Islamic scripture in addition to core subjects like reading, science, and math. Mosque attendance grew exponentially. Parents were enthused that someone else could watch and educate their children, for free. Yusuf came to learn that people embraced religion only when it served them, so he doubled down on providing social services and charity work.

Slowly, China was also letting its people see the rest of the world again. Under Communist rule, Beijing had at first isolated itself internationally, letting only a select few elite government officials travel internationally on brief and strictly monitored trips. The officials often savored these precious excursions abroad. For example, when French-educated Chinese leader Deng Xiaoping was allowed an official visit to France in 1974, he spent his $20 government allowance on two hundred fresh croissants to share with friends back in China.

After Opening and Reform, Beijing relaxed travel rules and even began encouraging Chinese students to study abroad and gain technical expertise from foreign experts. Yusuf seized his chance. He spent 1999 at Pakistan's Islamabad University, where he met imams and religious scholars from across the Middle East, South Asia, and China. To his surprise, his fellow students made no distinction between him and the Chinese businessmen who were slowly trickling into Pakistan. To a foreigner, all people—Hui or Han—were lumped into the same category of being "Chinese." Yusuf realized it was only Chinese people themselves who saw the two groups as different.

While in Islamabad, Yusuf was offered a chance to join a group of Pakistani friends to make the hajj, the annual pilgrimage to Mecca in Saudi Arabia. He jumped at the opportunity and headed to the Middle East.

Despite relaxations on international travel, Muslims who want to complete the hajj from China must, to this day, first obtain permission from the state-run Islamic Association, which awards only a few thousand slots a year. Hundreds of thousands of Chinese people apply each year, and many of those given a coveted spot on these state-organized trips have applied continuously for years. By the early 2000s, a robust gray market for private hajj tours had popped up, organized by people like Ma Yanhu, a Chinese Muslim writer I met who was also within Yusuf's orbit of Muslim intellectuals. The tours Ma organized to Mecca were popular with the Hui because he catered Chinese food for the entire journey, a plus for those unused to Middle Eastern cuisine. Ma Yanhu's other advantage was that, through dozens of trips to Mecca himself, he knew all the workarounds to get Chinese passport holders a hajj visa.

Soon, tens of thousands of Chinese Muslims like Yusuf were surreptitiously going to Mecca every year. They brought back with them new ideas about Islam. Historic mosques in China were mostly built during the Ming and Qing dynasties and, save for the prayer hall and *mihrab* facing Mecca, these mosques were usually painted red and gold, just like a Ming-dynasty palace. But as more Muslims went abroad in the 2000s, they started advocating for building Arabic-style minarets and onion-shaped domed mosques to remove the "sinification" Islam in China had accrued over the last millennium. At first, Chinese officials supported Arabic domes, because they were seen as modern and a sign that China's Muslims were joining a global religious polity. Muslim parents started playing up family lore about being descended from travelers hailing from the Middle East. One Muslim friend told me how he had grown up being told he was ethnically Central Asian and Persian. He did have curiously dark, bushy eyebrows. But when he took a DNA test, he was disappointed to discover that his genealogical makeup was 80 percent Han Chinese. The remainder was a mix of other Chinese ethnicities, plus Uyghur.

This emphasis on bringing out Islam's supposedly "genuine" foreign roots annoyed Yusuf. He felt too many Chinese people were deluding themselves with stories of exotic family lineages, because it made them feel special. Yusuf thought this was the wrong approach. The Hui were Chinese people who had embraced Islam, not Muslim foreigners who had settled in China. The whole point was to show that whether Hui or Han, they were all Chinese, regardless of religious belief.

This negotiation of identities, between Islam and China, was on Yusuf's mind as he boarded the plane from Pakistan to Saudi Arabia to complete the hajj. Most of the other passengers were also on their first-ever hajj, and they were so excited they spent most of the trip standing in the aisles and shouting their praise for Allah. The next day, his heart pounding, Yusuf walked into the Masjid al-Haram in Mecca, where a seething mass of humanity was already orbiting the Kaaba, a massive, intricately inscribed black stone cube that Muslims consider their holiest site. Yusuf felt the edges of his individual being blurring as he joined the thousands of other pilgrims in circling the Kaaba. The whirlpool of humanity brought him closer and closer to the holy artifact. On his fifth circumambulation, a Saudi Arabian guard spotted Yusuf and extended a hand, shouting a welcome to his "brothers from

China," hoisting him close enough to the Kaaba so he could nearly graze the base of the cube with his fingertips.

For the next twenty-four days, Yusuf virtually lived in the masjid rather than wasting time walking the one hour each way back to his hotel each day. When he grew tired, he found an empty patch of carpet and went to sleep, the silent silhouette of the Kaaba keeping him company. Never had he felt so connected to the broader, Islamic *ummah,* or community. Nor had he ever felt so unquestionably accepted as a part of the Chinese community. Yusuf was penniless after buying his roundtrip tickets to Mecca, so for food, he relied on the charity of other Chinese pilgrims who had the foresight to bring their own pots and kettles and electric stoves to prepare Chinese cuisine. Yusuf returned to China brimming with new inspiration. He would convince the rest of China that Islam was intrinsic to Chinese culture, and that being religious and being Chinese were not only perfectly compatible, but one and the same.

Upon his return to China, Yusuf decided to pay a long-overdue visit to his home city of Xi'an, the capital of Shaanxi province. There, he came across an angry crowd of fellow Muslims outside a hospital. Several days earlier, a low-level police officer had beaten a Muslim man to death during a workplace inspection gone wrong. The city had tried to give the family about $30,000 to hush the incident up, and when his loved ones protested the bribe, the police arrested them. Thousands of people were now gathering outside the hospital gate despite a police cordon. Just a few dozen yards inside, the man's shrouded corpse lay just out of reach, under police custody while the courts adjudicated the death. The police were later absolved. Yusuf felt cool rage. How could the Muslim community become strong enough so they could not be bullied ever again?

Their answer was to build up wealth. As economic growth lifted the stifling blanket of socialism from the country, entrepreneurs, many from the ancient city of Linxia, the cradle of Chinese Muslim culture, fanned out across China, then abroad to the Gulf states, where they ran lucrative import-export businesses. By the time I moved to China in 2015, mom-and-pop halal restaurants were a common sight across cosmopolitan cities like Beijing and Shanghai. Muslim businessmen built up million-dollar empires in Islamic food, clothing, and healthcare products. Luxury halal beauty products and halal meat even sold well among nonreligious Chinese consumers who associated the stamp of halal with cleanliness and quality.

As early as the ninth century, the port megacity of Guangzhou was home to tens of thousands of Chinese and foreign Muslims. Opening and Reform in 1978 allowed them to open private factories that churned out cheap goods then trucked to Yiwu, the famed wholesale market city in southern China where many of our global consumer goods and trinkets are sourced. There, China's Muslims could really play to their strengths. Their fluency in Arabic and Farsi gave them an advantage when negotiating with the legions of Southeast Asian, African, and Middle Eastern traders who descended on Yiwu every few months to buy huge shipping containers full of fast fashion and electronic devices for export. By the early 2000s, Yiwu was one of the fastest-growing Muslim communities in China. In 2012, Aisin-Gioro Baoquan, an intrepid Chinese-Manchu imam, finished construction on the country's biggest mosque in Yiwu, built with imported Iranian marble. Private Muslim wealth flowed into mosques through religious donations often totaling millions of dollars a year, as well as into funds directly controlled by powerful Sufi spiritual leaders who ran the various Islamic sects that are a hallmark of Chinese Islam.

Muslims' new wealth also created demand for new scholarship on Islam, and Yusuf soon made a name for himself by penning short, vivid essays about everyday Muslim life in China. His writing was distributed to a growing Chinese readership through an informal publishing network mostly run by fellow Chinese Muslims who found creative ways to skirt the censorship machine. The country's propaganda bureau still maintained control over print, television, and radio. To print books, publishers with state-issued licenses had to obtain ISBN codes that indicated the text had passed a state censor and could be distributed in mainland China. Even in the relatively carefree nineties, Yusuf knew that he was not going to convince any state-run publisher on the mainland to sell books on Islamic history and philosophy. So he turned to his old friend Yuhe.

While Yusuf was studying in Beijing, Yuhe had gone into business, making a small fortune exporting textiles. He began reinvesting those profits into a Hong Kong–registered publishing house that printed Yusuf's volumes and imported them back into the mainland. Yusuf was a prolific writer and could pump out up to two books a year, far beyond Yuhe's personal printing capacity, so Yuhe sometimes only did a limited run of a few hundred copies per volume. Third-party booksellers even pirated Yusuf's books as demand for Islamic literature grew, a practice that flattered Yusuf more than it bothered him. After all, he was not writing to make money.

In 2001, Yusuf started an Islamic education center in the Chinese city of Xi'an. The terrorist attack on the Twin Towers in New York City on September 11 shook Yusuf; it was evidence of how skewed Islamic teaching and a lack of cross-cultural empathy could be used to induce violence. China's Muslims had long emphasized education as a way to preserve the integrity of their religious practice, so there were already hundreds of "scripture halls," or mosque schools, across China. In Yusuf's hometown of Kaifeng, female-only mosques and scripture halls even gave women the chance to become heads of religious communities. However, Yusuf built his center outside of the mosque because he wanted the freedom to experiment with how Islam could be adapted to modern China. He believed women and men could worship together, preached tolerance for non-Muslims, and emphasized social work and self-improvement over scriptural familiarity.

Running the center was not always smooth going. In 2003, Yusuf briefly went into hiding after online critics accused him of publishing extremist articles. Sectarian divides among Chinese Muslims were coming to the surface again; some of his students felt compelled to volunteer as his bodyguards, shuttling him between speaking engagements for fear he might be pummeled by querulous Muslims who disagreed with his more liberal teachings. Yusuf's assertion that Confucius should be recognized as an Islamic prophet was particularly controversial. And the local authorities were also growing unhappy with his fame. Once, he endured a grueling month-long stint in a "re-education through labor" detention camp for running an illegal newspaper, a broadsheet he published twice weekly about his Islamic education center.

Islamaphobia, always present throughout China's history, was also coming to the fore. In 2004, clashes between Hui and Han in the central province of Henan were set off by a deadly traffic accident. Around 150 people died. Dozens more were injured in a separate incident in 2012, while trying to prevent the demolition of a Ningxia mosque. Authorities said the mosque was built illegally and later tore it down.

The internet amplified simmering religious and ethnic tensions. Bloggers like Xi Wuyi, a matronly Marxism scholar, used her retirement from Beijing's state-run social science academy to embrace a new hobby: battling what she saw as "religious fundamentalism eroding Chinese secular mainstream culture." Her biggest target was halal food. In 2016, a long-proposed law to standardize halal food certification in China looked like it was finally about to move forward. The measures would bring China's halal certification process in line with international practices and allow Chinese exporters to sell their halal products globally. Without such certification, entrepreneurs were paying for costly workarounds, like setting up factories in Malaysia or Thailand to process halal toothpastes and sauces that could be exported. The financial gains of such a legislative change were huge, as the global halal market is estimated to be around $1.4 trillion.

But Xi and her followers cried foul. The law was a Trojan horse for sneaking in a broader Islamification of an atheist country, they argued. That proselytizers such as Yusuf were gaining followers on social media in the battle of online ideas gave Xi even more cause for fear. She marshaled some 3 million followers—an impressive figure even in populous China—and initiated weekly name-and-shame campaigns to expose any companies she thought were being overly accommodating of Islam. The companies, often halal restaurants, soon found themselves inundated with death threats and harassing phone calls. Soon, the halal bill was dead.

In 2017, Yusuf started hearing rumors of mass arrests in the Xinjiang region, in China's west. His first instinct was to dismiss them. The idea of rounding up hundreds of thousands of Chinese citizens was ludicrous, and it smacked of Maoist purge techniques that had been officially ruled a mistake by the Communist Party. Besides, what happened to Uyghurs had nothing to do with Yusuf's community. Although many Uyghurs are practicing Muslims, the Hui saw them as different; because of the Uyghur's Turkic roots, they were not truly "Chinese" Muslims, in Yusuf's eyes. Conversely, Uyghurs sometimes called Hui Muslims *tawuz*, watermelon; green and Muslim on the outside, but red and Communist on the inside. To Chinese authorities, these distinctions didn't matter. Both groups were suspect because of their religious and foreign trade ties. First, they had gone after the Uyghurs. Soon, the Hui were in the crosshairs, too.

In April 2018, a secretive Communist Party organ called the United Front Work Department (UFWD) quietly absorbed the functions of SARA, the religion regulator, and also took over the portfolio of another state body that oversaw ethnic minority affairs. The bureaucratic shuffle had seismic consequences. For decades, China's ethnic and religious affairs officials had worked within the state system to enforce the Party's orders. But many of them were religious practitioners themselves or belonged to eth-nic minority groups, and at the grassroots level, the officials often did their best to tacitly protect religious activity. The UFWD had no such aims. Established nearly as soon as the Chinese Commu-nist Party itself was founded, the department gradually evolved into one that could co-opt diverse groups for its causes while neu-tralizing critics of the Party. Because the UFWD works under the Party apparatus and not the state legal system, they had far greater power than the state bureaucracy, with little formal oversight from state institutions like the courts or the State Council, China's cabinet.

Within days, a mosque-dome-removal campaign picked up speed in Hui Muslim counties of the Ningxia region, in north-western China. Red banners exhorted residents in big white char-acters to *"fan shahua, fan ah'hua"*—combat Saudi influence and Arabic influence. Newly empowered UFWD officials drew up plans to redesign hundreds of Arabic-style mosques to look more like Confucian temples. Soon, scaffolding was drawn up around any rounded rooftop in Zhengzhou, the capital of Henan and home to more than one million Muslims. This was notable be-cause the crackdown on Islam had previously been limited to more remote border regions like Ningxia and Gansu, on the pe-riphery of China's more populous east coast. However, by 2019, even Zhengzhou's historic Muslim quarters were littered with buildings sporting odd towers and forlorn stumps that previously had been capped with an onion-shaped dome.

In Zhengzhou, dome-removals usually happened over a sin-gle night, to give residents zero opportunity to protest and to videotape the demolitions. The UFWD was careful to hide writ-ten evidence. Flustered mosque employees were bewildered when district police suddenly ordered them to destroy their own domes and minarets, at the mosques' own expense. When they demanded a legal basis for the demolition orders, the police were equally helpless. One mosque caretaker recorded one such confrontation with an officer. In the recording, the normally gruff officer softens apologetically when he finally admits he himself had been unable to keep a copy of the official demolition documents by the UFWD.

Other mosques preemptively took measures to protect themselves. At one Zhengzhou mosque, a construction crew surreptitiously carved out Arabic inscriptions from clear plexiglass, visible only to the believers who knew where to look. They had also hidden the dome of their mosque with bamboo scaffolding, ostensibly in preparation to remove the dome, but the imam there confided to me that they were simply hiding it from view until their troubles passed. "The Hui people have been through one storm after another, and this is yet another storm that will pass," he reasoned. "Who knows how the political environment may change? We do not want to spend money to tear our dome down, only to have to pay to build it up again next year."

Muslims in other parts of China found ways, big and small, to resist these expanding controls on their way of life. In August 2018, the residents of the town of Weizhou would wage the most concerted display of defiance.

Set right in the middle of northwestern Ningxia province's scrubby Yellow River plains, the soaring Weizhou Grand Mosque, the heart and soul of the town, is impressively large for the small community of twenty thousand residents who live in a collection of low-lying courtyard homes made of clay bricks and mud walls.

Destroyed by Red Guards during the Cultural Revolution, the
mosque was painstakingly rebuilt in the 1980s, then renovated in
the Arab style in 2015, with arched doorways and gleaming
white-tiled domes. The destruction of the mosque in the 1960s
had been a symbol of shame. Its resurrection marked the community's resilience.

The latest trouble began with a leaked government notice explicitly calling for removal of the mosque's domes. This was exactly the kind of written evidence UFWD officials normally tried
to avoid, because such notices could be used to marshal public resistance. The notices reprimanded mosque officials for lacking the
correct permits to build the mosque as large and tall as they had.
Residents found this ludicrous, because architectural plans for the
mosque had been designed in conjunction with local officials.

Alarmed Muslims shared a screenshot of the notice on social
media, where it spread rapidly across China. Hundreds of furious
residents staged a sit-in in the mosque, sharing videos of their
protest through popular Chinese social media platforms like live-
streaming app Kuaishou and chat app WeChat faster than censors
could take them down. Muslims too far away to get to the mosque
sent "red envelopes" of digital money on WeChat to friends who
were there, so they could buy instant noodles and other provisions
for what they anticipated could be a long stakeout. In Xi'an, Yusuf
pulled an all-nighter, mesmerized by the shaky cellphone videos
showing a sea of white-capped Muslims laying out prayer rugs in
and outside the mosque. Their strategy was simple: they reasoned
officials would not dare tear the mosque down while people were
inside. Taken aback by the public anger, Weizhou officials and
county-level United Front officials called off the demolition.

But the victory was short-lived. Within months, each home in

Weizhou got a knock on their door from government work units fanning out to do "thought work." The confrontations followed a pattern. First, they asked Muslim families to sign letters agreeing to "renovate" the Weizou mosque by removing its main dome and domed minarets. Most refused. Then came the threats: state employees would be fired if they did not sign the letter. Their children could be denied spots at public universities. Weizhou officials were even dispatched to Yiwu, the coastal market town more than 1,200 miles away, to find the patriarchs of especially recalcitrant families and browbeat them into signing. Most did. By the time I snuck past police checkpoints into the town in September 2019, the mosque had been de-domed and replaced with traditional Chinese palace roofs. The next year, Ningxia authorities began closing down hundreds of village mosques that they claimed were not being used. The remaining worshippers were merged with larger congregations elsewhere.

The Weizhou mosque resistors proved to be an exception. By and large, few other Muslim communities were as troubled by the mosque dome removals. The Hui are masters of cultural adaptation, and their mosques reflect a diverse range of religious inspiration. They believed the latest de-doming campaign was simply another aesthetic trend that would soon fall out of fashion. For example, at Qinghai province's famed Dongguan mosque, Buddhist symbols are imprinted on some of the roof tiles, and Tibetan stupas adorn the main buildings. When it was first built more than seven hundred years ago, Dongguan exemplified the Sinophone style of Islamic architecture incorporating Confucian and Buddhist elements. It wasn't until the 1990s that the green-tiled roof over the prayer hall was swapped out for a dome. In 2021, Dongguan underwent its third major renovation in a century as officials pressured the imam to tear down the domes in favor of Chinese roofs once again. It was one of the last major mosques in northwestern China to be de-domed.

"Everything changes from one era to another." The owner of a store selling Muslim head coverings and halal beauty products just outside Dongguan sighed. "During Chairman Mao's time, they tore down all our mosques. Then they built them up. Now they are tearing them down again! Just follow whatever political slogan the country is yelling at the time." What bothered him was the assumption that mosques had to be forcibly renovated to fit the narrowing spectrum of what was considered Chinese. He laughed at the idea that policymakers believed a renovation would somehow change how the Hui identified themselves within the larger Chinese polity. "Our belief is not embodied in our buildings. It lies in our hearts," the shopkeeper said, thumping his chest.

Yet across Gansu, Ningxia, and Qinghai, religious officials were successfully playing different factions off one another to ensure no opposition would halt the march of "sinification" across the country's Muslim northwest.

The country's powerful security apparatus began planting informants throughout otherwise tightly knit religious communities in China and abroad. One elderly ethnic Salar man in northwestern Qinghai province told me how proud he was that his son was tapped to become the town's next imam. But the week before he graduated from university, public security officials approached him with what they thought was an irresistible offer: he could get a civil service job shuffling papers as well as a corporate advisory position. The plush monthly salary and pension would be a nice complement to his meager pay from the mosque. In return, however, he had to file reports on the religious beliefs and activities of his fellow Muslims. The father made his son turn the security officials down.

The crackdown divided the Muslim community along sectarian lines. Religious sects had managed an uneasy equilibrium for decades, but now officials were turning one clique against the other once again. In Gansu province, various Sufi orders blamed the crackdown on the ideological influence of fundamentalist Wahabist and Salafi ideas imported from Saudi Arabian madrasas: influences like having women wear full face coverings and emphasizing Arabic-language instruction over Chinese texts—ideas that were now the target of the campaign to remove foreign influences. In Ningxia, a mosque belonging to a dominant Jahriyya sect set off some disgruntled murmurings because of its close ties to the state-run Islamic Association. For decades, its imams held positions in the pseudo-regulatory body. But such brownnosing only went so far. By 2019, they, too, had to shut down their madrasa. During the Qing dynasty, Han Chinese generals exploited sectarian differences off one another to quell several Muslim rebellions. Now officials were employing the old imperial strategy again "to let the minorities control other minorities," by dividing communities.

Some Muslims blamed themselves. They had enjoyed a few decades of relative openness and tolerance, and some of them had flaunted their newfound power and wealth too openly. They had built too many mosques, stacked their minarets a little too tall, gilded their domes a tad too shiny, according to their telling. Centuries of modesty had given the Chinese Muslim community a false sense of security. Now, their gaudiness had put them on the authorities' radar again.

In Linxia, the son of a prominent imam suggested to me that the state's crackdown on Muslims could be beneficial to the community in the long run, because it pushed Chinese Muslims to reflect on how they could progress. Why, for example, are Muslim areas on average poorer than coastal Han cities? It was because religion distracted them from entrepreneurism and encouraged an unhealthy fascination with Arabic rather than Chinese culture, he thought. Rather than invest in social programs toward education or public health, Muslims wasted it on sectarian competition with each other to build bigger and fancier mosques. Personally, the man continued, he welcomed the state's involvement in religious affairs; it would finally motivate fellow Muslims to modernize. Within an hour of talking with me, he was picked up by secret police, questioned overnight about our meeting, and released the next day. It turns out, he was considered a security threat simply for being the direct family member of a religious leader, and his phone calls, including the one with me, were being tapped.

More than fifteen hundred miles outside of Xinjiang, Yusuf was also noticing changes to Muslim scholarship under Xi's rule in Xi'an. Chinese academics who study the history of Islam told me that Chinese online databases had made it difficult to access articles about the Hui, and large numbers of articles had been removed. Chinese academic journals that focused on Islam and the Hui were barely scraping along as papers and books once contracted to be written were suspended from publication. By then, most publishers refused to print Yusuf's books, so he started sending them to loyal readers as free PDFs.

The call to "sinification" was kickstarting even stricter policies.

Some mosques started to forbid children under the age of eighteen to enter. Bright red posters extolling the virtues of socialism and the merits of Xi Jinping soon plastered mosque doorways, even as the Islamic schools inside were being closed—at first for just the winter break, then permanently. Even if schools had been able to remain open, there would have been few teachers to staff them. A new rule required imams to undergo political training in "Xi Jinping Thought" to obtain the requisite licenses to work in mosques; an even greater number lost their licenses for working in a province different from the one their identification documents were registered in. One school was abandoned in such a rush, I found dog-eared textbooks and chipped cutlery abandoned in its classrooms. The urgency was real: one imam in Gansu province was sentenced to four years in prison for teaching nine children scripture "without authorization." Former teachers emphasized their aim was expressly in line with state objectives. "We barely taught any Islamic doctrine. It was about making sure these children were educated and would not become criminals or radicalized," a former teacher in Yunnan province told me. Her school was later accused of distributing drugs. (A common stereotype about ethnic minorities in China is that they peddle narcotics.) The school shut down soon after.

The state also seized much of the private wealth that powerful Sufi religious leaders had accumulated through generations of Islamic tithing. Some then parlayed those funds into lucrative real estate investments that sent the net worth of some religious figures ballooning into the tens of millions of dollars. Yusuf was among those who pushed for more financial transparency. Instead, the state-run Islamic Association requisitioned the funds and took control of every major mosque's finances.

What really shook Yusuf was the detention and questioning of

Islamic students. In 2019, dozens of Hui Muslims studying at Egypt's famed Al-Azhar University were pressured to come back to China's Qinghai province by security officials, where they were arrested and questioned for several months about their connections to Uyghur students and alleged extremist groups. Finally, the Hui began sounding the alarm. While previously hesitant to speak out on behalf of Tibetans and Uyghurs—people they saw as non-Chinese—they now understood their fates were the same. "The oppression I saw inflicted on Tibetans twenty years ago and the Uyghurs ten years ago has finally reached my people," Ma Ju, a Hui scholar and commentator, told me. "You have legs, but you can't run away," he says. "You have money, but it's of no use. You have a heart, but you cannot lift yourself up. This is a new kind of repression."

The controls on Islam in China were tied directly to Chen Quanguo, the Party secretary of Xinjiang. Chen made a name for himself as a ruthless executor of state policies designed to quash dissent. In Tibet, he pioneered tough, new surveillance methods that blanketed the region with a grid of police stations—a method he quickly instituted when he moved to Xinjiang. He then looked farther afield. In November 2018, Ningxia sent a delegation to Xinjiang "to learn from the latter's experiences in promoting social stability." Party officials from both regions signed an agreement to fight terrorism. The message was clear: Xinjiang's draconian policies to limit religious activities and to surveil suspicious populations were starting in Ningxia.

Buoyed at the prospect of replicating his success elsewhere, Chen hit the road to promote his agenda. In June 2020, he visited the famous Dongguan mosque, in the capital of Qinghai province. Gesturing expansively at the white marble building with its bright green domes, Chen briskly walked into the mosque without taking off his leather shoes, breaking a core religious taboo. His entourage of several dozen local Party officials were aghast, but fearful of contradicting their superior they, too, walked in with their shoes on.

Chen received a very different welcome in Qinghai's Xunhua county, the home of the Salar people, one of China's ten recognized Muslim ethnic minorities. Once again, he confidently strode up to Xunhua's Jiezi mosque with his shoes on. He found his path blocked by the mosque's ethnic Salar watchman, who punched Chen in the face. Chen doubled over as blood dripped out of his nose. Behind him, a few United Front officials gasped. Others had to stifle their delight. Attendants bundled Chen into a waiting car and whisked him away. The Salar man was briefly detained before being quietly let go the next day after a community outcry.

Amid this turmoil, Yuhe, Yusuf's dear friend and close collaborator, decided to leave China for good. Yuhe and his wife had the misfortune of having all their identity papers registered in Xinjiang. The crackdowns in the predominantly Uyghur neighborhoods in southern Xinjiang had just begun, and the "winds of change," as Yuhe called them, were blowing north, to the capital of Urumqi, where Yuhe was from. An imam from Yuhe's home village had been arrested after a surprise police raid of his home turned up dozens of prayer books. Yuhe knew the man personally; the man had a strong spirit, and he refused to admit any wrongdoing, even in detention. Police put him in a dog cage for months, where his wife would bring him halal meals each day. Yuhe was horrified, but like Yusuf, he shrugged off the story. "We reckoned only religious figures would be suppressed," Yuhe later told me regretfully. "There was no way of knowing everything that followed."

Still, Yuhe was cautious. He traveled to Malaysia regularly for business, so he moved his entire immediate family over to Kuala Lumpur. They were not planning to stay indefinitely: in a few months or years, the political drama in Xinjiang would end, they figured, and they could return home. Three months after their departure, his homesick wife and two daughters briefly returned to Xinjiang for a holiday. When police scanned their smartphones at border control, they found the family had installed the chat app WhatsApp while abroad. China blocks access to foreign apps such as Facebook and Twitter, especially ones that offer encryption, and the three were detained. The youngest daughter—then seven years old—was sent to a state orphanage until an uncle managed to retrieve her. The eldest daughter was soon released but was unable to leave China. Yuhe's wife was sentenced to more than two years in prison, then assigned a government job in a logistics warehouse. Yuhe had a heart attack the day he learned of her trial. He is still trying to bring his wife and daughter, who are banned from leaving China, to Malaysia.

Yuhe estimates about four dozen of his relatives disappeared into the maze of informal detention camps and expanding prison facilities that dot Xinjiang, all for relatively petty actions: vacations to Turkey, finishing Arabic language training, or posting about Arabic music or Islamic poetry in online chat groups. One relative was arrested for completing the hajj in Mecca on an unauthorized private trip—ten years before. Ma Yanhu, the hajj tour leader, was also arrested for running an illegal business. He protested the charges. "Islam enjoys the protection of our country's constitution, and completing the hajj is the most important of the Five Pillars of Islam," Ma handwrote in an appeal letter. "My country's official policy is to manage religion according to the law, but in practice, many citizens experience restrictions over legal religious activities, including the hajj." He is serving an eight-year prison sentence.

Each week, Yusuf and Yuhe heard of another Muslim family who paid cash for a new apartment and shelled out thousands of dollars in bribes to expedite paperwork that shifted their household registration from Xinjiang to neighboring Gansu province or Ningxia, where security measures were not as draconian. That simple bureaucratic switch in location likely saved tens of thousands of Hui Muslims from Yuhe's tragedy.

Not everyone who tried to flee Xinjiang was successful. I was walking with a friend through the streets of Linxia city, China's "little Mecca," in the northwestern province of Gansu. It was a balmy, early-autumn evening, and the twilight cast deep shadows in the alleyways between the city's many mosques. From the shadows, a white-capped man emerged, pushing his bike, and he began frantically motioning us to step into a more secluded corner with him. He had overheard us talking about the state of religious affairs in China, and he wanted to share his own story. The previous winter, the daughter of a close friend had knocked on his door. He recognized her immediately; a decade earlier, she had been a standout student in his scriptural classes. Later, she married and moved back to Xinjiang, where her new husband was imprisoned as authorities rounded up religious figures. Fearing her own arrest, she fled to Linxia with her newborn child and was now outside his door, begging for help. He took her in and gave them shelter in the mosque.

The mosque's evening prayer group quietly brought her food each day. Months went by—until the night about a dozen police officers sent from Xinjiang raided the mosque. Their phones had

been their downfall, the old man said, shaking his head. Xinjiang's anti-terrorism police had been able to connect the woman's
relatives to mobile numbers used by members of the Linxia prayer
group. The last shred of news he received was that the former student had been sentenced to seven years in prison for extremism.
Her baby was adopted by a distant relative. My friend and I
walked back to our hotel in silence after hearing her story.

Yusuf watched from a distance as his community withered under
the force of "sinification," or making minority groups more "Chinese." He listened to Yuhe's advice and moved to Malaysia as well,
in 2019. The police were frequently calling him in for questioning
about his writing, his sermons, and his publishing contacts in
Hong Kong. His dream of spreading Islam was in tatters. Rather
than growing the Muslim community, Yusuf felt he was cursed;
everyone he touched soon encountered trouble. Dozens of his
customers were being detained every few months because of the
free PDFs of his books he was emailing them. He hadn't spoken
in months to his relatives who remained in China. Yusuf still felt
deeply Chinese, but for the time being, he knew China would not
tolerate Chinese people like him. "Let only red flowers bloom,"
Yuhe told me by phone from Malaysia. "The state only wants its
garden to have one type of flower: the red ones. Green, blue, or
white flowers: if they are not red, they will be cut down."

A few months after moving to Malaysia, Yusuf learned that an
old publisher friend of his and Yuhe's had been released from a
five-year prison term. Like Yuhe, this publisher had been publishing books without the right ISBNs. Unlike Yuhe, he hadn't left
China in time. Yusuf considered risking a trip back to China to

visit him, but he knew that like everything he now did, it would only give his old friend more trouble. A few weeks after the publisher's release, Yuhe received a WhatsApp with an enigmatic essay from him, the short lines of prose radiating with suffering: "There was always the bleak night, full of ghosts gloomily wandering about in their strange death. Life had no sound or color. Amid the dust scattered on the ground, the pain of living and the liberation of the dead began to entangle so that the wonderful temptations of life disappeared."

A few weeks after his release, I went to visit the publisher's old Beijing bookstore at Yusuf's request. It was situated among the offices for shiny tech start-ups and upscale after-school tutoring companies. On previous trips to Beijing, during happier days, Yusuf spent hours in the store tearing open new book shipments with his publisher friend and debating Islamic philosophy. He wanted to see what the store looked like now, so I sent him a few pictures of the padlocked storefront, the unopened boxes of his books inside gathering dust.

CHAPTER 7

THE MODEL MINORITY

Adiya's first distinct memory of seeing Chinese script was on the food labels at the grocery store. An ethnic Mongolian, he was growing up in Horqin Middle Banner, "the most Mongolian" of Inner Mongolia's eastern banners—banners being the communities that still retained their names from when the region was organized around flag-carrying clans. Few Han Chinese families had yet to migrate into the banner, so when he was in elementary school, all his classes were taught mostly in the Mongolian language. Mandarin Chinese was spoken only as a working language, so he was taught Chinese characters at school. Still, seeing the food packaging in the neat, left-to-right pictographs he only ever used in class was jarring. To him, the store around the corner was part of his private sphere, and his private sphere—the inner world he, his family, and a few close friends inhabited—was purely Mongolian.

His parents made sure to teach him the Mongolian script,

which is written vertically, the curling symbols cascading down the page like a string of ribbons. Mongolians in China are intensely proud that they have retained their alphabet, whereas their relatives just across their northern border in Mongolia, the country, use the Cyrillic of the Russian alphabet. His parents were also careful to give him a Chinese name—Wu Guoxing, meaning "flourishing country"—but with everyone he knew and cared about, he was Adiya, the Mongolian boy with a big heart and big mouth.

In the grasslands of Horqin banner, nearly everyone around him was ethnically Mongolian, though Han Chinese families were starting to trickle in through his middle school years, attracted by the boom in mining-related and commodity extraction jobs popping up across the region. Adiya felt the ethnic distinctions keenly, even as a young child. He and his school friends instinctively segregated themselves away from the Han Chinese children in school. Boys from the two ethnic groups frequently got into fistfights, usually retribution for some other beating the week before. Simply being Han or Mongolian was enough grounds for a pummeling. But Adiya had to allow the new Han families moving into the banner some begrudging respect. Most of them spoke with a distinctive lilt, marking them as native to Sichuan, a large and populous province in China's southwest. They were economic migrants, savvy at business, and they brought with them new restaurants and grocery stores that proliferated across the scraggly grasslands of the east part of the Inner Mongolia region.

Adiya was also starting to familiarize himself with their language, Mandarin Chinese, something his parents strongly encouraged him to do. Their considerations were purely practical. In the 1990s, Horqin banner already had two types of public schools their children could enroll in: Mongolian-predominant schools (though Chinese was still taught as a subject) or Mandarin-predominant institutions, where Mandarin was the dominant language of instruction. The majority of parents chose the latter because they knew Mandarin would soon be the working language of the region. Being fluent in Chinese also allowed young Mongolians to apply to university fields of study that were only open to applicants who had gone through a Chinese-language curriculum. To Adiya, the logic was simple: more Chinese people emigrating meant he would need Mandarin to communicate with them. He did not begrudge parents like his own who had sent their children to Mandarin-dominant schools, because he saw language purely as a skill, like being able to do mental math or fix an engine.

Only as an adult did Adiya appreciate how language shaped identity. When communities suddenly come under threat, they tend to band together and make a last stand. For his community, the end was decades in the making, and ironically, with so much time to prepare, they had done nothing at all, Adiya reflected ruefully. "It was the feeling of a frog slowly boiled alive," he told me decades later, thousands of miles away from his beloved banner. Identity loss and suppression were not the work of a generation; they were the accumulation of decades of forced assimilation, he had come to believe. The "sinification" of ethnic Mongolians—becoming more Chinese per the state's definition—had happened so slowly, he barely noticed what was happening until it was too late. When a group's identity was chipped away bit by bit, no one seemed to care.

Adiya's last year of fully Mongolian-language education ended after elementary school, in about 2000. Even at his Mongolian-dominant school, teachers were now teaching every lesson in Mandarin Chinese, rather than their native Mongolian. Previously, classes such as Chinese literature and English language were taught in Mongolian. Adiya thought this teaching style was more effective; better to teach people a foreign language with the aid of their mother tongue, so they were not grappling with two unfamiliar languages. Now, teachers spoke in Mandarin throughout the entire lessons. At first, Adiya found the lessons laughable. His ethnic Mongolian teachers were themselves not native Mandarin speakers and so they made grammatical and pronunciation mistakes obvious enough that he, even with his playground Mandarin, could hear. Yet not a single student or their parents questioned the switch in curricular language.

To them, the switch was a normal part of modernization. Old buildings and narrow roads were being razed all over Horqin banner to make way for taller, concrete high-rises with elevators and six-lane highways. Perhaps the old language had to go, too. Moreover, teaching Mandarin reflected the region's demographics that year: according to China's national census in 2000, out of the region's 23 million plus residents, 79.2 percent of the population were Han Chinese. The titular ethnic group for the region, the Mongolians themselves, was only about 17.1 percent of the population.

Even when the other party was ethnically Mongolian and could speak the language fluently, people now insisted on communicating in Mandarin Chinese when discussing formal, administrative affairs. Adiya noticed his friends at school all watched Chinese-language dramas. It bothered him that all the men in the serialized rom-coms and historical dramas were Han Chinese, and there was no one who looked like him. When Mongolian men did show up, they were depicted as unreliable characters who swindled their friends and walked out on their girlfriends.

One of his most indelible memories from middle school was accompanying his parents to his school's parent-teacher conferences. The four ethnic Mongolians—him, his parents, and his teacher—sat in a small classroom and conversed privately in heavily accented Mandarin. A sense of surrealness crept over Adiya. Who were they all playacting for?

The open grasslands have long been the site of contestation over land, identity, and power among native Mongolians and emigrant Han communities. As early as the nineteenth century, China's ruling Qing dynasty opened up Mongolian territory for agricultural cultivation and lifted a previous ban on inward Han Chinese immigration. Han farmers poured into the region, butting up against a largely nomadic Mongolian population who relied on herds of livestock ambling across the open plains for sustenance. Inbound migrants snatched up plots of land for fixed houses and agriculture, putting them in direct conflict with Mongols.

The fall of the Qing empire in the early twentieth century afforded Mongolians a chance to carve out more autonomy for themselves, though they found their efforts hamstrung by the two, far greater powers they are sandwiched in between: Russia and China. Conflicts between various tribes and factions within the broader Mongolian diaspora weakened what could have been a more united negotiation position. Mongols living in the northern grasslands looked to the Soviet Union. By contrast, the southern grasslands had a closer tie to the Chinese political project through decades of Han migration inflows and geographic proximity to the collapsed Qing empire. The ethnic Mongolians there looked toward Beijing instead.

In 1947, even before a Communist victory, Inner Mongolia threw its weight behind Mao Zedong and his army. Their early loyalty won them limited cultural rights within the new Chinese people's republic state established two years later. "One very strong sense in Inner Mongolia on the part of Mongols is how much they've given up, compared to what they feel they were promised by the People's Republic of China from the 1940s," says the scholar Christopher Atwood, a professor of Mongolian and Chinese frontier history at the University of Pennsylvania.

The right to teach and speak their language was a consolation prize to assuage those whose nationalist hopes had been dashed. Article 4 of the Chinese Constitution states: "All nationalities have the freedom to use and develop their own spoken and written languages." That meant regions like Inner Mongolia, with their higher concentration of non-Han residents, were granted certain cultural and educational autonomy. On paper, for the next seven decades, China's ethnic Mongolians could attend school and take university classes offered in six provinces and regions taught exclusively in the Mongolian language; after grade three, Mongolian students also began taking Chinese literature and foreign language classes taught in Mandarin.

However, by the time Adiya was in school, Mongolian-language education was already naturally diminishing in scope. More and more parents voluntarily chose to send their children to Mandarin Chinese–only schools, whose education afforded better economic outcomes. Official statistics from 2017 show that about 30 percent of ethnic Mongolian students attended a school with some form of Mongolian-language education, down from an estimated 60 percent in 1990.[1] Ethnic Mongolians in China made relatively little public fuss over this backslide in bilingual education, with one exception in 1981. Emboldened by a wave of political and economic liberalization sweeping the entire country that year, thousands of Mongolian students marched in the regional capital of Hohhot and demanded an end to Han migration into Inner Mongolia. Their demands were ignored, and the students simply went back to class afterward. Periodic protests over land grabs continued over the years as the nomadic pastoralist way of life faded away on the steppes.

Few other sizable instances of rebellion occurred again. Much of this political passivity may be due to the fractious nature of Mongolian identity, where different tribes and dialects and the lack of overarching religious beliefs among factions impede efforts at organized dissent. Instead, by all conventional definitions of success, China's ethnic Mongolians have become highly accomplished within the Party's strictures. They consistently achieve higher rates of literacy and educational attainment, per capita, than the dominant Han population. These successes also make them a model minority—an example of a pliant ethnic community's smooth integration into the Communist revolutionary project.

As Inner Mongolia's pastoral way of life faded away, and the region became increasingly indistinguishable from the rest of China, language became the remaining identity marker setting them apart from Han Chinese. For Adiya, that made the Mongolian language all the more special. It was a portal into an alternate Inner Mongolia unadulterated by Party dictates, a shibboleth for the initiated. "If you don't speak Mongolian, it's all just a Chinese environment [in Inner Mongolia]. But if you speak Mongolian, suddenly it's like there's this secret walkie-talkie that allows you to tune into all of this, this language that is spoken by people who look just like other Chinese people but are speaking in Mongolian," Atwood told me.

Adiya decided not to go to college after high school graduation, opting instead for a vocational degree in computer software. He got a job in IT in Beijing, where the bustle of Chang'an Street, a broad thoroughfare, could feel even more overwhelming than the expansiveness of the Mongolian sky. The anonymity of the capital afforded him a strange sense of home. "Every kind of person was there," he told me. Being Mongolian did not stick out in the hodgepodge of migrant workers, students, expats, and government bureaucrats who lived side by side in densely packed neighborhoods circumscribed within the city's ring roads. Ironically, it was in Beijing, the center of political power and arguably one of the most tightly policed cities in China, that Adiya could fully appreciate China's inherent, albeit slightly hidden, diversity.

Returning home to Horqin banner was a disappointment each time. Adiya had met Christians and Buddhists; Hui and ethnic Manchus; people from Guizhou province, all the way in the country's southwest, to the tech hub of Shenzhen. They all considered themselves Chinese, but that had not come at the expense of having to discard their religious or ethnic identities in their private lives. Adiya begrudgingly found himself in admiration of Han people. "I thought the Han way of thinking was really good, and I kept telling my fellow Mongolians that we needed to learn from them. Many Han people want to protect their language, their identity group, and they have a strong sense of patriotism. But us Mongolians? We have nothing!" During this period, he also started calling Mandarin Chinese "the Han language," to indicate it was primarily spoken by China's ethnic majority, the Han. It was a way to remind people around him that China's borders contained a multitude of languages and ethnicities.

The problem was his own Mongolian was slipping. The street signs in Inner Mongolia are bilingual, a nod to the cultural autonomy the region is supposed to enjoy, but they obscured the fact that young Mongolians like Adiya could barely read many of the more complicated street names in the Mongolian script. "Even the Mongolian we did speak with each other was becoming Hanified," Adiya remembered later. "I had to start sprinkling in Mandarin words in conversation, because I could no longer use our own language to express my thoughts." By the time he graduated high school, he felt most comfortable in Mandarin Chinese. No one was punishing him for speaking Mongolian; he was forgetting how to speak it himself.

In 2016, Adiya quit his IT job in Beijing and decided to move back home. He had been away for too long, and he wanted to give back to the place he had grown up. He eventually decided to set up a school giving bilingual after-school computer and math classes to Mongolian children. His teaching style reflected his own patchwork linguistic habits; he tried to use as much Mongolian as possible, but he had studied computer coding entirely in Mandarin Chinese, so he lacked a technical vocabulary in Mongolian.

The elementary-age kids who came to his classes enjoyed playing computer games with him, through which he taught them basic programming logic. Their parents were pleased, because their children's grades improved after a few months with Adiya. As an added bonus, their children also came back speaking more Mongolian. Adiya found his students were so lacking in Mongolian that he needed to start from the basics, teaching them the

Mongolian alphabet and how to spell before they could progress to conversational lessons in the language. Far from being discouraged, his students found relearning the tongue fun, because Adiya was not afraid to make fun of his own linguistic shortcomings; he was the first to admit his own Mongolian was far from perfect. "My Mongolian is really a mess," he'd laugh. "I am a victim of China's language policies as well." Teaching his young charges made him realize he was not the only one who felt this way. His teaching work took on a greater urgency as he used a home-built VPN to circumvent China's internet controls and read in translation foreign news reports on the ongoing crackdown on ethnic Uyghurs, Kazakhs, and Hui Muslims farther west in the country. "You feel a certain feeling of connection to other ethnic minority communities, and there the thought does occur to you: if they go after them first, when do they come after me?" Adiya remembered thinking.

In 2019, anti-government protests in Hong Kong flared up, fueled by long-term dissatisfaction with Beijing's attempts at more political control over the region and a proposed law that would allow Beijing to extradite people in Hong Kong to the mainland to stand trial. Adiya was addicted to following news on the demonstrators, staying up late to watch video clips of young protestors throwing bricks and glass bottles at Hong Kong police. Their defiance shocked and then intrigued him. He could not imagine Mongolians ever pushing back so boldly, or so violently. The David and Goliath nature of their dissent against the Party drew him in. With its combative local media and uncensored internet, Hong Kong was an unfiltered window into how dissent co-existed with state suppression. Adiya had never been to Hong Kong, but he immediately felt a kinship to the people of the territory. He felt they were holding the line for ethnic Mongolians: "I knew if the protests in Hong Kong failed to achieve their objectives, then the Party would continue suppressing other minority communities on the mainland."

Authorities on the mainland were doing their best to stamp out any coverage of the Hong Kong protests. Journalists and tourists traveling between the Chinese mainland and Hong Kong were frequently stopped by border authorities and their electronic devices searched for images and videos of the demonstrations, which guards forced them to delete or face immediate deportation. Starting in 2019, I knew I had to gird myself for hours of questioning about my work at airport immigration every time I came back to Beijing via Hong Kong. To protect my sources and my reporting, I learned how to store my digital files so they could not be easily found when my computer was searched. Adiya was even savvier. He worked with computers for a living, and his self-programmed VPN was adept at jumping over China's digital Great Firewall even as commercial VPNs were being jammed. He downloaded hundreds of videos of the Hong Kong protests onto hard drives in Inner Mongolia, knowing the videos would be deleted within hours by online censors. He compiled some of the footage into a short video he shared with friends in private. He warned them that Inner Mongolia was the next Hong Kong. Most of them laughed at him; they thought he was being hysterical.

Unbeknownst to Adiya, changes to Inner Mongolia's limited cultural autonomy had been well underway for a decade. The changes began quietly, in the ivory tower of academia and bureaucratic maneuvering, but they would have far-ranging consequences.

Chinese ethnic policy is roughly modeled after that of the former Soviet Union, in which well-delineated ethnic groups were gathered into semi-autonomous territories. The approach had to be slightly modified in China. The Party first set about defining the four hundred or so ethnic and linguistic groups in the country in the early twentieth century, arbitrarily merging some of the smaller communities until they had simplified their classification system down to just fifty-six ethnic groups in total. The Party then set up territories for some of the larger recognized ethnic groups it identified and taught civic institutions, such as universities and public welfare systems, to differentiate based on ethnic classification. Certain ethnic minority designations on one's identity card granted you privileges: the right to have more children than existing birth restrictions allowed, for example, and preferential access to "ethnic" or *minzu* universities. The autonomous regions—Inner Mongolia, Xinjiang, Tibet, Ningxia, and Guangxi—were not actually independent and remained closely controlled by the central government, though they allowed communities to retain some control over cultural practices and their mother tongue.

However, a new, "second-generation" wave of ethnic minority policymakers started pushing for a subtle reconceptualization as early as 2011, as the scholars James Leibold and Gerald Roche have pointed out. These new policymakers argued for a drastic reorientation, ditching China's regional ethnic model and Soviet classification system in favor of a more concerted push for a shared Chinese identity based on Han ethnic culture and language. In their mind, the Party had afforded these enclaves too many privileges and allowed them to foster regional power bases. The Chinese government wanted all its citizens, regardless of ethnicity, to put Chinese culture ahead of ethnic group. This generation of policymakers were in part inspired by how diversity was conceptualized in the United States, where people both preserved their distinct identities but also identified foremost as Americans—the "melting pot" theory of ethnic policy.

Identity politics necessitate catchy analogies, and under Xi Jinping, policymakers trialed a new one: China's fifty-six recognized ethnic groups were like the many seeds of a pomegranate, they explained, but together they comprised a whole fruit. "All ethnic groups in China are closely united as family members, just like the seeds of a pomegranate that stick together," according to Xi. Once again, the leader's preoccupation with the divisions underpinning the fall of the Soviet Union played a role here; without a common national identity, Xi feared, China was vulnerable to disastrous divisions along ethnic lines. The solution was "Sinicization"—a state-led effort from the top down to create a uniformly Chinese population, per the Party's standards.

Interpreted generously, Sinicization or "becoming Chinese" could be seen as a parallel to becoming American—in theory, a process of accommodating and adjusting to a variety of cultural inputs in order to create a new, authentic national identity. In practice, this was not how it worked in China. "When people make this one-way argument of Sinicization, I think they're confusing that with Han-isization," the late scholar Dru Gladney told me, referring to China's dominant majority group. In other words, ethnic Mongolians and other ethnic minority groups in China were not being asked to assimilate into one big, diverse melting pot while still retaining their ethnic identities. They were being asked to shed their Mongolian identity completely in favor of one, homogeneous national identity as defined by the Party. Inner Mongolia was fertile ground to try out this revamped ethnic policy. Historically, most ethnic Mongolians under Party rule in China had gamely followed state directives before. And so, in June 2020, when ambitious language policy changes were blithely announced, no one expected there to be any trouble, including Adiya.

The new policy changes specified that schools previously allowed to teach nearly all subjects in the Mongolian language would now have to gradually start teaching two required classes—politics and history—in Mandarin Chinese. All schools also had to start teaching Chinese-language literature classes one year earlier, now beginning in seventh grade. Mongolian-language instruction would continue, but the number of hours was to be reduced by up to half. Further downgrades seemed on the horizon; some policy documents began mentioning Mandarin-language instruction beginning as early as kindergarten in the future. The reduction of Mongolian language instruction was modeled after similar "bilingual" education rules implemented in China's Tibet and Xinjiang regions, where—with the exception of one language class—Tibetan and Uyghur students were now studying in Mandarin Chinese at all levels, despite earlier commitments to have true mother-tongue language education.

Officially, the catalyst for these changes in Inner Mongolia was textbook reform. The region's textbooks were outdated and were due for an overhaul, authorities said. To improve curricular quality, the regional education bureau decreed that the revamped textbooks and teaching materials for these required classes would all be in Mandarin Chinese, even if the school was a Mongolian-dominant institution. For some reason, the new textbooks could not be in Mongolian, as they had been before.

To Adiya's surprise, the Mongolian community reacted with immediate fury to the language instruction changes. He surmised it was the bluntness and speed with which the new curriculum was forced through: "Sinicization does not happen all at once; it is a very subtle process. But this time it was different. Everyone could see the change immediately with their own eyes. It touched the lowest limit of what we were willing to accept." He found the new textbooks ridiculously bad in quality. For example, some of the new, Mongolian volumes were still in Chinese but phonetically spelled out in the Mongolian alphabet. A few months later in August 2020, authorities shut down the only Mongolian-language social media app in the region, after angry parents used it to complain about the language policies and called for protests before the school semester began in September.

For China's some 6 million ethnic Mongolians, the curricular changes felt like a betrayal. They had hewed close to Han-majority Chinese culture, learned Mandarin, and opened their region to extractive mining without complaint. They assumed they would be spared the repressive tactics used against other ethnic communities based on good behavior. Perhaps, some Mongolians started to contemplate, it was time to misbehave.

The public dissatisfaction came to a head on the first day of school, September 1, 2020. Outside of dozens of schools, Mongolian parents stood at the school gates and chanted their opposition to the new policies. Some held Mongolian-language posters expressing love for their native language. "Protect our mother language and culture," they demanded. "Foreign language is but a tool. Our mother tongue is our soul," declared other signs. Inside the schools, the classrooms were empty. Parents had pulled their children out of class at the start of the fall semester in an act of civil disobedience. Mongolian families did not have a say over education policy, but they could control where their children went that day.

Their efforts were rewarded with a show of solidarity from Mongolians on the other side of the border, in the country of Mongolia. In mid-September, hundreds of people gathered in the capital of Ulaanbaatar, north of Inner Mongolia, ahead of China's then–state councilor Wang Yi's visit to the country. "Wang Yi, go away" and "Let's protect our native language," they chanted. Influential Mongolian statesmen came out to express their support for the class walkouts being planned across the region. "No matter where you live, as long as you are a Mongolian, you should join this movement. Without Mongolian language, there is no Mongolian nation we can speak of," exhorted the former president of Mongolia, Elbegdorj Tsakhia, in a video.

The protests on September 1 lit a fire in Adiya's heart. The fiercest dissent was concentrated in Tongliao, a city in the east of the region, about a seven-hour drive south from Adiya's hometown, but he hesitated to join at first. His girlfriend was a public school teacher at a Chinese-language school, and she warned him not to attend; participating in the growing protests could cause her to lose her job if he were identified. He held himself back from attending, even though seeing high school–age Mongolian students—the same age as the students he taught in his afterschool classes—calling for language rights moved him greatly. Some of the students affixed their names in the flowing Mongolian script to written protest petitions, their names jointly fanning outward from a central protest message, a radial symbol called a *duyuyilang* in Mongolian, which, because of its circular, nonhierarchical shape, did not designate any one signatory as the leader.

Adiya was proud his students felt confident shouting and writing in Mongolian, but he feared their message was getting lost in translation among their intended audience: the broader Chinese populace, who did not speak Mongolian but who might sympathize with their plight. And while the protests continued for days, those outside of Inner Mongolia's cities had little idea of the scope of Mongolian fury. That was because the Chinese state was aggressively deleting all digital traces of the class walkout. Anyone who shared written posts or videos about the school protests or empty classrooms had their accounts deleted within hours on WeChat. The videos themselves were quickly scrubbed as well. Human censors working overtime even hunted down copies of protest videos and erased those.

I was still in Beijing during the first day of the school term, and as hints of the unrest in Inner Mongolia trickled out of the region and percolated even to the country's capital (the censors could not catch everything), I immediately prepared to travel to Tongliao. First, however, I tried contacting ethnic Mongolians through social media, including the blogging site Weibo, the country's domestic version of Twitter. Though a handful initially expressed willingness to talk and had posted strident calls to action to protect the Mongolian language just days earlier, they had all received police summonses for their outspokenness and were now terrified of being identified and jailed for giving even anonymous interviews. One hesitant source said she could see armored military vehicles rolling by her window and assembling in her city's main square. She believed, correctly, that authorities could listen in on her phone line and access her social media accounts and initially proposed meeting in person, but eventually called it all off; even venturing outside invited unwelcome scrutiny and potentially detention.

Meanwhile, Adiya decided to attend ongoing protests, despite his girlfriend's warnings. He sprang into action. He filmed a few short segments of the protests in the regional capital of Hohhot and posted them on Twitter, a site that is censored in China. As the digital record of the region-wide protests disappeared under heavy censorship, Adiya downloaded the remaining visual evidence he could find online and preserved it onto a personal hard drive. When this was all over—and there was only one way for this to end, he knew—he wanted to preserve this brief moment of collective resistance, so he knew that he had not dreamed it all up.

Authorities in Inner Mongolia did not back down from the language policy changes. They dismissed the thousands of dissenting parents as a fluke and argued the changes reflected popular will and "the inherent excellence of Chinese culture and advances to human civilization." State media outlet *Inner Mongolia Daily* called on every citizen to learn Mandarin Chinese well as a show of patriotism. "It is a concrete manifestation of love for the Party and country," the paper declared.

Just as swiftly as the civil disobedience en masse had silently rippled through the region, authorities cracked down. Their methods were swift and brutal. In Tongliao, the city of 3 million where protests were among the fiercest, the city banned all cars from the roads for four days in a last-ditch effort to stop parents from congregating. Even as protests dwindled and remaining participants were arrested, security forces steadily ratcheted up the social, economic, and political pressure on ordinary Mongolian families to comply with the new textbook and education policies. School authorities sent municipal notices to parents, requiring them to sign official statements promising to send their children to school or face punishment. "If you do not send your child back, the government

threatens to fire those with state jobs or to cut your social benefits," one parent there told me. In Bairin Right Banner, a region
next to the Inner Mongolian city of Chifeng, and in Sonid Right
Banner, to the west, authorities said elementary and middle school
students who did not return to class by this week would be
expelled. In Kangmian Banner, parents were asked to sign a statement pledging to return their children to school or face punishment, according to police notices shared online.

Security officials in Inner Mongolia issued arrest warrants for
hundreds of parents who had attended protests—complete with
their mug shots grabbed from surveillance cameras. The police
distributed posters and issued mobile hotline numbers, urging
people to phone in tips about the whereabouts of residents who
often had done nothing but shout slogans for a few hours. "On
August 31, 2020, a case of picking quarrels and provoking troubles
occurred in the jurisdiction of Horqin District, Tongliao City, and
we are now soliciting clues from the general public," the posters
read. "Anyone who gathers in public places will be thoroughly
investigated by the public security organs." At least 130 people
were arrested within two weeks of the fall semester, according
to public police announcements, meaning the true figure is likely
much higher. The Southern Mongolian Human Rights Information Center, an advocacy group, estimated as many as five thousand people were put under some kind of police surveillance or
temporary detention in the weeks following protests. Further retribution targeted people's wallets. The city of Xilinhot announced
that parents who sent their children to school would receive preferential access to government aid programs. Those who did not
would have their children expelled, and their livestock herds,
which many ethnic Mongolians still depend on for supplemen-
tary income, could be inspected and fined.

I made it to the cities of Hohhot and Tongliao just as state suppression of the class boycotts the week earlier was peaking. Some of that suppression meant controlling the message—and closely monitoring meddling journalists who tried to report the story. Upon landing in Tongliao, I noticed an unmarked car driven by two men dressed in black immediately began following my driver and me as we left the airport—a security tail. My driver, an ethnic Mongolian I had randomly booked the day before on a drivers-for-hire site, was befuddled as to why authorities cared so much about a foreign reporter covering a class boycott that had been rapidly snuffed out. He himself did not think much of the protests, was ambivalent about his Mongolian identity, and had not participated himself. He still spoke Mongolian as his mother tongue at home with his parents but did not plan to do the same when he had children. "We Mongolians will all eventually assimilate and become Han." He shrugged. "That is our destiny as a minority—to eventually one day become part of the majority." He felt ethnic Mongolians could be counted on to be good Chinese citizens—and perhaps that was why he was visibly irritated at the obvious security presence monitoring us. His foot pressed down on the gas pedal.

Soon we were flying across the flat Mongolian grasslands at more than a hundred miles an hour while I anxiously clung to my seat, imploring him to slow down. I didn't want to make him complicit in any trouble the authorities might give me, nor did I want to die in a fiery crash on the highway. He seemed only more incensed at the idea of turning myself in and suggested losing our tail by dumping his car at the next town, bundling me through the back door of a friend's house, and borrowing another vehicle as a getaway van. I told him that was a bad idea.

Our high-speed chase ended outside a Mongolian-language

middle school. Two police cars stopped us as we were finishing up interviews outside the campus. Officers pulled my driver into a nearby storefront and locked me inside the empty car. Two hours later, my driver emerged limping. He drove me back to the airport in silence. He gestured at his torso, then held a single finger up to his lips, motioning me not to speak. He had been bugged.

They came for Adiya, too. At first, the police visits to his after-school tutoring classes were ostensibly routine regulatory checks: they needed to inspect the quality of his curriculum. Someone tipped them off that he was teaching most of the classes entirely in Mongolian by now. Police officers went to his parents' home several times a week for two months, leaning on them to warn their son to stop his illegal behavior. Jittery parents stopped sending their children, and his business started hemorrhaging money. A few weeks later, Adiya was told to shut his business down. He never received a straight answer about what law he had violated, but the police were clear he would not be allowed to operate any longer. Adiya was distraught; he had invested his life savings into renovating his classrooms. The only thing he had left was his freedom. His troubles may have ended there, if not for the videos.

During their inspections, police had seized Adiya's computers and hard drives. They discovered the jerry-rigged VPN software he had installed for tunneling his way out of state internet controls. The police fined him RMB3,000 (about US$450) for the VPN. Then they discovered the videos of protests across Inner Mongolia he had archived, to save them from being erased completely by state censors. Worse, they unearthed a compilation video Adiya had edited in 2019 of the anti-government protests in Hong Kong. From there, it was easy to track down his Twitter handle and discover the reams of anti-Party and pro–Hong Kong content he had been sharing online under various aliases. To Adiya, the fight for Hong Kong values and the Mongolian language were linked. They were two of the many existential struggles for identity playing out across China. To the police, his obvious admiration for the Hong Kong protestors affirmed theories believed by China's security apparatus that these instances of mass dissent on Chinese soil had been purposefully instigated by "hostile foreign forces"—and Adiya was one of their agents. And so, like so many before him who had taken on a powerful Party state that would not tolerate who he wanted to be, Adiya decided to flee the country.

His escape out of China in January 2021 first took him to the Chinese port city of Tianjin, from which he took a flight to Cambodia. At immigration, as he left Chinese territory, he gestured at the camera slung as a prop around his neck and told officials he was a photographer on assignment abroad. To his surprise, his ruse worked, and he was let through to Phnom Penh. There, he paid a smuggler about $400 to take him by motorbike along the forested land border into Thailand, where Adiya's brother and family had already moved a year earlier. Within half a year, he had successfully applied for and received refugee status at the United Nations office in Bangkok.

His route was a common one for Chinese political asylum seekers before the global COVID pandemic locked down China's porous land borders with Southeast Asia. Yet even those who reached Thailand were not safe from the long arm of Chinese law enforcement. Nearly two years after he arrived in Bangkok, Adiya got a knock on the door from two Thai immigration officers, who cuffed him and told him he was a criminal wanted by the Chinese government. Two weeks later in detention, he was told his permit to return to China had been expedited and approved. Two employees of the Chinese embassy in Bangkok and two Chinese police officers came to visit him in jail and told him the embassy had applied on his behalf.

The stress nearly broke Adiya. He was sick after several weeks in a crowded detention cell he shared with about two hundred other people. A few of them were fellow Chinese citizens like Adiya, arrested in Thailand for running financial scams and telecom frauds. Unlike him, they were eager to return home. Their food was meager, bland soup and plain rice every day. He developed a wheezing cough and experienced flash fevers. Outside the detention center, Adiya's family was protesting for his release, but Thailand would not let him go. Thrice, the Chinese embassy booked a flight for him to China, but Adiya refused to board. Then, a month into his detention, with no explanation, he was suddenly let go.

After his close brush with extradition to China, Adiya left Thailand. He has since resettled in Canada. Since the class boycott in 2020, there are increasing signs that the use of Mandarin Chinese is being further accelerated in Inner Mongolia's schools. A leaked voice recording in 2023 shared by the advocacy group Southern Mongolian Human Rights Information Center shows a school principal notifying parents that soon all Mongolian-language instruction will stop, and classes will be taught entirely in Chinese.

Adiya knows he will never be able to return to Inner Mongolia, but he told me he had no regrets. We spoke entirely in Mandarin Chinese, his most fluent language, though he said he no longer considered himself Chinese. Now in Canada, at the age of thirty-four, he is trying to study Mongolian again.

CHAPTER 8

THE BOOKSELLER

On October 24, 2015, a Hong Kong bookseller named Lam Wing-kee crossed the border from Hong Kong to mainland China on foot. The crossing was usually quick: a short line, an exchange of documents, then a metro ride to mainland China. There, the Party governed strictly, but Lam always had Hong Kong. The region had been granted "special autonomous region" status to keep it the entrepot where everyone from financiers to dissidents could—until 2047, at least—do whatever they pleased, enjoying civil liberties and a raucous independent press protected under a British-style common law system.

Lam frequently and intentionally blurred that demarcation. Stringy and bespectacled, he had made the crossing between Hong Kong and China dozens of times before, surreptitiously carrying an assortment of salacious thrillers, political biographies, and pulpy romance novels, all printed in Chinese. His books were in high demand in mainland China, where speculative and investigative works about top Communist Party officials and sensitive parts of Party history were usually banned. He had just one close call in 2013, when he was detained for several hours after Chinese border officials discovered him smuggling the books. However, a bribe and some jokes later, they let him go. Afterward, Lam remotely shipped most orders from Hong Kong to a list of anonymized clients.

Lam's brick-and-mortar store in Hong Kong, named Causeway Bay Books, was squeezed next to a lingerie shop. The bookshop was a hot spot for visiting mainland tourists curious about the latest political gossip. Hong Kong was actually home to several bookshops that specialized in "banned books," but his store was one of the most popular. He regularly worked thirteen-hour days in his cramped offices, sleeping there overnight when tasks piled up. Despite the mainland's proximity, he felt safe doing his work. The One Country, Two Systems policy was a strong buffer, serving as an airtight legal firewall between the restrictions in mainland China and his thriving business in Hong Kong. He was confident China would continue to respect that buffer.

That sense of security was why he felt lighthearted that October day as he crossed from the Hong Kong side to mainland China. This trip was a personal one; he was visiting his mainland girlfriend who lived in Dongguan, a Chinese manufacturing hub just fifty miles north of the border. But as Lam swiped through the first set of gates at the border crossing to get into Hong Kong, the gates in front didn't open, trapping him between the two sets. He was suddenly surrounded by about a dozen Chinese officers. Lam recognized one of them, the one who had questioned him back in 2013. This time, the officer was much sterner. He and ten other officers pushed Lam into a waiting van, then drove him to the Shenzhen police station where Lam sat overnight with his feet and hands bound to a chair. Early the next morning, he was handcuffed, blindfolded, then taken on a thirteen-hour train ride. As he got off, the blindfold slipped a bit, and he could tell from traffic signs that he was in Ningbo, a port city on China's eastern coast, far to the north of Hong Kong. The police officers accompanying him ignored his questions. No one would tell him why he was there.

In Ningbo, Lam was brought to a large, padded room. His room had a window he could see the sky through. "I realized birds sounded different when you listen to them behind bars and when you are free," he remembered. Two security guards kept watch over him at all hours, changing shifts every four hours. He noticed everything was tied down—even the toothbrush.

He had already been forced to sign away his rights to see his family or request his own lawyer. He signed because he was dependent on his unknown captors to give him food and water. The security officers then finally introduced themselves; they were from the Chinese Communist Party's "central case examination group," tasked with investigating anti-Party activities, and they wanted to know about Lam's forbidden books. Why was he selling his books to mainland Chinese customers, and how did he send the books to them? How much money did he make a year on mainland sales? Selling books from Hong Kong, they impressed on him, was destabilizing China and defamed its leaders. Lam was astonished. He could not wrap his mind around why a Party state as big and powerful as China's would care about one tiny bookstore.

Evidently, they cared a lot, because the books—or rather, the fact that they could be published at all—were a symbol of the brash Hong Kong identity the Party had grown increasingly concerned about. The former British colony had begun as a rocky island, wrested from a feeble Qing empire after its disastrous loss in the First Opium War to Western powers, including Britain. In 1898, in order to accommodate a fast-growing population in Hong Kong, the British empire extracted a ninety-nine-year lease for the New Territories, a large expanse of forested hills and coastline across from Victoria Harbour and directly on China's mainland. The land lease dramatically expanded Hong Kong.

In the early 1980s, the impending expiration of that lease prompted China, its imperial days long behind it and now run by the Chinese Communist Party, to ask for political control over all of Hong Kong. After years of protracted negotiations from which the Hong Kong people were largely left out of, British and Chinese leaders agreed to a treaty transferring sovereignty, as well as a new constitution for the territory under Chinese control, later called the Basic Law. In 1997, the colony was formally "handed back" to China, and the British Union Jack was lowered in favor of the red and yellow Chinese flag amid a gunfire salute and a downpour so heavy it nearly melted the paper on which the Prince of Wales' speech had been written. Under the terms of the handover deal, the Party promised it would rule Hong Kong with a light touch, and Hong Kong could keep its independent judiciary and civil liberties under a principle called One Country, Two Systems—at least, for the first five decades of Chinese rule, until 2047, when both sides would reassess the situation. Privately, British diplomats hoped the rest of China would have liberalized by then to more resemble Hong Kong: culturally Chinese, but politically more aligned with Western democracies.

As the people of Hong Kong grasped for a new identity under Chinese control, they settled on the idea of "core values": freedom, human rights, democracy, rule of law, and transparent bureaucracy. From the start, Hong Kong's identity was aspirational and not based on shared ethnicity. The core values set the territory apart from both their mainland Chinese brethren, who enjoyed little of these values, as well as their former British masters, who had granted Hong Kongers few of these privileges. Under the new Basic Law, Hong Kongers still did not enjoy universal suffrage, though the Law's writers had dangled the possibility that one person, one vote was the "ultimate aim" for Hong Kong. Until then, the surest way to voice one's opinion was to take to the streets and march.

And march they did. From the 1997 handover onward, Hong Kongers protested en masse in 2003 to shelve a proposed national security law that would give Beijing more policing power; in 2012 to stop new school curricula that praised the Party and criticized multiparty democracy; and in 2014 to voice betrayal when Beijing said the hope for universal suffrage was dead in the water and the Party would preselect Hong Kong's chief executive candidates.

Through it all, Hong Kong booksellers like Lam sold their wares. They were like canaries in a coal mine; as long as they were allowed to exist, unfettered, Hong Kong still retained its core Hong Kong values. The city was a pressure valve for the mainland, a political loophole pressed right up against mainland China. Mainland tourists flocked to Lam's bookstore on vacations, where they plunged into an alternate world in which the illicit secrets of former top Communist generals and alleged sexual indiscretions of China's elite could be printed on the page. Historical archives and books excised from mainland university libraries ended up in Hong Kong, where they presented a darker, grittier, and more detailed telling of the Party's grip on power. Having worked with a long roster of mainland authors, Lam knew full well how China's

new leader Xi Jinping was bringing the mainland back to an ideological Party state, but like many other people, he believed that
change stopped at the One Country, Two Systems firewall—the
binding promise the Party had made to the British and to the
Hong Kong people just over two decades ago. That promise could
not be ignored; the law was the law. In Hong Kong, Lam believed
he was safe.

Trapped in his padded quarters in Ningbo, Lam did not know
that across Hong Kong, other booksellers like him were disappearing from their homes within weeks of each other. All of them
shared an obsession with banned books. One of the first to disappear was Gui Minhai, a paunchy writer who co-owned Mighty
Current, a Hong Kong–registered publisher that had actually ac-
quired Lam's bookstore.

Born in Ningbo, the city where Lam now found himself a
prisoner, Gui had escaped the intellectual backwaters of rural
China to attend Beijing's prestigious Peking University and study
history, launching him straight into a vivacious cohort of budding
intellectuals. But Gui was a poet at heart, and among these avant-
garde circles, he began exploring a charged, emotional writing
style. "He was writing really bold, exciting stuff," remembers Mag-
nus Fiskesjö, then a young diplomat posted at the Swedish embassy in Beijing who became a friend. But while many of his
classmates, caught up in the liberalization of the 1980s, stayed in
China until the bloody apex of the Tiananmen Massacre near the
end of that decade, Gui went wandering. He ended up in Sweden,
where he eventually became a naturalized citizen. China does
not allow dual citizenship, and Gui swiftly gave up his Chinese

nationality. Later, he briefly moved to Hong Kong and dove into publishing both bodice-rippers and political investigations. In 2015, he and employees at Mighty Current were purportedly editing a volume on the secret love life of Xi Jinping, the then–newly appointed leader of China.

The book was never released, because Gui disappeared while on vacation in Thailand. China had stepped up its secretive extradition of its citizens from third countries, but Gui's kidnapping was unusual because part of it was caught on camera. Security footage taken from his Pattaya condominium building in Thailand captured his last moments of freedom. The grainy footage shows a Chinese man intercepting Gui as he returns from grocery shopping. Gui gives his groceries to the condo's security guards, then gets back in the car with the Chinese agent and disappears from view. Two weeks later, the same cameras filmed a group of four other Chinese men who said they were picking up Gui's belongings for him, because he was gambling in Cambodia. One stubs his cigarette out in the lobby's plants as they wait for the elevator to Gui's apartment. By then, even though Thai immigration authorities had no record of Gui ever leaving the country, he had already been secretly whisked back to China. A week later, Lam was detained at the border. Then, like dominos falling, two other Mighty Current employees, Liu Por, Mighty Current's co-owner, and Cheung Chi-ping went missing. Their families filed missing persons reports with the Hong Kong police.

Lee Bo, a scholarly looking shareholder in the Causeway Bay Bookstore who also lived in Hong Kong, must have known he was in danger, too. That December, he sent Gui's daughter, Angela, then studying in the United Kingdom, an email expressing his fears. Using Gui's English name, Lee wrote: "I write to you concerning the whereabouts of Michael. I wonder if you have known that he has been missing for more than 20 days, we fear that he was taken by special agents from China for political reasons." (Angela would also later receive messages on Skype from her father's account but seemingly written by someone else, instructing her to stop her advocacy about his disappearance.)

Weeks later, Lee, a British citizen, became the last bookseller to vanish. He was last seen on December 30, more than two months after Gui disappeared, when Lee visited the company's warehouse in Hong Kong and never went home. Days later, his wife received a phone call from an unknown number. It was Lee. He explained he was in Shenzhen, across the border from Hong Kong, where he had gone to assist with a police investigation. Lee did not speak to his wife in his native Cantonese, which was the lingua franca of Hong Kong, but rather in Mandarin, the standard dialect spoken in mainland China. He asked her not to speak out about his case. Hong Kong immigration police confirmed with his wife they had no record of Lee leaving the territory, but somehow, he, too, had ended up in mainland China.

Chinese security agents crossing into Hong Kong to abduct a foreign citizen was the most direct assault on the invisible demarcation separating Hong Kong from the mainland. Until these abductions, Beijing had respected the separate identities since the handover. Kidnapping five booksellers signaled the end of an era, and that legal firewall disappeared altogether.

Five months into Lam's detention, he was given an extraordinary task. For weeks, he had needled his captors for one last opportunity to see his family and return to Hong Kong to bid his homeland a final goodbye. By March, worn down by waiting, Lam signed a guilty plea for illegal publishing. Then he was put on a train back to Shenzhen and whisked to a sumptuous compound called Kylin Villas, used as a regular meeting place for high-rolling delegations and officials. To his surprise, three out of four of Mighty Current's disappeared employees were also there: Lee Bo, Liu Por, and Cheung Chi-ping. No one dared ask openly about what had happened to Gui Minhai. Over dinner, Lee handed each of the three seated men wads of cash: HKD$100,000 (about US$15,000) to cover Lam's last few months of living costs and a final payout for the official dissolution of Mighty Current publishing.

Lam was being groomed. After the dinner, he was upgraded from his single room to an apartment that security officers had rented for him in a small city near the Hong Kong border. They even arranged a daily outing for him; every day, Lam could leave his apartment and peruse books at the public library, whose chief librarian would later remember Lam, normally skinny, as gaining "a lot" of weight during the three months Lam was a loyal patron.

Throughout, Lam's interrogations continued. His captors wanted to know who wrote the books Causeway Bay Bookstore published, but Lam told them repeatedly he had no direct contact with authors; he only published their books and their identities remained anonymous. Chinese security officers showed him a partial client list that Lee Bo had copied before leaving Hong Kong. They told Lam they would grant his wish and send him and his colleagues briefly back to Hong Kong so they could close the missing persons cases their families had opened with the Hong Kong police. But Lam had an extra task: to retrieve the remaining records from a company computer containing the bookstore's full customer and author information, then hand them over to authorities upon his return to mainland China. Lam knew this meant his readers would face prosecution and imprisonment, but he was broken down by months of psychological pressure. He accepted the mission, and in June, under the company of two Chinese handlers, Lam finally headed to Hong Kong.

While Lam had gone missing, the people of Hong Kong were in a panic about the fate of the five booksellers. Who could be grabbed off the streets next? The red lines were changing. What could be considered politically sensitive? How far would the Party go to stop even the smallest of dissenters? In mid-January, only two weeks after Lee Bo disappeared, they had their answer. All they had to do was turn on the television.

Gui Minhai was the first to reappear. In January, his weary visage appeared on China's state-run evening broadcast, which aired a marathon feature claiming Gui had voluntarily turned himself in for being the driver in a deadly hit-and-run in mainland China more than a decade earlier. "Although I am a Swedish national, I feel that I am still Chinese and my roots are in China," Gui says in halting Mandarin Chinese, appealing to the Swedish embassy to drop its demands for his release. Chinese officials brought up the bookseller's identity—claiming that he felt Chinese, even if his nationality was now Swedish—as justification for ignoring Sweden's consular requests to its citizens.

The next month, it was Lee Bo's turn to go on television. Seated in a genteel, dark-wood-paneled room with two people watching over him, the manager claimed he had smuggled himself into mainland China of his own accord, so as not to leave an immigration record because of a mainland police investigation he was assisting with under wraps. "I still believe Hong Kong has freedom of speech and the freedom to publish, but that does not preclude recklessly spreading rumors and making up lies," said Lee in front of the cameras. He also said despite his British passport, he felt he was ultimately still a Hong Konger and a Chinese person, and as such, was cooperating with authorities.

An estimated six thousand Hong Kong residents marched in protest of their detentions in January 2016, waving yellow umbrellas—a symbol of anti-government defiance—and warning onlookers that no one was safe any longer in Hong Kong. About five hundred writers and publishers signed a petition demanding Hong Kong uphold the freedom of publication.

Lam knew none of this when he returned to Hong Kong that June. As instructed, he promptly went to Lee Bo's apartment to retrieve the company computer. He checked into his local police station to close a missing persons case his wife had filed. He saw that his beloved Causeway Bay bookstore had been shuttered by its mysterious new owner, Mr. Chan. And then in the hours before he was mandated to return to mainland China, he committed his first small act of rebellion: he turned on his smartphone. Connecting to Hong Kong's internet for the first time since his detention, he scrolled through the uncensored web. The eight months he had missed came pouring in, including images of fellow Hong Kongers protesting on his behalf, a familiar scene that evoked the Hong Kong core values he once proudly upheld. The images snapped Lam out of the fugue state he had sunk into during his months under detention. He decided to make a call.

Lam dialed the number of Albert Ho, a pro-democracy lawmaker who once had been a frequent customer of Lam's. Lam hadn't slept in nearly two days since returning to Hong Kong, but within hours, Ho had him surrounded by a scrum of journalists in a blockbuster press conference. Lam was ready to tell his story, even at the cost of endangering his Mighty Current colleagues and his girlfriend, back in mainland China. "Out of us five [detained booksellers], I had the lightest burden," he told reporters about why he decided to disobey orders, stay in Hong Kong, and keep the company drives safe. By then, three other booksellers had popped up in Hong Kong, too, staying just long enough to close their missing persons cases, then beat it back to mainland China. Only Lam had deviated from the script.

Speaking slowly, in a voice husky from fatigue, Lam described his detention and mistreatment and the animal fear he felt in detention. He told reporters he had been forced to memorize and recite a confessional script on camera. Telling the truth was a way for him to reclaim his freedom. "I am happy I did as a Hong Konger what I should do," he later told Hong Kong's *South China Morning Post*, Hong Kong's English-language newspaper. He also resolved not to leave Hong Kong. The city was his home, and the attention he received there was his only protection from further Chinese control. Ho, the lawmaker organizing the press conference, agreed with Lam: "Most of us are not leaving Hong Kong. Where can you go? Hong Kong is our home. I myself won't. So we need to, like Lam said, have the courage to say no to hegemony, to pursue the truth, and protect each other."

In the end, it was a murder that set up the final blow to One Country, Two Systems. The killing in question was a lover's spat turned fatal: Hong Konger Poon Hiu-wing was just nineteen years old when her boyfriend, Chan Tong-kai, strangled her to death in a hotel in nearby Taiwan, an island China claims as its territory. Chan stuffed her body into a pink suitcase the couple had bought that day together, then went to sleep. The next day, he went shopping using her ATM card and flew back home to Hong Kong. Prosecutors in Taiwan wanted to charge Chan for murder but could not extradite him to stand trial, because Hong Kong—part of China—cannot honor such extraditions and thereby treat Taiwan as a separate country. Chan only served twenty-nine months prison time in Hong Kong on four counts of money laundering, because he used Poon's bank accounts to pay off his credit card bills.

That saddled another Lam—Hong Kong's chief executive Carrie Lam—with a thorny legal matter: how to bring Chan to real justice. Poon's distraught parents personally wrote letters to Lam begging her to punish Chan more severely, and the letters struck a chord with Lam, herself the mother of two boys. To close this legal "loophole," as Lam called it, Hong Kong proposed an amendment that allowed the territory to set up extradition agreements with any location. As it was proposed, such a mechanism would also allow the extradition of people arrested in Hong Kong to mainland China. This was a touchy proposition that several of Lam's advisors pushed back against, but Lam was obstinate.

Hong Kongers immediately launched protests against the proposed amendment, which they feared would create yet another legal loophole—one that China would take advantage of to extradite political activists to the mainland, where they enjoyed far fewer civil liberties in a justice system that convicts more than 99 percent of those tried. Lam Wing-kee, the bookseller, was not at those protests. He was packing. The extradition law was confirmation of his worst fear, that Beijing was rapidly turning Hong

Kong into an extension of mainland China. He was relocating to Taiwan.

Nearly four years after his disappearance, I met Lam Wing-kee in Taipei, Taiwan's capital, under the archway of a popular shopping complex. He had arrived at our appointed time, he explained, but was a few minutes late so he could observe from a distance whether we had brought any unknown guests or were being followed. His eyes darted left and right, though he relaxed as he eased into telling his story, his native Cantonese peppering the Mandarin Chinese we used to communicate.

The years since his detention were taking a toll on him, and his simple T-shirt hung loosely off his gaunt frame. Despite his promise to stay in Hong Kong, Lam said now that he would never return. He no longer felt the city could keep him safe. "You cannot imagine the pressure China can put on you. I still have occasional nightmares. Sometimes I wake up screaming in my sleep," said Lam. He didn't know what had happened to his former Mighty Current colleagues Lee Bo, Liu Por, and Cheung Chi-ping; they remained in mainland China where he could only assume they lived under heavy surveillance.

There were also more disappearances in Hong Kong. In 2017, China nabbed Xiao Jianhua, a well-connected financial intermediary for the Chinese political elite whose formidable acumen had helped him build up a personal fortune of an estimated $6 billion, sequestered within an elaborate network of holding companies. Xiao protected the family finances of the Party elite, including Xi Jinping's sister and brother-in-law as well as the son of a top official under Xi's predecessors. But Xiao, a naturalized Canadian citizen, was also a symptom of the rot within the Party and thus a target of Xi, the Party's new chairman by 2012. The baby-faced bagman moved into a luxury suite in Hong Kong's ritzy Four Seasons hotel, protected by a retinue of reportedly all-female bodyguards, to put some distance between him and Xi. That didn't stop Xiao from being abducted, drugged, then rolled in a wheelchair across the border into mainland China by Chinese security agents, reappearing five years later to be tried in a closed court and given a thirteen-year prison sentence for financial crimes. "The Chinese system has changed massively" since he was detained, Lam told me. "Then, perhaps in kidnapping Hong Kong people, China was a bit anxious because this matter would be made public. But now, they very likely would not be afraid at all."

He obtained residency in Taiwan and reopened Causeway Bay Books in Taipei in 2020, but it wasn't smooth going. The opening was delayed by a copyright lawsuit from a similarly named company in another Taiwanese city—an effort from a Chinese shell company to bury his store before it had even opened, Lam believed. A few days after finally opening his new bookstore, two men Lam did not recognize mobbed him in a Taipei cafe and splashed red paint all over him. The two assailants were never found.[1]

Gui Minhai's fate was a final warning to Lam of the dangers he faced in China and the potential stakes of an extradition agreement with Beijing. In 2018, released after two years of imprisonment, Gui was exhibiting early signs of a neurological disease, and he wanted to seek better medical treatment in Beijing. This time Sweden sent two of its diplomats in China to personally accompany Gui to the Chinese capital. The small group was sitting on the train bound for Beijing when some ten Chinese security officials forced Gui off the train. He has never been seen publicly since. In 2020, Gui was sentenced in a closed trial to another decade in prison, this time for passing on intelligence to foreign countries.

Lam believes he will never see his colleague, nor Hong Kong, again. His hope now lay in the young people who had chosen to stay in Hong Kong and who were now protesting the proposed extradition amendment, as well as a litany of other grievances over Chinese mismanagement, such as a severe housing shortage and extreme income inequality. He watched the demonstrations from afar, torn by conflicting impulses. He was not sure the protestors would succeed. He also knew if they did not protest, Hong Kong values would not get a second chance at survival. The city was about to explode.

CHAPTER 9

THE PROTESTOR

O n the day that would change his life forever, Kenny had
wandered over, mostly out of curiosity, to the hulking legislative council offices of Hong Kong. There were whiffs of rebellion
wafting around. The city's biggest trade union was calling for a
strike. Thousands of people were gathering for a "picnic" at a
nearby park—code for protest. They wanted to block a routine,
bureaucratic formality scheduled to take place within the government offices: the second reading of a legislative proposal.

The proposal was called the Fugitive Offenders and Mutual
Legal Assistance in Criminal Matters Legislation Amendment
Bill, proposed by Hong Kong's chief executive Carrie Lam. The
proposed amendment would allow Hong Kong to extradite sus-
pects to other places, including mainland China, to be tried. Hong
Kong residents, who had long prided themselves on their "Hong
Kong values" and their emphasis on civil liberties, were aghast.
The amendment, they argued, could be used to legalize the abduc-
tion of political dissidents. It had happened before, after all, with

the kidnapping of the five booksellers. To Hong Kongers, the city's leaders were intentionally blurring the line between what China directly controlled and what still remained of Hong Kong. The amendment was exactly what Lam Wing-kee, the Hong Kong bookseller, had feared upon returning to the city and breaking his Chinese security gag order in 2016, before going into self-exile in Taiwan.

But most Hong Kongers stayed put; they would march. Kenny marched, too. Three days before that fateful June day in 2019, he had joined one million Hong Kongers in the streets, the peaceful crowds shielded by multicolored umbrellas from the torrential summer rains as they snaked through the streets of Hong Kong Island. One million was an impressive number even for a city that loved to protest. Protesting was the only way the public could voice their preferences because there were no direct elections for Hong Kong's top chief executive position. Also, protesting worked. In 2003, peaceful crowds signaled their displeasure with national security proposals to amend the region's constitution to criminalize subversion against the central Chinese government. In 2012, popular opposition succeeded again, stopping a curricular overhaul citizens thought was too pro-Beijing.

This time, to Kenny's dismay, Chief Executive Lam pressed ahead despite public opposition and announced she would not shelve the Fugitive Offenders amendment. A second reading for the bill was scheduled, and then it would be up for legislative vote. That was why, by late morning of June 12, the day that changed his life, Kenny and nearly forty thousand other demonstrators were milling around the legislative council offices. They would block the legislators from entering the building if needed. Close by, more vigilantes were on guard, ready to swarm any vehicles ferrying legislators. Someone had hung a banner that said

"Withdraw the Extradition Bill, Defend One Country, Two Systems" off the side of a footbridge. The protestors were clear they were not revolutionaries. They did not intend to overturn the political system; they simply wanted their government to uphold the promise to preserve Hong Kong's legal buffer with mainland China until at least 2047.

Kenny showed up that morning in his normal office clothes, but he saw that hundreds of the younger, more hardcore protestors had donned black T-shirts and yellow construction hard hats. They seemed prepared for a violent confrontation. Hundreds of riot police, clad in black body armor and wielding a phalanx of body-length riot shields, streamed into the roads surrounding the legislative offices. By midafternoon, the bravest and the angriest protestors charged the police barricades. The police responded by tossing metal cannisters of tear gas back at the protestors. The acrid smoke spread quickly, choking anyone nearby. Throughout that afternoon, the police fired dozens more cannisters like projectiles, sometimes using them to drive away demonstrators holding nothing more than umbrellas. Police pepper-sprayed a cluster of passersby sitting down on the street next to a planter of decorative flowers, for no reason, it seemed to Kenny, other than that they were *there*. Their screams, the bright flowers, the surrealness of it all—it was enough to overwhelm him.

Any semblance of social order broke down. Ordinary Hong Kongers were digging up pavement tiles to throw at riot police and hauling cinder blocks into makeshift roadblocks. Kenny found himself in front of a glass skyscraper owned by China's state investment company CITIC. Protest organizers had applied for and received prior police permission to hold a rally in front of the enormous office building, and Kenny thought he would be safe there, but he could see that riot police were massing at both ends of the street in front of CITIC Tower, cutting off all escape routes. Suddenly, they fired tear gas from both sides at the peaceful crowd. It was the first time Kenny had seen such a projectile land so close. He could hear the percussive thump of the cannisters being launched, then a terrifying moment of silence during which he knew it was arcing toward him. He had nowhere to run—only toward the shining doors of CITIC Tower, but they were locked. No amount of shaking and banging could open them. The protestors were trapped against the glass doors.

Kenny heard screaming behind him. He couldn't breathe. The air was mixed with stinging tear gas, and the press of people was squeezing him painfully. The crowd was trying to push its way into CITIC Tower, trampling those in front of them as pure fear engulfed them. A trickle of people were making their way into the tower through a singular revolving door, nearly falling over each other as they were yanked into the lobby and beyond, into safety. Kenny thought he would die before he reached the revolving door. He was pressed up against the glass windows nearby, slippery with humidity and the slick of people throwing themselves against the thick panes. A handful of protestors who had managed to find their way into the tower lobby were laboring to smash the glass from the other side with metal cordon poles. Minutes later, he made it through one of the broken windows, drawing deep gulps of air into his burning lungs.

Something broke inside of Kenny after that afternoon. He no longer trusted the police or the city's civil service. Before, there had been a kind of understanding, a social compact, between Kenny and the Beijing-appointed order in the city. He tolerated them and occasionally, during protest movements, he pushed back against the state, but always within limits for the sake of safety and civility. Now those limits were gone. At his next protest,

Kenny did not wear his office clothes. He donned a helmet, a face mask, and bought some plastic goggles. He was ready to wholly dedicate himself to the cause.

He hid his nightly protest activities from his family. They did not see much of each other anyway, and he knew, save for a close aunt, that they would disapprove. Kenny was born in mainland China. When he turned two years old, just a few years before the former British colony was handed back to China, his mother ferried them both to Hong Kong, only several dozen miles from his birthplace. At the turn of the new millennium, the city was still far glitzier and richer than mainland cities like Shenzhen and even Shanghai. One of Asia's major stock markets was run out of Hong Kong, and it was the regional headquarters for dozens of major multinational companies. Economic opportunity beckoned, irresistibly, even under Chinese Communist Party rule.

Never forget that you are Chinese, Kenny's mother would remind him. The city was back under Beijing's control, now a Chinese city finally run by ethnic Chinese officials, albeit ones effectively chosen by the central government in Beijing rather than by Hong Kongers. Kenny's family felt this was better than living under British colonial appointees, when being ethnically Chinese felt like occupying a lower caste. In 2008, Kenny watched on television as the flag of the People's Republic of China—red with five golden stars—rose at a stately pace next to that of the International Olympic Committee. The Beijing Olympics filled him with pride because China was becoming a global power, and Kenny believed Hong Kong would be at the forefront of China's rise. The city already had a thriving financial services sector, a multilingual and highly educated population, and proximity to both China and the rest of Asia. Moreover, it enjoyed special political status that China promised would give it a "high degree of autonomy"—until at least 2047. Until then, Hong Kong was to be ruled with a gentle hand under One Country, Two Systems. Kenny vaguely knew that the Communist Party could be ruthless in quashing social dissent, but perhaps Hong Kong's success would prove to the leadership in Beijing that political liberalization and economic development went hand in hand. To Kenny, Hong Kong was a safe, stable place growing up, a place where he felt that if he worked hard he could succeed.

First, he had to make it to university. His mother had remarried after moving to Hong Kong, and Kenny frequently clashed with his stepfather over his commitment to his schooling. The family priority was to work and earn money, just like his older stepbrother was doing, even if he had to drop out of high school. On weekends, Kenny spent his time at charity houses, so he could find some peace and quiet and time to study. His favorite subject in high school had been liberal studies, a uniquely Hong Kong element of the mandatory curriculum that combined history and current events with critical analysis. His teacher discussed events censored on the mainland—the 1989 Tiananmen Massacre and the writings of Liu Xiaobo, a Chinese dissident intellectual and winner of the Nobel Peace Prize—and asked Kenny and his classmates what lessons these events had for Hong Kong. After taking the class, Kenny started attending the annual candlelight vigil in Victoria Park to remember the thousands of lives lost during the Tiananmen Massacre in Beijing. Attending was a privilege because he knew such a vigil would not be possible on the mainland. It only solidified his new conviction that Hong Kong could be the model of political opening for the rest of China.

Years later, when Kenny had graduated, gone to university, and gotten his first real job as a civil engineer building the gleaming skyscrapers and concrete blocks that dotted the city skyline, he still thought back to his liberal studies classes. Hong Kong's overheated property market, already constrained because of the region's small size, exceeded the budgets of most young Hong Kongers. The best plots were being snatched up by mainland Chinese buyers. Who were these buildings being constructed for, Kenny wondered, and how had Hong Kong become so inequitable? He himself could not hope to afford an apartment in the buildings he was helping build. He started to volunteer his time with a local political party, one that focused on providing social services to the city's poorer citizens and improving public resources within each city district. It also ran more pro-democratic candidates during legislative elections every four years.

Suddenly his older stepbrother, normally aloof, became very interested in his work. He wanted to know where the party's offices were located. Who were its senior officers? Kenny suspected his brother was not asking out of mere curiosity but had fallen in with one of the local gangs sympathetic to Beijing's politics and who attended the occasional pro-Beijing rally. He would not tell his brother where the party's offices were, but when his brother offered to buy the party's entire inventory of political leaflets, he let him. Kenny had no idea where his brother had suddenly gotten all that money.

By late summer 2019, the anti-extradition bill protests were ballooning into something much bigger: a demand for broader democratic reforms. Those demands had stalled after a series of protests dubbed the Umbrella Movement, which had started five years earlier in an effort to let Hong Kong voters directly choose their chief executive. The Umbrella Movement simmered into a standoff, as demonstrators occupied one of the city's main throughfares for more than two months. Eventually the encampment was torn down, the petition for universal suffrage largely ignored, and Beijing continued to prescreen all chief executive candidates. The end of the Umbrella Movement had seemed like a death knell for a more democratic future for Hong Kong. But this time around, as pushback against the extradition proposal picked up momentum, Chief Executive Carrie Lam backed down; she grudgingly shelved the extradition amendment in the face of increasingly violent protests.

The protestors now wanted more. About two weeks later, demonstrators stormed the city's legislative council. The date was no coincidence; it was July 1, the anniversary of Hong Kong's "handover" to Chinese rule. Dozens of masked demonstrators used metal carts as a makeshift battering ram to smash through the government office's windows. Hundreds of people poured in, ranging from floor to floor and vandalizing the portraits of council members, though they were careful to leave a room full of antiques and the legislative council's library untouched. The citizens of Hong Kong were "taking back the legislature," one protestor there later gleefully told me. Controversially, someone laid a British colonial flag on the raised main dais in the legislative chamber. Other people scrawled demands for universal suffrage on the smooth, oak-paneled walls of the chamber.

These graffitied demands became the core of the protest movement. "Five demands, not one less" was a standard chant at demonstrations that followed throughout August and September. Kenny and the tens of thousands of demonstrators who joined him on the streets wanted, among other things, an investigation into alleged police brutality during protests; amnesty for anyone arrested; and true universal suffrage to directly elect Hong Kong's legislators and chief executive. In other words, they were asking for a complete remake of the Hong Kong political system into a more representative democracy—and one that would last beyond the fifty-year term China had allowed during the handover. The protests that kicked off that summer in 2019 were Hong Kong's biggest protests yet, one over the identity of Hong Kong and what it should stand for.

By late July, Kenny had fallen in with a team of about one hundred people who kept in touch through Telegram, an encrypted messaging app. He would end up meeting nearly everyone in their chat group on the streets of Hong Kong, but it was as if he knew them in an alternate dimension. He didn't know anyone's real name. In broad daylight, he wouldn't have recognized them in their office clothes, sans face mask. But for the next four months, under the cover of night, they spent hours together nearly every weekend, working in tandem to build barricades, track police movements across the city, and graffiti protest slogans on bridges.

Although everyone was fully anonymous in the Telegram group, they each had carefully specialized roles so that together, they operated like one cohesive unit. Some of them were "fire magicians"—the moniker given to the pyrotechnic enthusiasts who rapidly assembled Molotov cocktails to chuck at oncoming riot police in case a diversion was needed. Then there was the *woh-leih-fei*, who comprised the vast majority of protestors. Cantonese for "rational, peaceful, and nonviolent," the *woh-leih-fei* usually showed up to demonstrations in their normal street clothes, carrying nothing but an umbrella, and staying well away from riot police. Their mission was to overwhelm with their sheer numbers. The unit's "information specialists" hung back at demonstrations, scanning narrow alleyways, and monitoring other chat groups for information on where the city's police were massing. They rapidly sent out texts and updated crowdsourced maps online that tracked police movement in real time.

Ordinary residents enraged by police brutality and seeming government indifference also began pitching in any way they could. Some donated goggles and masks or paid to import them as supplies in the city ran short. Being caught with goggles or masks—standard protest gear—could mean a brief detention or arrest, so other residents started a volunteer ride-hailing service to help demonstrators get to safety in the early dawn hours and avoid public transport. On long protest-filled weekends, Kenny and his Telegram group of volunteers rented an Airbnb to use as a safe house, so they would not have to return home and face their parents between demonstrations.

The front-liners like Kenny came the most heavily armored, in full face masks and sporting knee and elbow pads for dodging blows and protecting joints from the jagged edges of bricks they hurled at riot police. Most of them were young men like Kenny: strong and daring enough to be the "charge boys" that could hold off security for a few more minutes as everyone else fled. But not all front-liners were millennials. One of those I met, a hairdresser by day, was old enough to be Kenny's father. He was horrified by the police violence against protestors television stations had documented, and he believed the demonstrators were fighting to secure Hong Kong's future. In many ways, he told me, he felt like a guardian figure. When night fell, the young protestors became his children—and that sometimes meant convincing the most impulsive of them to retreat, for their own good.

One night, he found himself being chased by riot police with firehoses that shot torrential streams of blue-tinted water at protestors. The hoses were strong enough to knock people clean off their feet, and the water burned and stained their skin a bright blue for days, marking them for arrest afterward. He pleaded with the teenage front-liners around him, but they refused to flee. They didn't want to abandon their precious gear, expensive helmets, and gas masks, but keeping them would immediately incriminate them to police if they were caught while running. "I had to talk them down into abandoning their toys and run," the front-liner said.

By September, I was flying in from Beijing to spend nearly every weekend in Hong Kong. The contrast was head-spinning. I would depart in the morning from Beijing, the seat of political power in China and where anyone who dared to unfurl a protest banner would be bundled into a waiting van within seconds. By the same evening, I was in the chaos of a Hong Kong street battle, with residents young and old yelling insults at a phalanx of riot police. At that point, I had lived in Beijing for half a decade, but I had yet to see a protest in the capital. The defiance of Hong Kong felt utterly alien for someone from the mainland.

In the sea of black, the favored sartorial color of protestors, the trained eye could pick out makeshift symbols designating some of these specialized roles. Supply runners ferried everything from water bottles to bricks they had pried from the sidewalk to the front lines. Other demonstrators stalked the perimeter with purloined traffic cones at hand, which they used to quickly cover any smoking tear gas cannisters lobbed their way to stop the cannisters from spreading their painful contents further. Medics had crosses made of red duct tape stuck on their black canvas bags of medical supplies. Police were occasionally arresting hospitalized protestors, so they stopped going to hospitals. If someone was injured after a night of protest, they sought help instead from a quasi-underground network of sympathetic doctors and emergency medical technicians who could treat scrapes and contusions.

One August night, as the mass of protestors contracted and expanded, into and out of Hong Kong's commercial streets, using nothing but a few shouted, coded commands, it became an organic whole greater than the sum of its individual protestors. Suddenly I felt the mass shift; people behind me were running, pushing the rest of us forward. "Tear gas!" they shouted. I could see diners at a nearby restaurant run out, too, as the cloud of smoke crept toward their tables. Someone paused on the sidewalk to hand me several plastic squeeze vials full of saline for washing my eyes out, then dashed away before the police could get closer. A huddle of us found a quiet corner under an overpass and waited for the next confrontation.

One demonstrator had cut her finger in the melee. Immediately, protesters sheltered her from view with umbrellas and then crossed their arms in the air, signaling for help. Others repeated the gesture and yelled for assistance. Protestors farther away heard their calls and amplified them forward—a human telephone chain. In less than a minute, a medic came sprinting over. He knelt to the ground and immediately began bandaging the cut on the fallen protestor. His name was Calvin, a twenty-two-year-old trained EMT who had quit his job so he could be a medic full-time at nightly protests.

Later, he sat down on a curb as he told his story, weary from the night of running. At first, he had joined the anti-extradition movement as an ordinary protestor, but because of his medical training, he became a protest medic. During the day, he made house visits to people who were seriously injured the night before, treating them in private to minimize their risk of arrest. He was using his own savings to fund this work, including the gauze and bandages he carried with him to each demonstration, but he only had a few months in savings left before he would be unable to pay his rent. With the way things were going, Calvin suspected it would all be over in a few months, with either all the protestors arrested or full anarchy as Beijing's rule in the city collapsed.

Sometimes Kenny was out late enough that he finished a night of protest and went home only to shower before heading straight back to work. If he was slower or sometimes late at his job, his boss didn't say anything; Kenny believed he silently supported the protestors.

Kenny's strong moral code had been nourished by an adolescent love of Japanese anime comics and Chinese martial arts tales. He had been transported as a teenager by their grand narratives of good versus evil. He took comfort in the absolutes of those stories; even when the good guys lost, they did so with dignity and honor. He knew he faced David and Goliath odds in facing down the Hong Kong police, the chief executive's office, and behind her, the full force of the Chinese Communist Party. He was prepared to sacrifice his career, his youth, and potentially his freedom if it meant he had contributed to some larger good, just as his heroes in his favorite comic books had.

His fellow protestors took inspiration from martial arts films. "Be water," they reminded each other, a phrase lifted from a Bruce Lee martial arts flick. The idea was to decentralize protest. No one person was ever in charge. Like water, the protestors would be formless, adapting to whatever situation was at hand. Decisions about where to protest and when to retreat were made collectively, on the spot, in the street. They flowed like an unpredictable stream through alleys and thoroughfares, and when they hit resistance, they evaporated, a thousand black droplets of water scattering.

A thread of despair ran through the last of the demonstrations that year in 2019. The hopelessness made for a curious contrast to the fervency of the earlier anti-extradition protests, and it showed how different these protests were from other instances in Hong Kong's history of resistance. In 2019, Hong Kongers saw institutions honed over decades under both British and Chinese rule break down in the face of a massive loss in public trust. The turning point was in July, when dozens of white-shirted thugs beat journalists and peaceful demonstrators, then stormed a nearby metro station where protestors were on their way home. Bystanders and those watching online as the attack was live streamed placed some 24,000 calls to emergency services for help. The police took thirty-nine minutes to arrive—an eternity for a force once-renowned for its efficiency in monitoring the compact city.

Emily, a young social media editor at Hong Kong's most brash pro-democracy outlet, *Apple Daily,* was on her shift monitoring footage of the protests that day when the attack happened. She watched as reporters on the scene live streamed the frantic screams of those trapped underground. Having combed through dozens of hours of protest footage on previous shifts, she felt asphyxiated by the violence playing out on her screen that afternoon, the accumulation of weeks of secondary trauma overwhelming her. She told me she could feel the blood rushing to her head, dark spots crowding her vision. She fainted in her chair.

The incident also deeply divided Hong Kong over even the

basic facts of what had transpired. Shortly after the Yuen Long attack, named after the metro station in which it occurred, I wandered around the New Territories, a vast swath of lush land that shares a land border with mainland China. To get there, I ventured out on the one light-rail track that arced up north, the skyscrapers and multistory escalators petering out into three-story family homes, clustered protectively together. These were the "Indigenous" villages of Hong Kong, where family clans had farmed the land well before the British, and later the Chinese Communist Party, governed the region. Here, I was closer to the city of Shenzhen, on the mainland, than to Hong Kong's main island. The Qing empire, who was then ruling China, leased the New Territories to the British in 1898 for a ninety-nine-year term, and it was this lease's impending expiry that prompted negotiations for the eventual handover of Hong Kong back to Chinese rule. The people of the New Territories were used to living in the shadow of China. Permanently rooted to land temporarily lent out to the foreigners, their self-identification as people of China had not wavered.

I met a resident named Paul in the village of Nam Pin Wai. The village was just steps away from the infamous Yuen Long metro station, and after attacking protestors, the white-shirted assailants had retreated here, melting away into the narrow alleys. According to local media, the village is also the territory of a well-known triad group, Wo Shing Wo. Paul, a plump sixty-something man playing cards with several friends, eyed me suspiciously when I entered the village. He called out to me in fluent American-accented English occasionally clipped by his native Cantonese. He wanted to share his side of the story.

He said he had traveled the world, worked in the United States, and about a decade ago, decided to come back to his hometown in the New Territories. He was unapologetic about his fellow villagers beating the protesters. They did it out of self-defense, he claimed, as part of a nightly, all-volunteer patrol to protect the village from marauding protestors. "We are not going to be sitting ducks. We are not chickenshit," he spat out. Caught between an urbanizing, expanding Hong Kong and a rising China, the indigenous village was choosing to ally with the latter, even if that pitted them against thousands of anti-government protesters.

Paul and his friends saw no contradiction between Hong Kong's values and Chinese governance. "We are part of China. We were handed back [to China] in 1997," said Wong, sitting next to Paul. He reached over to snap up a clam on his plate. "We should not expect the United States or the United Kingdom to help us. We can only rely on China." But their affinity for Beijing was largely born out of fear, not love, of a powerful China. "We enjoy special privileges," says Paul, referring to Hong Kong's rule of law and access to international financial systems. He felt the protestors were playing into Beijing's hands by giving China an excuse to exact devastating revenge on the city: "I hope they value what we are. Don't screw it up. Don't spoil it."

Hong Kong's government—and behind them, the Chinese Communist Party—were not backing down. Two months of intense protest later, only one of the protestors' five demands had been met: the suspension of the anti-extradition bill. The protestors increasingly felt backed into a corner. Protesting was no longer about winning; protesting was about survival. In the end, it was all or nothing. Peaceful protest had clearly not worked in achieving their five demands. With nothing left to lose, some endorsed targeted violence. The city slid from cynicism into outright nihilism.

This attitude came to be called *lam chau* among protestors—literally translated from the Cantonese to mean "embrace burning." It was a philosophy of destruction: the harder Beijing tried to stamp out protests, the harder the protestors would hit back at the Party's tools of power in Hong Kong. *Lam chau* meant doxxing Hong Kong police officers on Telegram group chats, so they received hundreds of death threats. Adherents taught themselves how to make explosives and catapults and fought pitched street battles night after night, sometimes destroying storefronts, sidewalks, and vehicles in the process. This small group of militant protestors called themselves the *yuhng mouh,* "the valiant" in Cantonese, and they embraced violence with the assumption that their adversaries were even more willing to use violence against protestors.

The seeds of this political showdown between the prodemocracy and pro-Beijing facets of Hong Kong were rooted well before the region's handover to China in 1997. Hong Kong lawyer Martin Lee founded the city's first pro-democratic political party and was dispatched to Beijing in the 1980s to help negotiate the Basic Law, a constitution that provides the legal foundation for the region of Hong Kong under Chinese rule. He went to Beijing with high hopes; a joint declaration signed between China and the United Kingdom guaranteeing Hong Kong's independent courts, freedom of speech and the press, and the reform of the city's former colonial government into a more direct democracy.

Those promises were quickly chipped away under Chinese pressure. Proposals to introduce direct elections of legislative council candidates and the top chief executive were scrapped. Instead, pro-business lobbies would choose the city's top leader and most of its legislature. "Ten years after the Joint Declaration, however, and only three years before the handover, it has become clear that neither Britain nor China is going to honor the promises that each made in the Joint Declaration. Almost before the ink was dry on the treaty, the PRC Government began to backpedal from its promises of self-rule for Hong Kong," Lee wrote in 1994 in the academic *Journal of Democracy*. "As 1997 draws closer, the communist regime's threats and meddling grow stronger by the day." Lee finally quit his role on the Basic Law drafting committee in 1989, in protest over Beijing's decision to fire on its own citizens protesting in Tiananmen Square that year. The exact death toll of the Tiananmen Massacre is still not known, but thousands of pro-democracy protestors likely died. The tragedy was not a promising omen for Hong Kong's own prospects, but Hong Kong forged on with the handover and a hope that what remained of its autonomy would remain untouched.

Three decades later, *lam chau* adherents ditched that social compromise in favor of what was effectively a suicide pact. Their radical militancy alienated most of the city's well-heeled middle class and expatriate community who saw the protestors themselves as responsible for ruining their comfortable vision of Hong Kong. They decried the violence and called for police to reestablish law and order. But for *lam chau* protestors, that was the point: they wanted to create discomfort to remind the rest of the city of the existential battle it faced against Beijing and to preserve what was left of Hong Kong values.

As the anti-extradition protests soldiered on, it became less clear what the protestors were fighting for, other than for the sheer sake of confrontation, to make the arrests of thousands of previous demonstrators mean something. I felt this late one August night, the mugginess of summer already giving way to the hint of a cooler autumn, as I watched a group of several hundred people laboring to fence off a major city road from incoming police. They had painted over the lights on tram lines and drawn up barricades. Someone lit a pile of plywood on fire while others pounded on metal drums made out of sheeting torn off a nearby construction site. Green lasers crisscrossed the dark night sky—protestors liked to shine the laser pointers at police to deter them from snapping pictures of the demonstrators. The streetlamps cast a sickly tint on the full-face gas masks people wore as they worked to pry out bricks from the sidewalks for use as catapult ammunition. When the riot police inevitably came, a handful at the back of the retreating group of demonstrators lobbed empty beer bottles, which shattered and burst into flames. Then they ran off to another street, another confrontation, another close escape.

Their nihilism bred despair, which bred more violence. They fought every protest now as if it were their last. They would destroy as much as possible so there was nothing left when Beijing, inevitably, took over. I noticed the same phrases popping up over and over again in the English-language graffiti scrawled on bridge underpasses and building walls left by the nocturnal guerrilla fighters. *It was you who taught us peaceful marches are futile,* one read. Another was more stark: *If we burn, you burn with us.*

The central government issued a warning in response. "Those who play with fire will perish by it," said Yang Guang, a spokesman for the Hong Kong and Macau Affairs Office of the State Council. Anyone who engaged in "violence and crimes . . . will be held accountable." Kenny gave himself a deadline: if the Hong Kong government had not acceded to even just one more of the protestors' five demands by December, he was going to stop going out each night. His political activities were getting dangerous. He knew the police force was taking photographs and building up dossiers of information on the few hundred front-liners like him. If caught, he knew the consequences were harsh. Nearly 2,500 protestors, almost a third of them minors, had been arrested already and charged with rioting, and they faced up to ten years in prison.

In the end, his arrest came sooner than he expected. It was an October afternoon, and Kenny and some of the protestors in the Telegram group were wandering around a working-class neighborhood in northern Hong Kong. They had heard there would be a protest in the area and wanted to be on standby in case they were needed. As they were crossing the street, waiting for the demonstration to kick off, they were ambushed by a crowd of police from behind. The officers tried to knock Kenny down, but he dodged and kept running. Then he heard screaming; a young woman had fallen and was yelling for help as a police officer tried to drag her to her feet. Kenny sprinted back and beat the officer off, then hoisted the girl up as he started to sprint again. He almost made it.

A bystander stuck their leg out of the crowd and tripped Kenny. Sprawled on the sidewalk, he was tackled by several officers, then hauled into a waiting van. At the police station, one of the officers recognized him from a previous protest. They had nabbed a front-liner, the police officers realized. They beat him again, one officer punching him repeatedly in the back of his head. Kenny blacked out.

His hearing was scheduled for that same month, but Kenny never showed up. Instead, he went into hiding. His fellow protestors were still going out onto the streets, and he kept his hopes up that some kind of political armistice could be reached with the regional government by December. Once that happened, he would no longer be a fugitive. He hadn't given up on Hong Kong just yet.

That autumn flew past in a riotous blur of shattered glass and body armor, the touch-and-go of graffiti sprayed then erased, the lethargy of a city under siege broken by nightly protests. Increasingly desperate protestors turned to increasingly destructive means to voice their dissatisfaction with the growing economic inequality of Hong Kong, the rising property prices, mainland investment pushing out local control, and the influx of Mandarin replacing Cantonese use.

Kenny could only watch it from afar, observing in silence as one by one his team was picked off the streets and arrested during the nightly protests. By January 2022, police said they had arrested a total of 10,496 people for rioting, a charge that carried a maximum sentence of a decade in prison. He cut off all ties with the remaining protestors in his Telegram group to protect them—and to protect himself. He had already skipped his appointed court hearing and was now officially considered a fugitive. The best thing he could do for the cause right now was to remain invisible to the world, even as the world he had grown up with was rapidly changing around him. He silently rooted for everyone who remained free enough on the outside to continue demonstrating. The Party would not dare arrest everyone, he reasoned.

The Party never planned on arresting everyone, because they did not need to. They would leverage the power of the law to use people's own fears to control them.

I was sitting in my office in Beijing late one afternoon in June

2020 when the newsflash came through from a handful of local
Hong Kong media outlets: mainland China's rubber-stamp legislature was about to pass a law effective by midnight that day to
criminalize nearly all dissent in Hong Kong. It was called the Law
of the People's Republic of China on Safeguarding National Security in the Hong Kong Special Administrative Region, and it
was the culmination of years of effort from Beijing to end Hong
Kong's limited autonomy under One Country, Two Systems, once
and for all. Since 2014, Chinese policymakers and legal scholars
had been researching ways to wield "comprehensive jurisdiction"
over Hong Kong. But Xi was unwilling to wait for Hong Kong
lawmakers themselves to mount stricter laws to control dissent.
He decided to declare a tough new security law by fiat and passed
by the central government in Beijing, where it would brook no
opposition.

I frantically scanned through the final text of the proposed
legislation, reeling at the broadness of its terms. Its language was
succinct: the law would allow Beijing to establish its own national
security agency on Hong Kong soil to prosecute security cases and
operate according to mainland China's legal standards, outside the
scope of Hong Kong law. Beijing would also appoint an advisor to
supervise the local Hong Kong administration on national security issues. Those found guilty of the highest degree of subversion,
secession, collusion with foreign forces, or terrorism could face up
to life in prison. "The legal firewall, if you like, that separates the
two systems [of Hong Kong and Beijing] is now gone," said Alan
Leong, a former chair of Hong Kong's bar association and chair of
Hong Kong's Civic Party. "We are allowing the long arms of the
Chinese Communist Party to reach Hong Kong."

Hours after a slew of newspapers, including *Wei Wen Po* and
Ta Kung Pao, two pro-Beijing outlets that often signal official

Chinese policy, broke the story about the impending legislation, China's leader Xi Jinping signed the measure into law, vowing it would restore stability and safety to the region. The national security law was then incorporated into Hong Kong's Basic Law. The law's precepts were diametrically opposed to Hong Kong values, the core of its identity and what had separated it in spirit if not politically from mainland China. The four buckets of potentially treasonous behaviors—subversion, secession, foreign interference, and terrorism—were intentionally left vaguely defined so as to include acts committed outside of Hong Kong, like writing essays critical of China and printing protest slogans.

The city's chief executive Carrie Lam defended the new law, insisting that the sweeping new law was limited in scope and "will only target an extremely small minority of illegal and criminal acts and activities." Yet she also admitted that she, too, had been taken by surprise by the national security law; Hong Kong officials had not even seen the full proposed text of the national security law in the weeks leading up to its passage.

It was a flex of pure political power. The year before, millions of protestors had used the force of their bodies in Hong Kong to protest an anti-extradition law and the Party's inept governance of the city. The police responded with water cannons and rubber bullets; protestors fought back with bricks and glass bottles. But in the end, the Party did not need any physical force to win. Within hours of the law going into effect, at least two opposition political parties announced they had effectively dissolved themselves. The next week, Joshua Wong and fellow activists Agnes Chow and Nathan Law announced their resignations on Facebook from Demosisto, the youth political party they founded in 2016, but they resolved to continue their activism individually.

Andy Chan, an activist who advocates for outright independence from Beijing, also said he was disbanding the Hong Kong branch of his political party and shifting operations to Taiwan and the United Kingdom.

I noticed that hundreds of outspoken Twitter accounts run by Hong Kong residents were voluntarily deleted over the next few days as people rushed to clear any potentially incriminating web-browsing history and online political posts. Dozens of Hong Kong contacts opened accounts with Signal and Telegram, encrypted messaging apps, to shield their communications from national security authorities. I knew they were doing so, because I received a notification every time a person in my iPhone contacts registered their number with the apps. "Great changes are coming . . . no one can be sure about their tomorrow," Wong wrote on his Facebook page, in a post announcing his resignation.

A noticeable pall fell over Hong Kong, even before any arrests under the new national security law were made. Protestors in the anti-extradition movement were fair game; they could be charged with sedition. Most alarmingly, the law's scope was retrospective, meaning it could prosecute behavior committed before the law had been passed. The law also applied to actions committed outside of Hong Kong—meaning, under the most liberal interpretation of the national security law, writing an editorial in a North American newspaper that was critical of Beijing's policies in the region could be considered in violation of national security. Emily, the *Apple Daily* editor, told me she felt like a human filter for all the bad news the outlet was covering about Hong Kong. She was regularly seeing a therapist for her post-traumatic stress disorder. "We have nothing now," she lamented—nothing of their original civil liberties. The realization also emboldened her: "We have nothing to lose." She was already thinking about moving to Taiwan, an idea she shared with her manager. He was sympathetic. Everyone was looking for a way out.

Undeterred by the sudden pall after the national security law, Hong Kong's civil society organizations put up one last fight in anticipation of the delayed legislative elections coming up that year in 2021. They had reason to hope. Two years earlier, candidates from pro-democracy parties had made gains in the city's district councilor elections. These hyperlocal elections have little policymaking power and are largely concerned with neighborhood services, such as garbage disposal and fixing streetlights, though councilors had the power to appoint five seats on the city's legislative council. But after months of protests in the streets that autumn against the proposed anti-extradition bill, the councilor elections also became a barometer of public sentiment and an indication that if public anger were harnessed through systematic political organizing, there was momentum to attempt a pro-democracy majority in the legislative council for the first time ever.

One problem that has dogged pro-democracy parties in Hong Kong is their sheer number, meaning that competing candidates often undercut each other by splitting the vote. To address this problem, veteran activists including Professor Benny Tai and former lawmaker Au Nok-hin proposed an unofficial primary where Hong Kongers could come out and vote on which pro-democratic candidates they wanted on the final ballot. The election was nonbinding but the symbolism of the city's remaining pro-democratic factions uniting was powerful. Authorities warned casting a vote in the primary could be considered secessionist under the national security law; more than 600,000 Hong Kongers turned out anyway that June, in defiance of such warnings. It was more than three times the number organizers had been hoping for.

The national security hammer came down half a year later. On the morning of January 6, 2021—as most of the world was transfixed by the images of Trump supporters attacking the Capitol in Washington, DC—Hong Kong authorities sprang into action. They arrested forty-seven people for taking part in the unofficial poll.

In February 2021, Hong Kong began requiring civil servants to take loyalty oaths professing their support of the Communist Party and its policies in the city. Anyone who refused to take the oath or did so in a manner deemed insufficiently sincere would not be able to take up office. To be a patriot in modern China meant supporting the Party both intellectually and emotionally, to show one's allegiance in a bit of choreographed political theater—with a raised voice and a shaken fist. "The administrative power in Hong Kong must be maintained in the hands of patriots," Xia Baolong, then China's top official in charge of Hong Kong affairs, said in a speech justifying the largely performative new requirement. For the Party, however, performance matters: it wants to see the loyalty embodied in observable action and speech. "You cannot say that you are patriotic, but you do not love the leadership of the Chinese Communist Party, or you do not respect it," added Eric Tsang, a senior Hong Kong official, a day after Xia made his comments. "Patriotism is holistic love."[1] Holistic, in that political loyalty should percolate through all facets of a civil servant's life.

This put Hong Kong's some thirty thousand civil servants in an awkward position, though many viewed the oath as a routine, regulatory step, and awkwardly read out loud their lines when needed to continue their jobs. The region's officials were also in a difficult spot, as they now had the hazy responsibility of determining whether a civil servant was sufficiently sincere when announcing their Party loyalty. "Your question is very interesting—whether a civil servant or any person in taking the oath is genuine," Carrie Lam told reporters. "I don't think I have an answer for that. Ultimately the test lies in the behavior. If somebody who has taken an oath to swear allegiance and pledge loyalty has subsequently done something which is in breach of the oath, then appropriate actions will have to be taken by the authorities."

Hong Kong has never had an electoral democracy, but under the city's Basic Law constitution, residents did have the right to vote for local district councilors and directly elect half of the region's legislators. After the anti-extradition protests, Party bureaucrats believed this system suffered a surplus of autonomy. "Some of the chaos in Hong Kong shows that there exist obvious loopholes and deficiencies in the current electoral system and mechanisms which provided opportunities for anti-China and anti–Hong Kong forces to take over management in Hong Kong," Wang Chen, then–vice chairman of China's legislative elite standing committee, declared in the spring of 2021. The Party needed to thread the needle of preserving the illusion of political choice even while guaranteeing its preferred outcome.

Once again, Beijing neatly solved this issue by shaping the law to fit their purpose. That March, Beijing unveiled sweeping new electoral changes to the way Hong Kong chose its legislators and chief executive. The proposal suddenly appeared on the agenda of

China's National People's Congress literally hours before it convened for a week of annual political meetings that spring. Under the new measures, all legislative candidates would now be effectively vetted and approved by an election committee, a tool to ensure a pro-Beijing majority each time in the legislature while keeping Hong Kong's cosmetic democracy. The five seats chosen by district councilors were eliminated altogether.

Back in 2014, when Beijing announced it would vet future candidates for the chief executive post, the move prompted large, peaceful, and ultimately unsuccessful protests—the Umbrella Movement. There was no such opposition this time, seven years later—in large part because nearly all of the opposition parties and leaders were facing criminal or national security charges. And the blows kept coming. That November, China's National People's Congress Standing Committee passed yet another resolution that gave Hong Kong authorities the power to bypass local courts and summarily remove politicians seen as a threat to security. Four Hong Kong lawmakers who supported the territory's pro-democracy movement—and were thus barred from running for reelection—were immediately unseated, as stipulated in the resolution. Hong Kong's remaining fifteen opposition lawmakers quit in protest. Now, no opposition parties had representation in Hong Kong's legislative council, and by packing the committee that appointed the city's next chief executive, Beijing could now ensure that "only patriots" could run for office.

On June 24, 2021, just under a year after the security law came into effect, *Apple Daily* was shut down. The brash, freewheeling paper founded by former clothing tycoon Jimmy Lai was forced to close after much of its editorial masthead and management officers, including Lai himself, were arrested on national security charges. Authorities also froze its bank accounts, meaning the outlet could not afford to print more editions of the paper, ending its twenty-six-year run. Beloved by readers for its feisty prodemocracy editorials and its investigative reporting, *Apple Daily* was also fun to read, delivering chatty gossip and opinion columns while also being one of the few independent Hong Kong outlets that dared to publish hard-hitting coverage often critical of Beijing. Lai had come to Hong Kong when he was a child as a political refugee, before building up a billion-dollar fortune through textiles and fast fashion that he then used to fund pro-democracy activism as well as *Apple Daily*. His rise through the business world and media establishment was a Hong Kong fairy tale and proof of the region's dynamism and diversity. His fall was a nightmarish tale for how much the region had changed under the security law.

The day after *Apple Daily*'s closure, people began queuing at newsstands and breakfast shops for the paper's last print edition. *Apple Daily* printed over one million copies, knowing that as soon as the paper hit the stands it would become a collectible—the physical embodiment of an era when Hong Kong had been home to a rambunctious, independent press corps. All one million copies sold out by 8:30 a.m. that day.

Its physical operations may have ceased, but the spirit of *Apple Daily* still lives on as a digital ghost. Within days of its closure, a ragtag team of volunteers had assembled online to save what they could of the twenty-six-year-old outlet. The police raids on *Apple Daily* meant that many of the outlet's servers had been seized and access to their internal drives cut off. Its website was taken offline by authorities. No other central repository of the paper's journalism existed—something an anonymous group of volunteers hoped to rectify. "Imagine the central library of your country is burning. That is exactly what's happening in Hong Kong. So at this point, we just want to save as much content as possible," said one of these volunteers, who went by the online moniker Mr. Ho.

To assemble a complete, digital version of the now-defunct paper, Mr. Ho and other volunteers were soliciting loyal readers to send in scanned physical copies of *Apple Daily* they had saved, especially copies of older editions that were never digitized. The papers were then scanned and saved on an online archival platform called Arweave that distributed the data across thousands of hard drives around the world. "We like to think of it as kind of a Library of Alexandria 2.0. That is what we're aiming for," Sam Williams, Arweave's founder, told me. "Except instead of being in a centralized place, which can burn down, it's spread all across the world, and it's kind of replicated in hundreds or even thousands of copies so that any one of those copies can go missing, and the other copies just kind of take its place."

One by one, each of Hong Kong's independent news outlets folded under legal pressure. In December 2021, seven editors and board members at *Stand News* were arrested for national security crimes, causing the outlet to shut down. *Citizen News,* another outlet, said it was voluntarily dissolving days later. These outlets published editorials and essays distributed internationally that were critical of the Party and the anti-extradition law, activity that could be labeled as colluding with foreign forces. No one blamed them for closing; their publishers and top editors had reporters to protect. They might be willing to risk their freedom to continue reporting, but they could not ask all their employees to do the same.

Emily, the young social media editor at *Apple Daily* who had fainted after witnessing the Yuen Long metro attack, had been battling depression and anxiety since the incident, with symptoms that became so crippling she had to take a leave of absence from the paper. On the night the paper closed she went out for a despondent drink with her colleagues. "I can't see any hope that would keep me in Hong Kong," she told me sadly. We were talking on the phone a few days after one of her close colleagues at *Apple Daily* had unexpectedly announced he was moving to the United Kingdom. She knew he was considering emigration, but she hadn't expected him to move so soon. At their goodbye, however, she didn't feel sad. "Moving away from Hong Kong is a very reasonable choice," she told me matter-of-factly.

What had been unthinkable a year ago for her now had a cold, hard logic to it. In fact, she was now considering applying for a master's program in the U.K. herself. She was gladdened someone she cared about was getting out before her, especially when she concluded they could be targeted for their past jobs. "The Hong Kong government has decided that the place you work is not a safe place to work," she realized. "And they have been the ones to make it an unsafe place to work." Everyone she knew was debating internally about whether to leave at this point. Some harshly criticized people leaving: "They think it is an act of irresponsibility. They say, if you leave Hong Kong, then there will be no one left to continue to protest. But some people like me who want to leave just think it's just a personal choice," Emily continued. "There's nothing we can do now to stand up to the Chinese Communist Party here, but overseas, we can still do things like that, outside of Hong Kong."

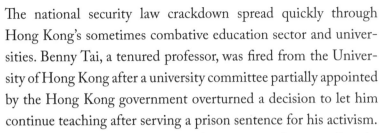

The national security law crackdown spread quickly through Hong Kong's sometimes combative education sector and universities. Benny Tai, a tenured professor, was fired from the University of Hong Kong after a university committee partially appointed by the Hong Kong government overturned a decision to let him continue teaching after serving a prison sentence for his activism.

Universities also hurried to rid themselves of potentially subversive symbols. In the early hours of Christmas Eve of 2021, authorities quietly removed a faux bronze sculpture known as the *Goddess of Democracy,* which had stood on the campus of the Chinese University of Hong Kong for eleven years. Made by Chinese-born artist Chen Weiming, the sculpture was done in the likeness of the papier-mâché sculpture that had anchored Beijing's Tiananmen Square during the pro-democracy protests there in 1989. Another Hong Kong institution, Lingnan University, dismantled a bronze relief Chen had also sculpted depicting the Party's crackdown on those same pro-democracy protestors. By then, Hong Kong University had also removed a towering bronze statue entitled the *Pillar of Shame*—an imposing eight-meter column of twisted, grotesque faces and figures entwined in postures of agony that had been created by Danish artist Jens Galschiøt and bequeathed to the university right before the Hong Kong handover in 1997.

In particular, education authorities targeted liberal studies, a compulsory subject unique in Hong Kong. Teachers pride themselves on developing critical thought and argumentation skills in students so they can examine their own society, and it was this discursive, open-ended nature of the course that had made it Kenny's favorite subject in high school. He credited it with honing his sense of right and wrong and his interest in social justice issues, which ultimately pushed him to join the anti-extradition protests in 2019.

Keenly aware that the class was correlated with raising political awareness among its younger citizenry, Hong Kong officials moved to broadly reorient the entire public education system. "National security education is a part of, and inseparable from, national education," an education bureau circular declared in February. Defining a common identity of what it meant to be Chinese was now a key priority and a part of a country's security. "The fundamentals of national security education are to develop in students a sense of belonging to the country, an affection for the Chinese people, a sense of national identity, as well as an awareness of and a sense of responsibility for safeguarding national security," the circular explained.

I spoke to Hong Kong secondary school liberal studies teachers scrambling to parse through their curriculum, removing and substituting certain sections last-minute before the fall semester began. They knew they needed to be ultra-careful in the classroom the coming year. They not only had new and unfamiliar national security rules to comply with, but also were fearful nationalistic students and their parents could report them for alleged violations. "We will not be allowed to teach about civil disobedience [in the fall semester], but we are expected to teach about the national security law," said one secondary school teacher, who told me her principal put her under investigation after parents alleged that she described Hong Kong police as "riot police" to students in an online lecture. She was cleared after providing a video recording of the lecture. Her case was among the nearly two hundred cases the Hong Kong Professional Teachers' Union said were opened against teachers by the city's education bureau after anonymous individuals reported comments the teachers made on their private social media accounts in favor of the 2019 anti-government protests.

"My anonymous accuser sent complaint letters to my workplace and shared [the complaints] online. They claimed to have sent the information to the Chinese Communist Party as well," said a second Hong Kong secondary school teacher then-currently under investigation by the education bureau for allegedly insulting police on his personal Facebook account. "There is a sense of terror among teachers," said Fung Wai Wah, president of the teacher's union, who tracked the cases.

Kenny, the young protestor, was still in hiding in Hong Kong. His family was adamant that he should stay in the region, despite the national security law. His brother assured him it would be all right. Kenny didn't agree. The enforced confinement was stultifying, and his own inaction was weighing on him. Like many millennial and Generation X residents, he felt his future in Hong Kong was bleak. He made up his mind to leave. The only question was how.

CHAPTER 10

THE FUGITIVE

The weather was perfectly clear and sunny—ideal for someone trying to leave Hong Kong forever. Kenny was walking
toward a pier in the city where he had been told, just a few hours
before, that a fishing boat was waiting for him and four other passengers. He had no idea who was driving the boat and or who
would be on it with him. All he knew was that it was his last
chance to get out of Hong Kong.

He had not slept well the night before, contemplating how he
had ended up here: holed up in a stranger's home, a fugitive now
preparing to leave his home, perhaps forever. Rather than toss and
turn for an extra hour, he grabbed his bag and decided to head
over to the pier early. At five in the morning, the normal hustle
and bustle of the waterfront was replaced by an eerie stillness. He
repeated the code phrase he had been taught to say over and over
again in his head—something nonsensical about an animal, he
remembered—and nervously scanned the docks for anyone who
looked like they, too, might be looking to escape.

Some days earlier, he had turned the last of his savings over to a smuggler: some HKD$120,000 (more than US$15,000) in savings and donations from friends. The smuggler promised Kenny he could take them out of Hong Kong. Kenny did not have much faith in his words. He had already tried four times to leave the city, and all four of his attempts had failed. Thrice, the smugglers got nervous the police had caught on and canceled the escape attempts. Once, the person who promised to sail Kenny out never showed up; Kenny did not know if the person had scammed him or had gotten arrested themselves. Either way, he was thousands of dollars poorer and running out of hope.

This last chance to leave came through last minute. A friend who he met protesting on Hong Kong's streets during the past autumn got in touch to offer Kenny a position on the boat. His friend had actually been designated the spot first, but he decided he was not yet ready to go into permanent exile. By circumstance, Kenny now had one last chance to get out of Hong Kong. He no longer wanted to live in hiding. He had already spent ten sunless months sequestered in various apartments across the city, and he had nothing more to lose. If this escape attempt failed, he would turn himself in to the Hong Kong police.

Kenny spotted another figure ambling up the dock in the early-morning sun. Something about the look on the teenager's face—tight, emotionless—told Kenny they were here for the same thing.

The teenager gave his name simply as Tommy. They were about to risk their lives together in an ocean crossing to an island hundreds of miles from Hong Kong, but they knew to be distrustful of each other. Together, they bought a cheap breakfast at one of the few kiosks opening early, Kenny munching on a ham and cheese sandwich as he tried to make small talk to pass the time. He was queasy from a night of bad sleep, but he scarfed down the thin sandwich. It could be the last warm thing they would eat all day.

Over the next two hours, the three other passengers arrived. They were all young men. The youngest was just eighteen years old. Kenny, now twenty-six, eyed them up and down, appraising them silently. What had they seen on Hong Kong's streets that made them want to leave so badly? Did they, too, have bounties on their heads? Families who loved them and who, by tomorrow, would be grieving their departure?

None of them were carrying much, and they hopped easily aboard the small fishing vessel that would hopefully ferry them to freedom. Kenny had packed a small backpack with his identification documents and some food. He noticed one of the other passengers, named Ray, was carrying a fishing pole and some tackles and suppressed a chuckle. He was not sure how much use the pole would get out in the deep ocean, but it reinforced their disguise as wayward fishermen.

At seven in the morning, the five men got into the small fishing vessel. They were silent and unsentimental. There were no tears, no grand goodbyes. They loved Hong Kong, but now they had to leave; it was as simple as that. Kenny looked back one last time at the landscape of blue sky and shining metal, of creeping banyan trees covering dull concrete. He knew that even if he were ever to come back, it would not be to the same Hong Kong he was leaving. It had already changed so much.

Their destination was Taiwan. An island only sixty miles at its closest point from the coast of southern China, Taiwan (or the Republic of China as it is officially known) had charted a very different political path from its far larger neighbor, the People's Republic of China. Kenny was fleeing a Hong Kong that had tried to reject the Party's vision for what Chinese rule and being Chinese should mean; he was sailing now toward an island that had spent more than seven decades creating an identity that drew heavily from Chinese culture but was not limited by it, in defiance of Communist Party threats.

The tension between China and Taiwan traces back to 1949, when, after a bruising civil war for control of China, the losing Kuomintang army fled to Taiwan along with as many as 2 million troops, allies, and their family members. They shifted their seat of government to Taipei, but they did not give up their claim over the rest of China. The island refuge was meant to be temporary, providing a defensible base that bought the Kuomintang Party (KMT) precious time to regroup and amass an eventual attack to retake China from the ruling Communist Party. Chiang Kai-shek, the KMT's mustachioed leader, set about building an authoritarian state on Taiwan. When the island's local population revolted, Chiang imposed martial law and ordered the secret arrests and executions of an estimated 28,000 people over four decades of what Taiwanese call "the White Terror."

Across the Taiwan Strait, Chairman Mao Zedong and the now-ruling Chinese Communist Party (CCP) had not given up on their mutual animosity. For the next two decades, the two Chinese armies under Chiang and Mao dueled over their competing claims of sovereignty of who really represented the true China. Throughout the 1950s, the KMT and CCP's troops fought active skirmishes on a string of small islands that dot the narrow strait of water separating eastern Taiwan from China, but neither side was strong enough to invade the other.[1]

For decades, the KMT Party, on the island of Taiwan, continued to claim it rightfully governed all of China from Taipei. Operationally, the Republic of China (Taiwan) had no control over China. However, it was not until 2018 that Taiwan defunded its last provincial government office representing its historical claims to territory in the province of Fujian, across the strait in China. Not to be outdone, the Chinese Communist Party continues to appoint political delegations to represent Hong Kong and Taiwan at annual legislative and political meetings held in Beijing, as if Taiwan is a Chinese province.

This unresolved question of sovereignty haunts Chinese leaders. Mao was thinking of Taiwan even on his deathbed, according to notes of one of his last meetings in 1975 with then-American secretary of state Henry Kissinger. Mao must have realized the chances of taking Taiwan were slipping away with the years; however, he told Kissinger that China would settle the issue of Taiwan "in a hundred years," and not in the present.[2]

Unlike Hong Kong's, Taiwan's sovereignty status remains ambiguous. The island is not under China's control, and it functions as an independent country, with its own central bank, legislature, and army. It elects its own president and formulates its own foreign policy, despite Beijing's vociferous claims to govern the island, and unlike China, Taiwan is now a democracy. In 1987, the ruling KMT lifted martial law. Over the next few years, political reforms rapidly transitioned the island away from authoritarian, one-party rule into a vibrant but also chaotic direct democracy. Every two years now, the island is engulfed in noisy political campaigns for local or national elections in which each political party invariably accuses the others of vote-buying and corruption.

All this made Taiwan Kenny's top choice for emigration. Nearly all of the island's 23 million inhabitants speak Mandarin Chinese, a language Kenny had learned in school in addition to his native Cantonese. On top of that, within the larger Chinese-cultural sphere that encompassed Hong Kong, mainland China, Singapore, and beyond, Taiwan was a cultural powerhouse. Taiwanese soap operas are televised in Hong Kong, its pop ballads beloved for decades in Hong Kong karaoke rooms, and drinks like boba tea were widespread in the city's malls. Geographically, Kenny would be out of China, but culturally, he would feel close to home. As to whether Taiwan would take him was another question.

On the boat, the five Hong Kongers ignored the heat and kept themselves busy with a multitude of tasks, including keeping the deck clear and their belongings dry. Kenny spent a full hour scraping the serial numbers off the side of the boat so the vessel and its owner could not be identified if they were apprehended by the Chinese coast guard.

The weather was clear, but that also meant the sun beat down ferociously on their exposed heads. There was no cover on the small boat, so they could only stand or sit on the prow. Kenny's hat had blown off from the strong winds and he was getting a bad sunburn. The waves got bigger as they plowed their way through open ocean. Tommy started quietly throwing up.

Mostly, the boys sat in silence, contemplating their fates and all they were about to lose if they successfully escaped and what they could suffer if they failed. None of them had told their family members they were leaving Hong Kong. They themselves had not even known the exact time and location they were departing from until the night before. The journey was already too risky without more people knowing about it, and if they were caught, their loved ones could be incriminated for abetting their escape. Better to slip out anonymously and without a trace.

On the boat, Kenny deliberately repressed the excitement that fluttered in his chest. After months of boredom in hiding, he did not want to disappoint himself yet again if they were stopped. He mentally tabulated a list of apologies he would deliver in person if he ever got the chance. He felt sorry for his mother, who had taken him to Hong Kong as a young boy, hoping for a better life. He knew he was disappointing her by leaving. The list was a mental rosary he ran through repeatedly with each skip of the fishing boat as it crested through successive ocean swells. The guilt of abandoning Hong Kong was already becoming an obsession.

Hong Kong was originally where people in China fled to—not away from. Some of the people who came were economic migrants: people like Kenny's mother who heard wages were higher in the then-British colony and planned to send remittances back to family members living on the mainland. Decades prior, during the tumult of a Chinese civil war in the 1940s, waves of hundreds of thousands of war refugees streamed into Hong Kong, hoping British imperial control there might shield them from the starvation and turmoil on the mainland.[3]

After mainland China came under Communist Party rule, the majority of people crossing into Hong Kong were fleeing the excesses of Chinese authoritarianism. From 1950 to 1961, the Soviet Union's state media claimed about one million Chinese people had fled to Hong Kong. Some were driven out by political purges, but most of these people were escaping a famine that had decimated rural areas after Mao spearheaded an ill-advised attempt to leapfrog the U.S. in industrial production. The British set up border patrols, but people still filtered into Hong Kong. The land crossing between Hong Kong and mainland China, whose porousness would later ensnare Hong Kong bookseller Lam Wing-kee, was a pressure valve for the flow of people trying to leave China, intertwining the fates of the people of the two places for centuries.

The national security law in 2020 reversed this flow into Hong Kong. Now people were desperate to leave Hong Kong. The first to leave were those who, by dint of higher education or wealth, could easily relocate elsewhere. Residents sold their apartments and homes as they liquidated their assets and prepared to emigrate. One real estate brokerage reported dozens of owners who sold their property at a loss, because they were in a hurry to leave, a phenomenon previously unthinkable for cramped Hong Kong, which is home to one of the most expensive real estate markets in the world.[4] In the year immediately following the implementation of the national security law, 113,000 residents left Hong Kong.[5] The drop was the largest since 1961, the year the then-colony started keeping such records. Most of those leaving were fresh college graduates, the core of the city's future workforce; the number of twenty- to twenty-four-year-olds plummeted 15 percent in just one quarter in 2022, compared to the year previous. Emily, the young editor at *Apple Daily*, was preparing to leave Hong Kong as well, as were many of her former co-workers. She now planned to study in the United Kingdom, get a master's in an English-language program, and find a work permit that would let her stay out of Hong Kong.

For those who had been active in the protests and were facing charges, however, it was becoming harder to leave. Hong Kong police arrested more than ten thousand people over the course of the anti-extradition movement, and nearly three thousand of them had already been prosecuted. Kenny, who had skipped bail and never showed up for his trial, was almost certainly facing an exit ban, meaning he couldn't just purchase a plane ticket and jet away. The city's new national security department was also fanning out across the city, keeping tabs on people they believed would try to leave and claim refuge internationally.

One of their first targets was a twenty-year-old activist named Tony Chung Hon-lam, who was taken from a coffee shop across from the American consulate in Hong Kong by unidentified men. Police publicly announced his arrest afterward, because they believed he was planning on filing an asylum application. Hours later, four other young Hong Kongers from the same student activist group as Chung tried to talk their way into the American consulate, only to be rejected from the premises. Street cam footage shows three plainclothes officers gently leading one of the young men away by the arm. He does not resist. A Hong Kong court later sentenced Chung to forty-three months in prison for money-laundering and secession, because Chung had sold playing cards and sweaters with the phrase "Hong Kong is not China" printed on them.[6]

Escape was thus not a decision one made lightly. Ray, the Hong Konger who had brought fishing gear on the trip, told friends before his trip that he gave himself a fifty-fifty shot at surviving the ordeal ahead of him. He accepted these odds: either he would make it out of Hong Kong or die trying.

Like Kenny, he had spent months couch surfing with sympathetic protestors after participating in a police siege on Polytechnic University. In the months after that standoff, Ray closely tracked the fates of the one thousand or so student protestors who had been arrested from two university campuses and felt their charges were systematically exaggerated so prosecutors could give them the maximum prison sentences. His parents suggested he turn himself in, but Ray refused. It was not jail he was afraid of. He feared facing an unfair trial for crimes he either did not commit or felt had been justified given the brutality of Hong Kong's police.

Now, floating in the Pacific Ocean in a fishing boat, Ray was most afraid of being nabbed by Chinese authorities. He knew that fugitives who were caught leaving could face even harsher punishments from Chinese authorities, a fate that would later befall their fellow protestors.

Indeed, a few weeks later, another group of Hong Kongers trying to sail to Taiwan were intercepted at sea by the Chinese coast guard in the South China Sea, about fifty miles off the coast of Hong Kong. The coast guard ferried ten of the twelve escapees to mainland China under criminal detention. The men were not "democratic activists, but elements attempting to separate Hong Kong from China," a foreign ministry spokesperson in Beijing declared. Their families tried to visit them, but Chinese authorities denied all communication with the escapees. The families petitioned their loved ones' cases in Hong Kong, but they were so terrified of being arrested themselves, they would only appear in public at press conferences fully masked, their hoods pulled tight over their heads and large sunglasses covering their eyes.

Few mainland lawyers were willing to take up the defense of the arrested men. In the end, only two lawyers persisted, despite the political risks. One of them was Ren Quanniu, the stocky lawyer I had met earlier in China.[7] Contrarian that he is, Ren told me he was attracted to the case precisely because of its political challenges. The former opera singer in him liked a bit of a show and a chance to take on a case with legal flair. This one, straddling two very different systems, could be precedent-shattering and give his legal career a significant boost.

The case could also bring significant risks. "I received several calls from national security officers. They said they had high-level orders from Beijing that I had to drop this Hong Kong case or my lawyer's license might be affected," Ren told me from his office in the central Chinese province of Henan. Chinese authorities were hypersensitive about anything touching upon the Hong Kong protests, keenly attuned to any sign of social unrest it might trigger.

Despite these threats, Ren immediately agreed to take up the defense for Wong Wai-yin, one of the twelve detained Hong Kongers, when approached by Wong's family, and I met him as he was in the throes of preparing for their trial the next year. Ren was meticulous in his prep work, because he knew mainland authorities were looking for any tiny slip-up or oversight to disqualify him from representing Wong. Ren had Wong's family film a video for him and handwrite a letter, stating that he, Ren, was Wong's personal lawyer. Despite that, he never was able to meet his client in person. Shenzhen prison guards barred Ren from speaking to Wong, saying he couldn't prove the detainee had hired him. Later, they said Wong had hired another lawyer for himself.

Stymied from being able to prove he was legally contracted to represent his client, Ren spent months petitioning the mainland justice ministry to recognize the family's statements hiring him as their lawyer. Meanwhile, ten of the twelve Hong Kong escapees sat in a detention center in the southern Chinese city of Shenzhen—the same city where Lam Wing-kee, the bookseller, had been nabbed only six years earlier—at the whims of an opaque Chinese court system. Only a year earlier, more than one million Hong Kongers took to the streets to protest Beijing's proposed control over their judicial system. Now a small group of their fellow citizens were living through that nightmare.

The twelve escapees were tried in December 2020. Seven of the men were given shorter jail sentences in China of between seven months and three years. For taking part in their defense team, Ren and another lawyer, Lu Siwei, were stripped of their legal licenses to practice in mainland China. The threats had not been bluster, Ren realized, but very real.

"At least I do not have a mortgage to pay off," he joked with me in the months after he lost his license. He tried to appeal the decision, faxing off stacks of letters and petitions, just to give the provincial justice ministry more work to do. I knew he was putting on a brave face though. With no hope of getting a new license soon, Ren was forced to take on lower-paying paralegal work, helping other lawyers prepare briefs and conduct research. His career as a swashbuckling human rights lawyer was over.

For nearly half a million people, there was one legal way out of Hong Kong, but it required being born at the right time. The ticket out was called a British National Overseas passport, or

BNO, an unassuming booklet just a shade darker blue than the Hong Kong passport.[8] The British government had issued an estimated 2.9 million of these BNOs in the last months of their rule of Hong Kong. At the time, the BNO only granted six-month visits to the U.K., with no right to work. Now, in response to Beijing's crackdown on Hong Kong, the U.K. would allow BNO holders and their direct family members (another 2 million or so Hong Kongers) to come to the United Kingdom and work for up to five years before applying for British citizenship. The BNO had become, by decree, a permanent pathway. The catch was, one had to have applied for the BNO right up to (but not including) the date of handover back to Chinese rule. Anyone born on July 1, 1997, or after could not apply for a BNO—an unalterable line in the sand for many of the young demonstrators in the 2019 anti-extradition protests. Perhaps that was why they fought so viciously and so fearlessly toward the end; they had nowhere else to go but Hong Kong. "I just feel trapped in Hong Kong because I can't do anything about the Hong Kong situation. But it's OK. It's just. I accepted my fate," one former protestor told me. She had been born just a few days after July 1.

The United Kingdom said it was deluged with more than 100,000 applications for its BNO visa program in 2021.[9] But two days before the visa applications opened, China said it would not recognize the passports, and those attempting to depart Hong Kong with a BNO would be denied boarding. "The British side's attempt to turn a large number of Hong Kong people into second-class British citizens has completely changed the nature of the two sides' original understanding of BNO," a Chinese foreign ministry spokesperson argued. The fight over the legitimacy of the BNO was, in other words, a fight over the definition of who was considered a Chinese citizen.

Hong Kong citizenship has always been a shaky concept. After all, where does a colonial subject sit in relation to empire, or the residents of a "special administrative region" to the mainland? And which identity takes precedence? The Chinese identity, Beijing declared, in a legal interpretation of its nationality law. Beijing declared that from 1997 onwards, the Hong Kong passport was akin to Chinese citizenship and overrode any other dual citizenship.

That, of course, begged the question of who counted as "Chinese." For example, did that term expand to include ethnically non-Chinese people born in Hong Kong who possessed Hong Kong passports but who also held British or European citizenship? In negotiations for the territory's return to China, Beijing declared such people were not Chinese and were to be barred from the higher levels of civil office in Hong Kong's local administration. "Britain wanted to turn the future Hong Kong into an independent or semi-independent political entity under its influence," Chinese diplomats wrote.[10] Chinese-ness had thus both a legal connotation ("persons born in Chinese territories") but also an ethnic dimension ("of Chinese descent").[11]

In Beijing's eyes, the U.K. was sneakily staking out a nationality claim on ethnic Chinese citizens of a Chinese territory through the BNO. But for Hong Kongers, the BNO made sense: Chinese ethnicity did not define "Hong Kong" as an identity. Being a Hong Konger was about a liberal set of political values and a shared, though loose, constellation of cultural and linguistic qualities. "Whenever there are forms, like when I discover there's no other field than Hong Kong, then I might choose 'other' instead of forcing myself to choose 'Chinese,'" a young woman named Ellen grumbled to me. She had been born just a few weeks before the handover in July 1997—just in time for her parents to secure her a BNO, but late enough that she had only ever known Hong Kong as a Chinese territory. Yet she felt not the slightest bit Chinese.

Like so many other Hong Kongers, her grandparents had been born in mainland China, fleeing during the Great Leap Forward, a political movement in the late 1950s that had resulted in mass famine. Now, more than seven decades later, Ellen was preparing to leave Hong Kong. She viewed her emigration as a continuation of her family's flight away from the Party's reach. "I think in the future, the Chinese government would take over this place completely," she said of Hong Kong.

Ironically, the BNO's cut-off date at handover meant that an entire generation of young Hong Kongers who perhaps felt most strongly that they were solely Hong Kong in identity and not Chinese were excluded from an easy emigration out of the territory. One of those people was a young student I met named Marco, born in October of 1997, mere months after the cut-off for a BNO. He felt like he had been born with a ticking time bomb set at five decades, the period of limited autonomy China had agreed to give Hong Kong. "It feels like a counting down, like fifty years. So I would be exactly fifty years old by then," he mused. In the end, he hadn't had to wait that long for his city's temporary lease on freedom to end. He feared many of the city's civil liberties were already gone, and he hadn't even celebrated his twenty-fourth birthday yet.

Living in the shadow of a promise, one ultimately not kept, didn't give Marco a sense of free rein. Instead, the expiration of that promise overshadowed all of Marco's major life decisions—what to study, where to work, who to love—in case one day he had to throw that all away and leave. "It is always, like, a time limit to force you to think, do you have to plan it earlier or is it too late to wait till, like, around five to ten years near that deadline? Is it ever going to be too late?" he asked me. Handover meant being born into a place you were destined to abandon. Through chance, he had been born to parents in Hong Kong on the eve of handover, designating him as the generation that would have to live through its last remaining years of true autonomy.

None of the five Hong Kongers trying to get to Taiwan on Kenny's boat had a BNO. As fugitives, they were forced to take a more unconventional exit. The waters around Hong Kong and China were surprisingly busy. The large shipping freighters petered out as they sped farther away from Hong Kong, giving way to smaller fishing boats like theirs. Almost all of them sported the red and gold–starred flag of the People's Republic of China. To get to Taiwan, their fishing vessel needed to skirt the northern edge of the South China Sea, a large body of water ringed by China, the Philippines, Vietnam, and Brunei, among other countries. Each of them had conflicting claims to parts of the sea, and China now routinely sent out patrols of coast guard boats to accompany the Chinese fishermen sailing through their claimed waters to defend their territorial claims.

For one heart-stopping moment, Ray thought he saw a Chinese coast guard ship approaching them while accompanying a small group of fishing boats that clearly displayed Chinese flags. This ship was far larger than a normal fishing boat, and the deck looked crowded with communications equipment a commercial vessel would not need. The five Hong Kongers onboard sat still and kept their eyes on the horizon. Ray let out a pent-up breath after the boat passed them by without slowing down.

In the monotony of the open ocean, their eyes started playing tricks on them. The men thought they saw land multiple times, but they were just imagining things as the hours bled into one another, each the same as the last. Ray steadily ate through the store of energy bars he had packed. He had even packed hand sanitizer for everyone on board.

After six hours of sailing, the five Hong Kongers crossed into international waters. Their navigator cut the engine in celebration. An immense pressure lifted off Kenny's chest, and he took a deep breath. They were no longer in China's orbit. His fellow passengers cheered. With about two hundred miles behind them, they were still no more than halfway to Taiwan. Yet for all intents and purposes, Kenny knew they had already succeeded: he might never go back to Hong Kong again, but at least he would not be sitting in a Chinese prison. The possibilities for the future, like the ocean in front of him, suddenly seemed infinite.

At hour eleven, a lush speck on the horizon appeared. It was the eastern coast of Taiwan. The major port city of Kaohsiung was only a few dozen miles away. The boat operator stopped the engine and hailed the Taiwanese coast guard in Mandarin Chinese, one of the main languages spoken in Taiwan. They were fishers blown off course with a bust engine, he explained; could they get a tow back to land?

When the Taiwanese coast guard arrived, Kenny and his travel group confessed everything. These Cantonese-speaking Hong Kongers were clearly not Taiwanese fishermen. They asked for political asylum, handed over their identity documents, and hoped for the best. All five of them were swabbed for the novel coronavirus; it was still the height of the global COVID-19 pandemic, and Taiwan's borders were closed to most foreigners. Once declared negative, Kenny and the boys were taken to a Taiwanese military base in Kaohsiung. He tried to hide his elation in the company of these stoic Taiwanese soldiers. Soon, he hoped, he could begin his life all over again in Taiwan.

CHAPTER 11

THE ASYLUM SEEKER

On a college campus on the island of Taiwan, Li Jiabao took a deep breath and prepared to go live online. It was March 2019 and he was about to go ahead with the most important, and perhaps most reckless decision he had ever made in his twenty-one-year-old life.

The first shot in his eighteen-minute live stream is shaky, and Li points the cellphone camera at the gray brick path in front of him. In the video, he giggles with casual abandon, his voice bright with excitement as he settles on a suitable place to make his big announcement. Behind him, the trees on the campus of National Tsing Hua University, in the northern Taiwanese city of Hsinchu, are already lush green with foliage. "China's modern-day politics are just a kind of continuation of the thousands of years of Chinese dynastic rule," he begins, taking aim at a 2018 constitutional amendment that allowed leader Xi Jinping to remain president indefinitely. He pitches his voice higher as he barrels into a prepared speech he has printed out, taking aim at a litany of abuses he blames on China's ruling Communist Party. "I have faith that one day we can stand in Tiananmen Square in the years after Communist Party rule and tell the rest of the world that we feel the rays of freedom and democracy again," he announces in Mandarin Chinese, pumping his fist to underscore his point. No one around him on campus seems to notice him. At one point, Li has to shout over the engine of a campus bus driving past him.

Li vaguely knew that such speech was politically subversive and could spell danger for him if anyone on the Chinese mainland saw it, so he wore a purple bandanna loosely wrapped around the lower half of his face to obscure his identity. "I apologize for being forced to make this speech anonymously as I live under oppression," he told the handful of viewers. Perhaps because of these dangers, positive reactions from online viewers started to come in immediately. Li watched in disbelief as the retweet count on the published version of his video shot up to hundreds of viewers within hours. Years later, he would realize how paltry that number was (a popular TikTok video in China can garner tens of millions of views in an hour), but to a boy from a small town in rural Shandong province, abroad for the first time in his life, the attention was thrilling.

Encouraged, Li went out the next day and filmed a second video. This time, he left his face uncovered, looking earnest behind his round wire-rimmed glasses and a pompadour of permed, wavy hair. He also stated his full name and hometown in case his identity was at all unclear. His appearance stoked a fair share of bewilderment. For one, Li had none of the trappings of a traditional Chinese dissident. He was young and had been born in a China already constrained by online content controls and censorship. He also did not fit any of the usual subgroups (religious, ethnic minority, or petitioner) targeted for persecution under the Chinese

Communist Party. He had no history of previous public activism. For more than ninety minutes, Li gently answered questions on Twitter from suspicious Taiwanese and Chinese users. He wore a bemused, polite smile to show he meant no harm. Within days, some ten thousand people had watched his second talk.

Li was exhilarated. He had dreamed of being a political dissident since he was a teenager, and now, on the cusp of full adulthood and away from the suffocating blandness of his parochial hometown, he felt vindication that his political beliefs, derided in China, were welcomed, if not celebrated, in Taiwan. Separated only by a channel of water from its much larger and more powerful neighbor, Taiwan nevertheless felt far, far away from China and its authoritarian Communist Party. Li had a vague sense his denouncement of the Party would cause some trouble when he returned home, but after studying in Taiwan he felt he could say what he pleased. "I hope my children can live in a society where they have the power of free expression without censorship and wake up to a free future, just as Taiwan already has," he told his viewers in his first live stream. Like Kenny and other young Hong Kong protestors who pinned their hopes on finding refuge in Taiwan, Li felt he was safe on the island.

The Chinese authorities reacted more quickly than Li expected. Within hours, his accounts on Chinese social media sites, where he had also posted his video lectures, had been permanently frozen. He could no longer sign into his Chinese bank account. State security officials called his parents, warning them their son was being corrupted by his studies in Taiwan. When he called his parents, he could hear they were in some kind of office, with police officers in the background instructing them to ask Li to return home to China. Li knew the full force of the Chinese security state could come down hard on prominent dissidents, but he had not imagined they would care enough about his short videos to give him much thought. In a way, it was flattering.

The threats also reinforced Li's desire to leave China. Plus, given these clear signs of intimidation, he might have a case for asylum in Taiwan. He took careful screenshots of the threatening messages Chinese national security agents had sent him on Telegram and Twitter. He photographed the pop-up error messages on his bank account and documented how his account on WeChat had been blocked. Then he turned in all his evidence to the Mainland Affairs Council, a Taiwanese government body that oversees the complex relationship between Taiwan and China, politely requesting legal residence in Taipei.

There was one big problem for Li: Taiwan does not have a formal asylum law.[1] While the island usually does not return asylum seekers back to countries where they might be at risk of torture, the island has no legal framework for granting them permanent residence, leaving political migrants floundering in limbo for years without a clear legal pathway to becoming a citizen and gaining the right to work. Asylum is instead granted to individuals based on their merits, on a case-by-case basis.

Li was hopeful that Taiwan would imminently loosen its immigration laws. Only an hour's flight away, in Hong Kong, anti-government protestors were being arrested by the thousands, and Taiwan's president had taken a strong, public stance welcoming these pro-democracy figures, though she stopped short of offering them formal residency. In 2019, Tsai Ing-wen was Taiwan's president and then also head of the Democratic Progressive Party (DPP). She issued a statement in which she "expressed hope that the people of Hong Kong would be able to feel strong support from the shared concern of Taiwan and the international community, and that they would know they are not alone in their pursuit of further democracy and freedom." Not only would Taiwan not extradite any Hong Kong protestors back to Chinese territory, she also hinted that Taiwan would look for ways to allow young Hong Kongers to stay and study. "Taiwan's government and civil society are cooperating to give the people of Hong Kong our utmost support," Tsai's office said.[2] Embracing outsiders in this case paid political dividends: surging sympathy with the Hong Kong protesters and fears of a more autocratic China boosted Tsai's flagging poll numbers during the island's 2020 elections. Tsai handily won a second term as president, beating a more China-friendly candidate.[3]

Li hoped to ride this wave of Taiwanese public support for welcoming in democratically minded outsiders. He went on Taiwanese talk shows to plead his case. He patiently repeated his story: how the Chinese police had interrogated his parents, cut off his funds, and continued to send him threats on social media. He kept up an intermittent correspondence with veteran Chinese dissidents, hoping to emulate their activism and to seek reassurance he had chosen a meaningful path. "I think it is very good that there are young people like Li who are willing to stand up and speak their minds," Zhou Fengsuo, a longtime activist and former student leader during the Tiananmen pro-democracy protests in 1989, told me from his home in New Jersey. With respected figures like Zhou vouching for him, Li felt he had proved his dissident credentials to Taiwan. Yet the responses back from the Mainland Affairs Council were dishearteningly brief, bland legalese masking the stinging rejection each time: try again later.

Just in case, Li submitted several applications to academic programs in Taiwan, but since he had dropped out of his Chinese vocational college degree program after airing his live-streamed denunciations of Xi Jinping, he did not qualify to attend most higher education institutions in Taiwan. One academic program made an exception for him, through which he obtained a student visa to stay a semester longer. With a student visa, he did not have the right to work, so he relied on handouts of charity from Taiwanese well-wishers and friends. He routinely sent messages to Taiwan's Mainland Affairs Council, hoping for progress on his asylum case. Then he waited. Weeks turned into months, and months into years. He was stuck.

Chinese citizens seeking political refuge have been seeking safe haven from Taiwan for decades, sometimes through audacious means. In 1993 alone, desperate Chinese citizens attempted ten separate hijackings of commercial planes taking off from China. During one hijacking that year, a married couple and their eleven-year-old son brandished a box connected to some wires, which they claimed to be a bomb, forcing the flight crew to divert the flight to Taiwan.[4] Taiwan promptly arrested the couple upon landing. "We want to go to a place that has real democracy and respect for human rights," Luo Changhua, one of the hijackers, told Taiwanese reporters after disembarking. He said Chinese authorities had forcibly demolished their home in China, leaving them destitute. For years after, embarrassed Chinese aviation authorities opened all luggage on southbound commercial flights to search for knives or toy weapons, fearful their passengers were planning a hijacking to escape to Taiwan. (Defections happened both ways; Taiwan forbade its citizens living on Kinmen islands, close to China, to own inflatable balls after a Taiwanese soldier named Lin Yifu swam to China using a basketball as a flotation device. Lin later became China's chief economist at the World Bank.)

For decades, Taiwan actively recruited Chinese political defectors, especially those with military skills. It set up three-story-tall speakers outside military garrisons on Kinmen Island, whose rocky beaches are only less than two miles from China's southern shore at certain points. The Taiwanese military then hired female broadcasters to voice hourly propaganda segments and to play Taiwanese Mandopop music, especially ballads sung by singer Deng Lijun, known as Teresa Teng abroad. Radio amplifiers strengthened the broadcast signals and blasted them across the water to lusty young Chinese soldiers on the other side of the Taiwan Strait. To those raised on the austerity of Communist aesthetics, Deng's crooning was almost dizzyingly liberating and sensuous, and her music became a serious tool of Taiwanese soft power.

Chen Xiaoping, a former state radio broadcaster, hosted an hour-long radio show for Chinese audiences called *Teresa Time*. The show only played Deng Lijun songs, the singer's dulcet voice interspersed with promises of up to seven thousand taels, or the equivalent of US$800,000 (in 1970s prices), to be paid in solid gold for any Chinese military pilot who successfully defected to Taiwan.[5] All the radio scripts were inspected by Taiwan's intelligence agency. Chen dutifully read them out loud at a carefully prescribed pace, and the recordings were checked by military censors before they were beamed via shortwave into the mainland. China did its best to block *Teresa Time* by playing raucous Peking opera over Deng's songs. Taiwan's military countered by flying balloons filled with snacks and little plastic tchotchkes that played Deng's song "Sweet on You" after pressing a button. "We knew we definitely could not outfight [the People's Liberation Army]. Militarily, they had more people, so we relied on these psychological warfare tactics to change popular sentiment," Chen told me from her office in Taipei, nearly four decades after she had put down the microphone at *Teresa Time*. "Of course, at the time we really thought our compatriots in China were suffering, and we really felt in our hearts we could help them and lift their spirits."

A handful of Chinese pilots did defect. One of them, a forty-one-year-old Chinese air force veteran named Fan Yuan-yen, left behind his wife and three children. He safely landed in Taiwan in 1977 after being chased by several Chinese-flown, Soviet-made MiG-19s across the Taiwan Strait. "Life on the mainland is too miserable. I cannot stand it any longer," he told Taiwanese military officers.

This was exactly what many Taiwanese government officials wanted to hear. Even in the depths of Taiwan's own authoritarian years, the island called itself "Free China"—in contrast to "Red China" on the mainland. The island's ruling Kuomintang Party (KMT) officially considered itself the true sovereign of all China—defined as Taiwan, the Chinese mainland, and even Mongolia. After losing a bloody civil war against China's ruling Communist Party in 1949, it retreated to Taiwan, in a Mandarin Chinese–speaking exodus that was frequently at odds with Taiwan's indigenous communities and non-Mandarin-speaking ethnic Chinese population.[6] For the first few decades after their defeat, Taiwan's political capital in Taipei was seen as a temporary base from which the KMT would eventually mount an overwhelming military assault across the Taiwan Strait and re-move the Communist Party from power in Beijing. Chen, the radio host, now laughs at the absurdism of those ambitions: "We laugh at North Korea now, but we forget that we were once like North Korea!"

The KMT traced its political lineage back to the Chinese re-public, founded after a 1911 revolution on the mainland. In its telling of history, Communist Party rule of greater China is a po-litical blip, an interlude the KMT would eventually end. These two Chinas—the KMT and the Communist Party—continued to fight each other, even after the KMT retreated to Taiwan. Thou-sands of Chinese soldiers died trying to take Kinmen Island in 1949. Fighting carried on intermittently around Kinmen and sev-eral other Taiwanese islands close to China, followed by the con-stant shelling of Kinmen. Both sides continued bombarding each other until 1979, though in later years, China and Taiwan settled on a tacit equilibrium where they would only bomb each other on alternate days, sometimes with loud explosives filled with propa-ganda leaflets. Only in 2014 was Kinmen completely de-mined of explosives.[7] (Local artisans now turn the spent shells into excel-lent cooking knives.)

Taiwan ended martial law in 1987. Over the next decade, Lee Teng-hui, the island's first democratically elected president, nudged Taiwan into a new status quo, formally giving up the government's ultimate goal of reunification with the mainland, yet deliberately leaving unclear which government—Taipei or Beijing—represented China. For example, Taiwan's citizens born in Kinmen are still issued national identification cards that list their place of birth as "Kinmen county, Fujian province"—a prov-ince Beijing controls but which Taiwan has never officially ceded.

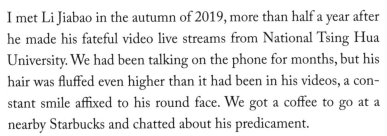

I met Li Jiabao in the autumn of 2019, more than half a year after he made his fateful video live streams from National Tsing Hua University. We had been talking on the phone for months, but his hair was fluffed even higher than it had been in his videos, a constant smile affixed to his round face. We got a coffee to go at a nearby Starbucks and chatted about his predicament.

Li was still upbeat about his prospects. He had his supporters among Taiwan's civil society groups and among student groups who had sympathy for any Chinese-speaking person yearning for freedom. One of his supporters had lent him his apartment, in a quiet part of Taipei, in a concrete building losing its battle with mildew. The oily smell of cooking lingered in the dingy kitchen, blown in from his neighbors upstairs. Li's room was so small he could barely fit a twin mattress inside. A battered secondhand dresser contained a few volumes of borrowed books—volumes on Taiwanese democracy and Hong Kong history. His only personal effects were a pillow and lamp, which he used during late-night reading sessions. He said he was happy. "I do not miss home at all," he said, widening his eyes as if surprised by my question. "Perhaps I miss my mother's cooking sometimes, and my old bed," he laughed. His bed in China was wide enough to roll around in without falling off the edge.

Overall, Li embraced his decrepit conditions with a bohemian zeal. The whole thing was still an adventure for him, and the future still full of possibility. What mattered most was he had made it out of his dead-end small town in northern China, where he had been ostracized by his classmates and reprimanded by his own parents for his political ideas. He told me he had been born with a deep yearning to be better and to see more of the world. Taiwan was his gateway to bigger and better things.

Meanwhile, he was doing his best to prove he had no ties to China, but he was now caught up in the political eddies that complicated the island's tense relationship with China. In China, Li was not Chinese enough—unwilling to be blindly loyal to the Chinese Communist Party and too liberal to fit in with his more nationalistic classmates and parents, who were bewildered at their son's rebellious streak. Yet in Taiwan, he found he was regarded as *too* Chinese. Caught between the changing identity politics of the two opposite sides of the Taiwan Strait, Li found himself rejected by both. "Being Chinese is like an original sin," Li told me. Everyone had already decided for him that he was Chinese. It was a stain that he could never wash away.

A major turning point in China-Taiwan relations came in 2014, when China-friendly legislators in Taiwan's parliament proposed a new trade treaty that would open dozens of Taiwanese service sectors to China, including communications, tourism, and transportation. The legislators argued that Chinese investment was a necessary boost to Taiwan's thriving but small economy. The proposed treaty, called the Cross-Strait Agreement on Trade in Services, provoked immediate controversy because of the opaqueness with which it was rushed through the legislative approvals process. Mass, peaceful protests and sit-ins in front of Taiwan's legislature from civil society groups and student organizations eventually shelved the treaty, but the peaceful demonstrations—dubbed the Sunflower Movement—prompted a broader rejection of Taiwan's gradual drift over the last decade into China's economic and political orbit. By 2024, only about 3 percent of Taiwanese considered themselves exclusively culturally Chinese in identity.

Any remaining illusions that Taiwan could keep its way of life if Beijing took control ended with the sudden invocation of the national security law in Hong Kong in 2020. Beijing had long promised if Taiwan "unified" with the mainland into one China, under Communist Party control, the island would get to keep its courts, civil liberties, and some independent democratic functions. That idea was codified into the concept of One Country, Two Systems and would be trialed in Hong Kong for at least fifty years after the territory was handed back to Chinese rule. The experiment failed with the imposition of its national security law and the arrests of all prominent dissidents in Hong Kong. Trust in Taiwan that Beijing would respect any legal buffer dissipated.

Taiwan was also undergoing a minor identity crisis. In a nod to American discourse, some Taiwan commentators dubbed it a culture war: a tug-of-war between those who felt more Taiwanese as opposed to those who felt more culturally Chinese. Under the governance of the Democratic Progressive Party, the island was decentering its identity away from simply being "Chinese," defined as Mandarin-speaking and ethnically Han. This identity had been forcibly imposed with KMT rule in 1945. In reality, an underlying Taiwanese identity already existed, an identity that draws profoundly from Chinese culture, but also embraces waves of immigration, an indigenous Austronesian community, and Japanese colonial history. The KMT did its best to obliterate these layers of identities, leaving only the elements they believed to be the most "Chinese" behind.

As a result, under KMT occupation, Taiwanese people could be jailed for speaking their mother tongue, which included Chinese-adjacent languages like Hakka or Taiwanese Hokkien, rather than Mandarin Chinese, the language the KMT brought with them from the mainland. Much as the Communist Party would try to erase the Uyghur and Mongolian languages on the mainland decades later, the KMT also started its language campaign with residents at a young age.

"They suppressed the use of our mother tongue and cast Mandarin Chinese as more highbrow," remembers Wang Wenhong, a native of the southern Taiwanese city of Kaohsiung, who was born shortly after KMT rule began. "Local offices and administrators would ignore you if you spoke Taiwanese Hokkien to them." His father, Wang Ping-shui, a Japan-trained politician, was among the estimated eighteen thousand to twenty thousand people disappeared and executed by the KMT during violent protests against KMT rule beginning February 28, 1947. The bloody purge eliminated many of Taiwan's civil society leaders, as well as its educational and cultural elite. Wang himself was just over one month old and grew up never knowing his father. "The Ming, Qing, and Han dynasties were all like this. When a Chinese society switches emperors and changes dynasties, it is a Chinese tradition to kill off the previous society's elites and intellectuals," Wang mused while we talked at Taipei's National 228 Memorial Museum. Wang, now in his seventies, sits on the institution's board.

Growing up, Wang and his family practiced a quiet rebellion at home by speaking his mother tongue, Hokkien, with his mother and brother. His mother also spoke Japanese fluently, having been educated under the island's previous colonizers, and she struggled to assimilate to the Mandarin dominant discourse under the KMT. Wang also had to endure public humiliation. His Chinese teachers forced him to wear a heavy plaque around his neck whenever he was caught speaking Hokkien at school. The KMT also leveraged an extensive radio broadcast system set up by Taiwan's former Japanese rulers, originally built to transmit wartime propaganda and communications, and used it to air daily Chinese classes and lectures extolling the greatness of Chinese culture.

Now a democracy in the twenty-first century, Taiwanese are discovering a once-censored history of colonial oppression under KMT authoritarian rule. After being elected president in 2016, Tsai Ing-wen authorized sealed government archives to be opened so academics could finally investigate the full scale of arrests, forced labor, and executions during the island's martial law period. Taiwanese were empowered to peel away the layers of state "Chinese-ness" imposed on their Taiwanese identity. Statues of Chiang Kai-shek, the KMT dictator who started the party's rule on the island, were taken down from their pedestals and consigned to a park at the urban fringe of Taipei. The island's indigenous communities, once pushed out of their ancestral lands and forbidden from teaching their Austronesian languages, were allowed to set up mother-tongue nursery schools that are taught exclusively in indigenous languages.

These policy moves have grated against Taiwan's more culturally Chinese communities, many of whom are descended from Chinese war refugees and who still feel connected to their lost ancestral home on the mainland. This includes Taiwan's former president Ma Ying-jeou. In 2023, he visited China for the first time, stopping by his father's birthplace, where he delivered a tearful speech in the local Chinese dialect. "They were very surprised that [for] someone whose parents left mainland China more than seventy years ago and their son can speak fluent Hunanese!" Ma, his eyes glistening with the memory, recounted to me in his office. A shared language and culture, he maintained, were "the root of people in Taiwan and in mainland China, as Chinese" and the key to lasting cross-straits peace.

The Party was also watching closely from Beijing. It was keen to ensure Taiwan remained "Chinese" as well, blasting what it called the de-Sinicization of Taiwanese society under the Tsai administration. In particular, they pointed to a new set of public education textbooks the island's education ministry released as part of its reckoning with its brutal KMT and Chinese colonial past. Beijing was especially upset at the shortening of a textbook chapter on the overthrow of the Qing dynasty in 1911, from the original six thousand word-length to three hundred words. "Distorting history, diminishing, or even expunging the great achievements of Dr Sun Yat-sen and the revolution are just one part of the de-Sinicization and 'Taiwan independence' agenda," a Chinese spokesperson said.

Yet Taiwan and Beijing have never given up their competing claims of who is truly "Chinese," both politically and culturally. Taiwan maintains its government (called the Republic of China, or ROC) is the real China, not the government in Beijing (the People's Republic of China, or PRC). Taiwan had preserved the traditional Chinese script and sequestered some of the finest Chinese jade and ceramic imperial relics in its national museum. Though the Communist Party in Beijing was modernizing its military and threatening to "unify" Taiwan through invasion, Taiwan maintained its cultural high ground. It congratulated itself for having preserved some deep kernel of true "Chinese-ness" lost under Communist rule from Beijing.

The start of the global COVID pandemic in 2020 cut much of the remaining cultural ties between China and Taiwan. The steady stream of Chinese tourists and students who once thronged the streets of Taiwan stopped coming. Taiwanese businessmen who had factories in China stopped traveling there because of China's onerous quarantine requirements. Hearing a mainland Mandarin accent in Taiwan became an oddity, and anyone who even spoke with a distinctly mainland accent faced more suspicion and sometimes outright hostility from Taiwanese communities. Li Jiabao now realized he had been mistaken in expecting Taiwan to offer him unconditional political refuge. He shared their political values, but that was not enough to become Taiwanese. He would never be allowed to fully shed his Chinese identity.

Li patiently did what he could to adapt to these political winds. He remained active in liberal Taiwanese student groups, staying abreast of environmental justice issues and China-critical debates. He enrolled as a student, but with no work papers he could only take on short-term gigs that paid him in cash, under the table. He even began modifying his northern Chinese accent, dropping the rounded consonants he had grown up pronouncing in favor of a more sibilant, nasal lilt in his spoken Mandarin and adding emphasis on the last syllable of each sentence. I realized he was trying to sound more Taiwanese.

Li's immigration struggles mirrored a broader social reckoning in Taiwan, which was finding the mantle of Asian democracy a weighty responsibility to bear. Political constraints and xenophobic attitudes were making it difficult for the island to live up to its liberal promises—especially any commitment to take in political asylum seekers. For many Chinese dissidents living in exile in North America or Europe, the island was proof that the dream of a Chinese democracy for which they had sacrificed so much was already a reality for 23 million people. Yet Taiwan had to figure out how to protect its fragile democracy, especially with a much more powerful, hostile neighbor like China just across the Taiwan

Strait. Open societies are inherently vulnerable to the influence operations of less-forgiving and more closed-off authoritarian countries. It is a conundrum that democratic societies the world over, including the United States, are struggling with.

Detractors arguing against a more liberal refugee policy argued the sheer volume of people Taiwan anticipated would allow China to send informants and spies, and the island's intelligence services would not be able to adequately vet all the Chinese refugees. As a result, vetting of Chinese nationals became even stricter; Taiwan's national security agency blocked several immigration applications from Hong Kongers who once worked for auditing firm KPMG and the territory's airline, Cathay Pacific, on the grounds that their employers were too financially connected to Chinese investors.[8] Roughly a third of residents on the island believed taking in asylum seekers hostile to China would worsen Taiwan's own relationship with China.[9] "China will take advantage of that kind of freedom, liberty, and democracy," Luo Chi-cheng, a lawmaker with Taiwan's Democratic Progressive Party, told me in 2018. "A democracy like Taiwan has different concerns, sitting next to authoritarian China, than other ordinary democracies."

Contemplating an influx of Chinese refugees to Taiwan also triggered historical traumas the million-strong KMT exodus had brought in 1949 to the island from mainland China. A deep-seated anxiety permeated Taiwanese communities who still remembered how that influx had displaced an entire generation of Taiwanese and brought with it four decades of martial law. "They only have to send one million more mainland Chinese over, and our democratic values would be disrupted. We need to have strict screening methods towards immigrants and especially political refugees," Guan Jianren, a newspaper commentator, told me after penning a column in Taiwanese media arguing for Li Jiabao's deportation.

Moreover, officials were afraid open acceptance of political refugees from China would spark an unmanageable wave of Chinese immigrants that would overwhelm Taiwan's generous social services system. The island's excellent healthcare services remain heavily subsidized for citizens, even for those who live abroad. Protecting Taiwan's scarce resources and a strongly ethnicity-driven conception of national identity meant the island had historically made naturalization extremely difficult. Opening Taiwan up to Chinese citizens could be catastrophic, anti-immigration advocates argued. Plus, the island had come to heavily rely on Southeast Asian migrant labor; if Chinese residents begin claiming citizenship, what was to stop Vietnamese, Thai, and Indonesian workers from doing the same?

Despite president Tsai Ing-wen's encouraging words to would-be asylum seekers, the reality was that at least hundreds of political refugees were struggling to receive permanent residential status on the island. Even Hong Kongers who had once regarded Taiwan as full of promise were becoming disillusioned. This included Kenny and the young Hong Kong protestors who had risked their lives to smuggle themselves on a fishing boat into Taiwan. The Hong Kong Five, as they had come to be known to the Taiwanese public, were still stuck on the Kaohsiung military base since being intercepted by the island's coast guard in August 2020.

Unbeknownst to Kenny, the Hong Kong Five's arrival had triggered a miniature political crisis in Taipei. Within the first few days of their quarantine, the Hong Kong Five's presence leaked to the Taiwanese press. A furious public debate broke out over what to do with the young men. One side argued they immediately be given asylum to signal Taiwan's commitment to democratic ideals. Another side pushed back; why should these five men be granted an exception to stay, especially if it invited reprisals from Beijing?

The Hong Kong Five had also unwittingly found themselves running up against the KMT's concept of the Republic of China (ROC), an archaic concept that is very much alive in the geopolitical discourse around Taiwan and is constitutionally embedded in its own bureaucracy. Formally, Taiwan is called the ROC, and the name is still retained on the island's passports and official documents. Yet while it has given up any pretense of aspiring to take back or control this territory, Taiwan still officially considers the Republic of China to include mainland China and Hong Kong. This claim has necessitated strange political contortions. Hong Kong's anti-government protests in 2019 began because Taiwan was unable to extradite an alleged murderer back to Hong Kong—for the simple reason that Hong Kong is officially considered part of the Republic of China (Taiwan) and thus a domestic territory. Even after Beijing made its political control of Hong Kong painfully clear by passing the national security law and sending waves of Hong Kong political asylum seekers to Taiwan, the Republic of China in Taiwan did not—indeed, could not—consider these people as foreigners eligible for asylum. To do so would be to admit that Hong Kong belonged to Beijing.

To the Hong Kong Five, this immigration conundrum was immensely frustrating. They had evaded Hong Kong national security police for months and braved the high seas to sail to Taiwan in a small fishing vessel, only to be tied up by Taiwanese bureaucracy and domestic politics. Kenny passed the days by establishing a routine. He went out for morning walks and watched Taiwanese soap operas at night. The soldiers on base were polite and warm, and they sensed the boredom of their young charges, periodically bringing them Taiwanese delicacies and night-market snacks. Then, just like Li Jiabao, he waited. The others struggled under the weight of monotony. Tommy, the youngest of the group, broke first. He tried to escape the military base. He made it as far as the gates of the base, where he was caught trying to hail a taxi to the airport.

One of the most vocal lobbyists on their case was Lam Wing-kee, the dogged Hong Kong bookseller. He had immediately moved to Taiwan after Hong Kong proposed its extradition treaty with mainland China. Although the treaty was shelved, Lam never again returned to Hong Kong. The fiction of One Country, Two Systems was over, and he no longer felt safe there. Instead, he set about trying to reestablish his bookstore in Taipei, at the juncture of one of the city's most popular tourist spots. He was also spending a lot of his free time helping young Hong Kong protestors seek temporary residence in Taiwan. Most of them had come on student visas that were set to expire when their school terms ended. "They were not prepared at all. They are so young," Lam lamented.

Displaced Hong Kongers opened a handful of cafes and stores across Taipei, creating spaces where—even if just during a cup of coffee—they could recreate a feeling of home. In 2021, Aegis restaurant, one of the most popular gathering spots in Taiwan for Hong Kongers, burned down.[10] The spot's demise was a harbinger for many young Hong Kongers, who were eventually forced to look beyond Taiwan for a new home, one that carried less historical baggage over identity and fewer bureaucratic hoops to jump through.

Lam is now running Causeway Bay Books from its new Taipei

location, but he is still on edge. In 2023, a Chinese-born publisher named Li Yan-he had been detained in China after returning from Taiwan to see family and to cancel his Chinese passport. Chinese authorities then said Li was being investigated for endangering national security. Li was a prolific founding editor at one of Taiwan's best-regarded nonfiction publishing houses. His detention was different from Lam's own case; unlike the Hong Kong booksellers, Li was not kidnapped but had returned to China on his own. But his detention was a bone-chilling reminder to Lam that the Party was paying close attention to Chinese-language writers and publishers all over the world, even in Taiwan.

Nearly three years after making his fateful live streams, Li Jiabao was now living in southern Taiwan. He had met a Taiwanese woman on Facebook, and they had fallen in love. The couple were planning to get married.[11] With a marriage certificate in hand, he would also finally be eligible for citizenship after three years of residency on the island.

The three of us—Li, his fiancée, and me—met up over spicy hotpot in a Taipei mall. Li had grown up in the last few years, displaying a broadness in his torso and face that had not been there during our first meeting. He had tampered his enthusiasm for Taiwan as well. He had spent the last three years watching other Chinese acquaintances receive asylum in the Netherlands, the U.S., and Canada, while he had yet to enroll in a Taiwanese university or get a job. He calculated he would be well over thirty years old by the time he finished a college degree and could begin job hunting. His gambit for political freedom had cost him his twenties. "How could I not regret my decision?" he told me, a rueful smile flashing over his face. Cynical Taiwanese continued to pile on him every few months, accusing him of making the live streams solely to obtain Taiwanese citizenship. "If I wanted political asylum, I would have applied for a visa to the United States and applied there," he shot back. It probably would have been easier than the life he was now forced to eke out in Taiwan.

After months of back-channel negotiations, the Hong Kong Five were told they were being offered a chance for asylum. Taiwan would not keep them, so the United States was taking the five young men instead and letting them apply for asylum status there. In January 2021, the five men flew to New York City.

Boarding the plane and leaving Taiwan was less dramatic than Kenny anticipated. The Hong Kong Five learned there was Wi-Fi on the plane, and they all immediately fell into a silent frenzy messaging their loved ones. It was the first time they could talk to their families without endangering their own safety since their boat escape from Hong Kong. Furiously typing thumbs distilled half a year of adventures and heartache into a few lines of text hastily sent over before the plane ascended into open sky. For Ray, it was also the first time he had ever been on a plane. When he closed his eyes and reclined in his plush seat, he could almost pretend he was going on a vacation. This flight meant a chance to start over, but also a chance to continue his fight for Hong Kong.

Before flying to New York, volunteers had given them winter clothing, which the men had never had to purchase before in balmy Hong Kong. Unused to the heavy clothing, Ray put on all his clothes at once, layering the pieces until he was sweating on the plane. They landed in New York during the dead of winter, in the afterhours of a wet and dismal snowstorm. It was the first time the five men had ever seen snow. Delighted, the five men began rolling in the white stuff, which quickly turned gray as it mixed with the filth of New York City streets. Kenny didn't care. After so long living in uncertainty, caught in limbo between competing claims of sovereignty and national borders, he had finally found a home. In the months to come, however, he would discover that China was not as distant a topic in the U.S. as he had hoped for.

CHAPTER 12

THE DIASPORA

The United States Kenny arrived in was deeply divided over whether—and how—to confront China's growing influence. The Chinese diaspora, numbering more than 5 million people in the U.S., is central to this debate. Their identity is being tested by Chinese extrajudicial operations on American soil. They are subject to rising anti-Asian racism. And their loyalties are questioned by their fellow citizens—though none more viciously than by their fellow diaspora members.[1] The sculptor Chen Weiming knew this better than anyone.

More than thirty years ago, he left China and emigrated from his native Zhejiang province to New Zealand, before finally settling in the United States. However, China remains central to his artwork and activism. Chen has exhibited from Hong Kong to New York, creating both monumental statues and ephemeral performance pieces criticizing perceived injustices committed by the Chinese Communist Party. During one performance, to condemn China's 1989 violent crackdown on protestors in Tiananmen

Square, he set up a skull outside the Chinese consulate in Los Angeles, then invited other Chinese dissidents to throw sixty-four eggs at it, the number representing the date of the military crackdown, June 4. The year before that, he locked himself in an iron cage for seven days and seven nights on the Hollywood Walk of Fame in Los Angeles. Most famously, he created the *Goddess of Democracy*, one of three sculptures removed from the grounds of Hong Kong universities in 2021 in the wake of the national security law. (Chen made headlines in 2010 when he tried to visit Hong Kong to see his statue, but authorities deported him. Chen is still trying to get Hong Kong authorities to release the *Goddess of Democracy* and let him ship it to the U.S.)

In short, he hadn't set foot on Chinese soil in years, and yet he had never stopped caring about the country that continued to break his heart. Chen was committed to the project of political reform in China, despite having given up his Chinese citizenship as a young man. He was preoccupied with questions of how to best love a country that did not love you? How to continue being proudly Chinese, without having to be a citizen of China? One way Chen sought to answer these questions was through his art. In 2017, he started Liberty Sculpture Park on a patch of land he purchased in the Mojave Desert outside a sleepy town named Yermo, an unincorporated settlement in California and a former gold mining town. Chen described the park as "a commemorative garden for the victims of the CCP's tyranny."

The park's first artwork was a bust of Crazy Horse, the famed Lakota chieftain and warrior, whose tribe Chen believed originally inhabited the park's desert lands. Other sculptures soon followed along more familiar themes. They included a shackled statue of Li Wangyang, a persecuted Chinese labor activist. Chen followed with a work called *Hong Kong, Revolution of Our Times,* a sculpture of Hong Kong protestors sheltering behind a wall of umbrellas, and then a bronze plaque depicting former House Speaker Nancy Pelosi's 1991 visit to Tiananmen Square, entitled *The House Speaker Speaks Out.* But the park's centerpiece was a twenty-seven-foot-tall fiberglass gray bust of Chinese leader Xi Jinping, his skull adorned with red coronavirus spikes and a hammer and sickle splattered with red paint adorning one side. Chen called this piece *CCP VIRUS.* "The left face is the evil skull, the black ruthless eyes and the hideous big teeth; the back is the giant virus and the sickle and axe," his artists catalogue describes the piece.

Chen was incensed by the initial cover-up of the emergence of the coronavirus in Wuhan in 2019, and he hoped the piece would raise attention over what he believed was the Party's culpability for the ensuing global pandemic. The piece was large and sufficiently bizarre enough—rising out of the empty California desert—that curious drivers on the way to Las Vegas sometimes pulled over just to see what was going on. Chen was thrilled by the sporadic public interest. "If all these tourists stopped to take a look at my sculptures, they would see the inconsistencies and untruths in what the Chinese Communist Party says," he enthused.

The park was still very much a work in progress. A small sign along a dirt road dwarfed by the natural expanse around it indicated where the park began. Mobile homes and a U.S. Marine Corps depot stood nearby. Inside the park, the sculptures stood on bare ground, a few dozen yards from each other. Visitors had to walk through the ankle-high sand that pooled in small drifts alongside the artwork. A few minutes exposed to the desert elements was enough to fill both my boots and hair with a fine grit.

Despite the harsh weather, Chen was at the park at least a few days a week, sporting a paint-stained flannel shirt, his boyish face and easy smile covered by a cloth bandanna to block out the piercing sun and sand as he painted over rusty patches and repaired chipped-off corners.

In the summer of 2021, China was once again on Chen's mind as he drove through the Mojave Desert of eastern California, his car shuddering slightly as it plowed on against the heavy gusts of wind that threw up spires of gritty sand. He ignored the wind, the sand, the speed, his hands gripped on the steering wheel. He was in a hurry to get back to Yermo, because he had received frantic calls from a sculpture park employee and the park's neighbors: *CCP VIRUS*, his best artwork yet, he believed, had burned down.

Chen pulled up to Liberty Sculpture Park on a Saturday morning, parking in the unpaved parking lot, then jogged over to where the large sculpture once stood. He adjusted his baseball cap as he grimly surveyed the scene. All that remained of his artwork were a few charred remnants of the fiberglass sculpture, though the cinder-block pedestal it once stood on was mostly untouched, the red words "CCP VIRUS" emblazoned on one side still legible. Chen had sunk thousands of dollars of his own money into buying the materials and financing the labor to put together the piece. All that had gone up in smoke.

Yet he was not surprised by the piece's destruction. He had been steeling himself for weeks at the possibility someone might try to sabotage his campaign to hold the Party to account for a global pandemic he believed China was responsible for. These views were not widely shared among the Chinese diaspora in the

U.S. Chinese Americans and Asian Americans feared connecting COVID-19 with the ruling party in China exacerbated anti-Asian discrimination and violence in the U.S. Chen was careful to distinguish between the Chinese people and the Communist Party; unlike former president Donald Trump, who dubbed the novel coronavirus the "Chinese virus," Chen called it the "CCP virus," which he believed would prevent anti-Asian hate. "Chinese people are the ultimate victims of the CCP!" he told me. "People who visit here are very moved when they see us Chinese people ourselves speaking out, when even our current president [Biden] won't dare say it was China that caused the virus! They won't discriminate against us. In fact, they will respect Chinese people more for speaking out. They will see we are a people capable of self-criticism and self-reflection—all marks of a great people."

However, for many Asian Americans, the reputational damage was done. Chen's distinction was irrelevant to them as anti-Asian violence climbed, spurred on by racist assumptions that they had started the virus. An academic study published in the journal *Nature* estimated that traffic at Asian-run businesses decreased by 18.4 percent during the pandemic because of racist misconceptions about COVID-19.[2] For Chen to call out the Chinese Communist Party so vehemently by erecting a monument with an ethnically Chinese face covered in coronavirus spikes struck some Chinese Americans as counterproductive, even a betrayal. In short, there were many disgruntled Chinese Americans who might have hated Chen's statue so much that they would burn it down.

Chen's suspicions grew when he reviewed the last few weeks leading up to the ultimate destruction of *CCP VIRUS*. On one of his nightly patrols of the park, he had noticed two unfamiliar vehicles parked on the periphery. When he drove up to the cars, they sped away, their taillights fading away into the desert night. Just weeks before the fire, while Chen was away on a business trip to San Francisco, one of his employees found a metal cable wrapped around the sculpture. The perpetrators also sawed a square hole into the piece. Alarmed, Chen and his employees rotated night watch shifts in the sculpture park. They guarded the *CCP VIRUS* statue by taking turns sleeping in their cars with a Glock pistol balanced on the gearshift. Their patrols became more regular in the run-up to the June Fourth Tiananmen anniversary in 2021— always a perilous time for those involved in democracy work both in and out of China. The month after, with the anniversary over, they relaxed and paused their patrols, and that was when someone burned down *CCP VIRUS*. When Chen tried to review the security footage of his sculpture, he discovered that all the cameras around the sculpture had been disabled, the wires powering the surveillance system cut clean through.

Chinese diaspora politics has always been equal parts influential, litigious, and bloody. Ardent Chinese nationalists, patriots, and political reformers have long fomented their revolutionary plots outside of Chinese borders. The most famous of these diaspora leaders is Sun Yat-sen, a founding father figure revered in both China and Taiwan to this day. Born in Guangdong, Sun briefly lived overseas in Hawaii, London, Malaysia, and Japan, where he began collecting funds through a network of secret societies and diaspora networks to realize his long-held dream of founding a modern Chinese republic. To do so, he would need to overthrow the ethnic Manchu leaders of the Qing dynasty, which ruled the China empire with increasing ineptitude. Then, Sun planned to strengthen China to resist European imperialism. Most of

Sun's funders were ethnic Chinese living outside the empire like himself—scattered across Europe, London, and Southeast Asia. Sun's organizing helped form the backdrop to the Xinhai Rebellion in 1911, which finally ended Qing dynasty rule and is the date that Taiwan's government still considers its founding day.

Nearly a century later, another political movement—this time a failed one—created another wave of diaspora Chinese. The Party's brutal crackdown in 1989 on the pro-democracy protest in Tiananmen Square traumatized a generation of Chinese activists who would spend the rest of their days driven by a singular mission: the overthrow of the current ruling Chinese Communist Party and the rapid democratization of China. At least hundreds of surviving activists from the 1989 crackdown were smuggled out of China and sought refuge in the United States, Canada, and Europe. From their new homes outside of China, they continue to shape the political discourse about China.

Chen considered himself part of this 1989 generation, though he had already moved to New Zealand the year before the crackdown. From afar, he watched, aghast, as television footage showed tanks rolling through Beijing's Tiananmen Square, the skeletons of cars ablaze, and the faces of bloodied students fleeing on bikes through the capital. The events of 1989 never left him. He refused to forget the bloodshed, and he did not give up on the China that he envisioned, the one that could have been had China's leaders listened to the protestors who they chose to gun down instead.

By 2021, yet another generation within the Chinese diaspora was forming. This generation consisted of internet-savvy millennials and Gen-Z fluent in Western cultural ideas like identity politics and systemic racism. They were also more diverse than the Tiananmen generation. This generation included Hong Kongers, displaced and disillusioned by illiberal Party governance in the region and spooked by the national security law. After the law, Hong Kongers with the means and the ability to emigrate sold their apartments, emptied their bank accounts, and started new lives in the United Kingdom, Europe, and the U.S., where they have populated dwindling hamlets, revived shrinking church attendance figures, and become regular attendees at frequent anti-Party rallies held in Western capitals, alongside diaspora Uyghurs and Tibetans.[3] More than 150,000 Hong Kongers applied to settle in the U.K. alone during the first two years of the special long-term visa program for those with British National Overseas (BNO) passports.[4] Exiled activists and protestors, like Kenny and his fellow Hong Kong escapees, continued their advocacy against the Party-led governance of Hong Kong from new homes in the U.S. and Europe.

Joining them are a small number of young, mainland Chinese citizens who have grown disaffected by the Party's clampdown on civil liberties and civil society, its hostility toward LGBTQ communities, and the disappearances of any remaining academic freedom. These are the students of *runxue*, "run philosophy"—a pun on the English verb "to run," designed to evade online censors—sharing tips online on how to emigrate out of China. Born and raised in the age of the internet, these *runxue* adherents are increasingly outspoken in their criticism of the Party once abroad, harnessing their bilingual cultural and linguistic fluency to create their own narratives of what being Chinese can mean outside of China's state boundaries. This new generation of Chinese diaspora makes sleek podcasts about Chinese pop culture; holds live performances supporting Chinese feminists; and organizes talks with people and screenings of films banned in China.

Of course, not all of the new Chinese diaspora are so well-off or well-educated. Some pay smugglers to help them walk overland through the dangerous Darien Gap in Panama before crossing the Mexican border into the U.S.[5] U.S. Customs and Border Protection said they apprehended 37,000 Chinese nationals at the U.S.-Mexico border in 2023 alone, double the figure for the entire decade before.

The diversity of the Chinese diaspora, now numbering some 60 million people, has led to literal clashes in Chinese identity politics on American college campuses and cities. With free speech muzzled and advocacy muted within the borders of China proper, Chinese people living abroad are increasingly working through fractious identity issues in the U.S. and Europe instead. For example, in 2022, when some Chinese-born Georgetown University students hung up posters critical of the Chinese Communist Party and the upcoming winter Olympics being held in Beijing, other Chinese-born students tore the posters down, claiming they provoked anti-Asian hate.

These identity conflicts can be fatal. In one especially tragic instance in 2022, a Chinese-American man attacked a Taiwanese church in Orange County, California, shooting to death one person and injuring five others.[6] When police arrived on the scene, they found the shooter had glued together and chained shut the doors of the California church, then shot the elderly congregants inside. Before the mass shooting, he had mailed his handwritten diaries to a newspaper in Taiwan, titling his screed, "Diary of an Angel of Destroying Independence"—formal Taiwanese independence from China.

China is well aware of the power, past and present, of the diaspora. It has worked hard, to mixed results, to woo the diaspora through all-expenses-paid junkets to China, tried to co-opt Chinese American community leaders through a mix of coercion and economic reward, and funded overseas media outlets.

Chinese-Canadian publisher Jack Jia experienced this firsthand in 2005, when he was invited, all expenses paid, to a conference innocuously called the World Media Forum held in the Chinese river city of Wuhan. There, high-level Chinese editors dangled a tempting offer: free content from China News Service, a Party-controlled wire service aimed predominantly at Chinese-language readers in the diaspora. "When we took a look at their content, we saw it all read like Xinhua, the government mouthpiece," Jia told me. He refused the offer to collaborate with China's state news agency. Not everyone took Jia's position; in 2017, I found that Party-controlled outlets like the flagship *People's Daily* had active content partnerships with more than 220 Chinese diaspora outlets. "Chinese-language media and the Chinese people are one," Lu Hao, the managing editor of the American newspaper *Sino-US Times,* told editors at a forum promoting China's Belt and Road infrastructure initiative.

The Party's outreach comes from its ethnically centered conception of Chinese identity. It sees all approximately 60 million members of the Chinese diaspora—no matter if they do not have Chinese citizenship, feel no affinity to Chinse culture, or barely speak Mandarin Chinese—as part of a broad Chinese polity with a duty to support Chinese state interests. This narrow understanding of identity only fuels anti-Asian discrimination globally, by creating false suspicion that all ethnic Chinese are sympathetic to the Chinese state. Conversely, the Chinese state also attacks diaspora members with extra ferocity over perceived betrayals of their supposed motherland. As an ethnically Chinese, American-born journalist working in China, I was frequently attacked online by nationalist writers for being a *hanjian,* or race traitor.

Under pressure from both Chinese long-arm surveillance and harassment and rising anti-Asian discrimination, the diaspora began to turn on themselves. Distrust permeated activist circles in the U.S., with the diaspora pursuing potential moles within their ranks with an almost-fundamentalist zeal, reputationally tarring their peers as spies for the Party and waging protracted campaigns against perceived enemy factions.

In one particularly bizarre instance in 2021, disgraced Chinese tycoon Guo Wengui accused dozens of prominent Tiananmen-era activists and journalists of being double agents on behalf of the Chinese Communist Party. Guo had fallen out of favor after Xi Jinping's anti-corruption campaign purged one of Guo's political backers, the former chief spy Ma Jian. Fleeing to New York, where he ensconced himself in the penthouse of Manhattan's Sherry-Netherland Hotel, Guo claimed he had explosive kompromat on top Communist officials in China. Instead, he devoted much of his time to stirring up intrigue among the diaspora community. In daily lectures broadcast on his YouTube channel, Guo issued lists of supposedly compromised individuals, which included democracy activists like human rights lawyer Teng Biao and his former supporters, like Chinese American journalist Sasha Gong. Guo then directed his millions of viewers to accost the alleged turncoats. The wrongly accused, living in Canada, Australia, and the U.S., woke up to swarms of Guo-affiliated protestors on their lawns. (Guo was found guilty in 2024 of defrauding investors of more than $1 billion.) Figures like Guo split the already-fractured Chinese American diaspora. They squabbled among themselves about who represented the true interests of the community, weakening the diaspora's ability to distinguish real threats from manufactured ones.

The sculptor Chen Weiming was painfully familiar with this

intra-community fighting. He was an immigrant twice over because of such divisions. In 2007, he departed New Zealand for the U.S., after a bitterly fought defamation case against his newspaper in Auckland. As usual, his biggest detractors were his fellow Chinese. Upon arriving in New Zealand, Chen had come to believe the case for Chinese democracy needed to be fought in the court of public opinion. In the spirit of winning hearts and minds, he founded *New Times Weekly*, a Chinese-language paper for the Chinese diaspora of his new home of Auckland. *New Times* was unabashedly anti-Party. Every June, it ran commemorative essays on the 1989 Tiananmen crackdown, and it published scathing editorials against individuals Chen and his brother, the paper's co-founder, deemed Communist Party sympathizers.

One of their primary targets was the *Chinese Herald*, a rival diaspora publication that hewed close to the Party line. The founders of the two outlets came to blows—literally. Chen was accused of assaulting the *Herald*'s owner and damaging his eyeglasses. "The newspapers did not express their conflicting ideologies in the Western tradition of restraint," a New Zealand court dryly noted. The outlets also ran a proxy war of words, fielding ad hominem attacks against each other. From one of Chen's legal briefs: "*The Chinese Herald* subsequently wrote an article referring to [my wife] as having a 'twisted face' and said that she was 'as fat as a pregnant woman.' My wife has a slight facial disfigurement, which is a result of a childhood illness. We have had three children and my wife has not regained her former figure . . . I found the *Chinese Herald*'s description of her facial condition and her physical appearance generally to be unwelcome." The *Herald*, meanwhile, filed an injunction against any additional *New Times* editorials that lambasted them for being "cheats, abductors, forgers or falsifiers of deeds, are enemies against democracy, swindlers, slanderers, are human trash or make malicious remarks about employees behind their backs."

Behind the plaintiffs at the *Herald*, Chen thought he detected the puppet strings of the Party. He told me Chinese security agents had contacted him during his family trips back to China in the early 2000s, requesting he plant pro-Party content in his news outlet—a request Chen refused outright. "The Party felt we were a constant thorn in their side. When they realized we would not listen to them and accept their authority, they found another newspaper through which to suppress us, by going to court against us," he told me. In other words, he suspected—without any concrete proof—that the *Herald*'s defamation case was merely a front created by the Party. Though the case was eventually settled, Chen felt he needed a new start after his legal troubles. He escaped to the frontiers of the American West, where he would begin anew in California.

And he had a resourceful patron for his work now in the U.S.—a wealthy American businessman named Matthew. Matthew had come calling at the exact right time in March 2021, just as Chen was putting the finishing touches on the *CCP VIRUS*. The artist was cash-strapped but angling to do more ambitious pieces. For that, he needed a backer with deep pockets. Matthew pitched himself as an independently wealthy businessman with an abiding love for art. His taste in the visual arts had gotten him noticed by then–House Speaker Nancy Pelosi—a politician Chen had long admired and had dedicated a bronze plaque in his park to. Matthew claimed Pelosi was planning to start a new art institution and was in the market to collect subversive pieces like Chen's. A few days after getting in contact, Matthew flew to California to meet Chen.

Matthew had some strange requests. He wanted to watch

every step of Chen's sculpting process, but he lived in New York most of the time. Could he trouble the artist to install a video camera in the corner of his studio, so he could watch the sculptor work, from afar? Chen acquiesced. "I thought the request was totally reasonable," he later told me. A few days later, Matthew called again and asked to install yet more cameras, because the sculpture was three-dimensional, and one camera alone didn't capture the artwork's every angle. Chen was impressed with the broker's exacting standards, and he happily let him back in one more time to put in a full video surveillance system. Chen might have been more suspicious had the art broker been one of the Chinese diaspora, whose constant infighting and mutual suspicion frustrated the sculptor to no end. But Matthew checked all the right boxes: he appeared politically well connected in the U.S., and he was not Chinese.

In the U.S., the fissures in the Chinese diaspora ran deep, resulting in an intensely polarized debate within the U.S. over the country's complex bilateral relationship with China. It also created a curious alliance between those who profess to love China and those who fear it. As bipartisan rancor in the U.S. against China's rise intensifies, the executive and legislative branches have implemented an ambitious package of sanctions against Chinese companies and individuals. Perhaps surprisingly, the most aggressive policy proposals to counter China's influence are being championed by members of the Chinese diaspora.

Take the effort to ban TikTok and WeChat in the U.S., part of a broader effort to stop American users from relying on popular software made by a Chinese company. Detractors of TikTok, which is run by a Chinese unicorn headquartered in Beijing called ByteDance, argue it siphons away valuable big data on what Americans like and watch on the platform, giving the Communist Party in China unhindered access to the private lives of tens of millions of Americans. Meanwhile, they argue WeChat—run by Chinese tech giant Tencent—could provide the Party with a free channel to quietly push propaganda or misinformation to users and to subtly tailor the algorithms that govern the types of videos people can or cannot see.

WeChat is ubiquitous in China. It began as primarily a messaging app but has since evolved into an online payment platform with functions that let users hail taxis, order products from e-commerce stores, buy financial products, and reserve train and movie tickets. Its ease of access means anyone with friends, family, or business contacts in China must download WeChat to stay in contact with them. Distrustful of state media outlets, more and more readers in China turn to *zimeiti,* "self-media"— self-published blogs published on social media sites, especially through WeChat accounts and within large chat groups. None of this content is edited for accuracy, and disinformation about everything from vaccines to American presidential candidates is rife on the platform.

Given how much happens on WeChat both inside and outside of China, the Chinese state also actively censors and manipulates the platform. Security officials closely monitor the accounts of dissidents, petitioners, and journalists, vacuuming up entire conversations on WeChat, so they can block protests and interviews well before they happen. Citizen Lab, a research institute at the University of Toronto, found WeChat's parent company Tencent has compiled lists of sensitive keywords, which the app will automatically flag and filter if they crop up in private conversations.[7] The app then blocks the message from being received by Chinese-registered users. As WeChat censorship became increasingly heavy-handed, users in the U.S. began to sit up and notice. Some users realized their posts to Chinese users in group chats were being censored. Others who posted sensitive stories found their accounts blocked altogether. When then-president Donald Trump tried to ban both TikTok and WeChat, a group of Chinese Americans penned a petition to the White House supporting the measure.[8] The petition garnered 104,225 signatures.[9]

Curious about why Chinese immigrants to the U.S. wanted to ban one of their key communication links to China, I reached out to one of the petition organizers. Although he now lives in Texas, he has direct family who still live in China and didn't want to give me his name, for fear that the Party might punish his loved ones in retaliation for their activism in the U.S. China's ability to coerce members of the Chinese diaspora because of their kinship and financial ties to the country is one reason why this man felt so strongly about banning WeChat. Having made the U.S. his home over the last three decades, he had grown accustomed to the idea that suppression of political dissent and rampant censorship were common in China, the country of his birth—but not in the U.S., his adopted home.

Then, in March 2019, he noticed friends in the same WeChat groups he was in weren't receiving his messages. Shortly after, his account was suspended: he thinks it was because he voiced criticism of the Party to some WeChat friends. "The shocking piece is not even what's happening in China. The shocking [piece] is that China is exporting censorship to other parts of the world. It is exporting the Great Firewall of China," he told me, referring to the array of internet censorship controls China employs to filter what its citizens can see online within mainland China. Previously politically inactive, he described this realization as "a turning point . . . Tencent is doing business in the U.S., and they are not following American law here. It's just mind-boggling."

He wrote letters asking for WeChat to be taken off app stores and sent them to congressional representatives. When he didn't hear back, he began his White House petition. Although born in China, he saw himself as an American first and foremost, and he was determined that his fellow Chinese transplants should follow American rules. Like Chen, he believed speaking up against WeChat and other symbols of illiberal Chinese technology was a necessary performance of patriotism. He needed to show his fellow citizens just how American the ethnic Chinese diaspora was, in order to head off growing anti-Asian racism.

In response to Trump's efforts to ban WeChat, an opposing faction of Chinese Americans assembled to fight the executive order in court. They registered a nonprofit called the U.S. WeChat Users Alliance, and they argued the executive order was unconstitutional on First Amendment grounds because it fell heaviest on ethnically Chinese users who relied on the app to talk with family in China.

The main force behind the alliance was Clay Zhu, a plucky Chinese American lawyer. Born to a family of rice farmers in China's Hunan province, Clay got his lucky break through his academic prowess, snagging a scholarship to study law in the U.S., then worked on land rights policy in China, before starting his own successful law practice in California. Though WeChat is Chinese-run, Clay saw defending WeChat as a uniquely *American* thing to do—a defense of free speech that would not be tolerated in Xi Jinping's China. Clay gave interviews in Chinese-language blogs published on WeChat about how even geopolitics came secondary to rule of law in the U.S. He pointed out how fears that China hypothetically could leverage WeChat to sway hearts and minds globally did not mean an American's First Amendment right to free speech and the Fourth and Fifth Amendment rights to due process could be suspended. He worked for the next two months on preparing a case against Trump's executive order, putting aside his usual caseload.

When Clay finally received the Justice Department's evidentiary materials, he pulled an all-nighter and read through the twelve hundred pages of evidence before going to bed the next afternoon. "I went to sleep with a big smile on my face. I knew we would win," he told me later, over buttermilk waffles in California. "There was no smoking gun that Tencent was collecting Americans' data illegally, only speculation. The First Amendment had to prevail." In October 2020, a federal judge in Northern California issued an injunction against Trump's executive order against WeChat. The summer after, in his first term as president, Joseph Biden officially rescinded the executive order issued by his predecessor, though his administration has backed an order for TikTok to sell itself to American owners or face a ban in the United States.

After Clay's legal victory, Chinese legal scholars quietly contacted him. They were asking him, "How does a low-level judge issue an order against a sitting American president? That is unthinkable in China." Clay laughed. He accepted every single Chinese media request he received: "I was so passionate to talk to Chinese media because with this case, I had a perfect way to explain how freedom of speech works in a democracy." To prevent their articles from being censored and deleted, the Chinese journalists who interviewed Clay cast the WeChat case as a legal battle to protect Chinese interests from American hegemony. Clay disagreed with the characterization. As he saw it, he was not fighting on behalf of China but rather to protect the U.S. Constitution.

Meanwhile, Chen plowed on with his artistic work. He wrote off 2021 as his *annus horribilis*: it was the year his statue *Goddess of Democracy* was taken down in Hong Kong, his Tiananmen frieze was confiscated, and the *CCP VIRUS* burned to ashes. He grieved his loss through defiance: "In a very free society, where one doesn't experience oppression, one doesn't have such drive," he told me. He vowed to build a new version of *CCP VIRUS* and exhibit it on the anniversary of June 4 in 2022. Yet he knew from fellow activists in Chinese pro-democracy circles in the U.S. that the global shadow of Chinese politics was growing ever longer, and he knew he was on the Party's radar. China is increasingly leveraging its economic and political influence to clamp down on activities outside its borders that it wants stopped. The year before, Chen received a call from an FBI agent who advised him to be careful; they believed the Chinese state security ministry was monitoring his activities in the U.S. Chen was unfazed; he expected Beijing would be keeping an eye on him, and he continued making his art.

This time he was on his own, however. Matthew, the art-loving businessman who had promised to finance his work, was giving him the cold shoulder. After the *CCP VIRUS* sculpture burned down, Matthew seemed to lose interest in the museum project and eventually stopped taking Chen's calls and returning his texts. Chen took it as a lesson in self-reliance and began the lonely work of rebuilding.

In March 2022, Chen received stunning news: three men had been accused of spying on the sculptor and conspiring to burn down his beloved *CCP VIRUS*. To Chen's dismay, one of the men at the center of the conspiracy was Matthew. In reality, Matthew was not an art-loving businessman but rather a former Florida prison guard and private bodyguard. He was also an agent in a bungled, Chinese state–directed scheme to stop Chen's art.

According to the FBI, the plot against Chen began in earnest in January 2021, six months before *CCP VIRUS* went up in flames. A Long Island resident named Frank Liu had sent out feelers to a local private investigator: Could the investigator get the home address and names of the housekeeper and assistant of two Chinese dissidents? Liu, the founder of an overseas media outlet called Congress Web TV Station, offered to pay $3,000 in total for the information. Over the next months, Liu followed with more requests, including the federal tax returns of several dissidents, including Chen, explaining that he worked for a Chinese company with state links that needed to conduct due diligence. Unbeknownst to Liu, the investigator informed the Federal Bureau of Investigation (FBI). By now, Liu had also hired Matthew Ziburus. This was the "businessman" Chen would later meet. Blond and clean-shaven, Ziburus would handle in-person interactions with Chen and Liu's other targets without immediately raising suspicions.

Liu's directions to Ziburus, dictated in broken English, are at once highly detailed and ludicrously unrealistic. In March 2020, Ziburus flew to California, posing as the businessman-turned-art-dealer Matthew, to meet with Chen. "When you sit down together have table meeting or lunch or dinner, they will ask your background & who your boss, you can say: my is very rich Jewish man & head of Jewish community, he Donate money to support few democratic presidents & speaker of House, especially Nancy Pelosi who is very strong support democracy!" Liu texted Ziburus.

"Nancy want him to build up a democratic museum in NY or DC. That make him google & find out these sculptures are relate to democratic, for his ideal museum, that is why asking you go to see & negotiations." Qiang Sun, a Chinese security agent, and Chinese state intermediaries wired Liu and his wife more than $3 million for the operation. Ziburus was paid about $100,000 for his work.

As a handler, Liu was also meticulous about deadlines and budgets. He even advised Ziburus on how to haggle for the price of the commission, a ploy to get Chen to identify for the agents which pieces he believed to be the most important: "Tell them your boss is low key rich man but don't want to explore his name, the deal structure is buy if he give good price, he is not Picaso, why so expensive?" Liu texted. "So you can let him explain each sculpture to you & you shooting for boss to let boss under[stand] why so much value?" Ultimately, Ziburus offered Chen $125,000 to rent the molds for *CCP VIRUS*, an offer Chen refused, though he did allow Ziburus to install his cameras inside his studio. He did not know Ziburus had also surreptitiously placed a GPS tracking device on the underside of his car.

An FBI investigation found both the camera footage and his real-time GPS location were being sent to Qiang, who was likely operating out of Hong Kong. Back in New Zealand, Chen had had no evidence to prove his suspicion that the Party was bankrolling the defamation suit against his newspaper. This time, there was no doubt the Party's security apparatus intended to manipulate the full weight of the U.S. legal system to crush him. "After obtaining evidence, spend money for court and attorney fees to totally get rid of him," Qiang told Liu. Qiang was also adamant that Liu and Ziburus get rid of Chen's artwork, especially *CCP VIRUS*. "Destroy all sculptures and things that are not good to our leaders. Record videos. Make the media promotion/propaganda clear," he texted Liu. Liu pushed back; destroying the artwork would only raise Chen's public profile, but in the end, Qiang and his bosses in China won out. A few months later, Chen's virus-studded Xi sculpture was set on fire.

More FBI arrests of Chinese state–linked actors operating on U.S. soil followed. In 2023, the Department of Justice (DOJ) charged thirty-four officers in the Ministry of Public Security in absentia for creating and using thousands of fake social media accounts on Twitter and other platforms to harass dissidents abroad.[10] Another DOJ case concerned a local branch of the Chinese Ministry of Public Security that was secretly operating inside an office building in Manhattan's Chinatown neighborhood. Two men were arrested for taking orders from the Chinese state. Further arrest warrants were issued in absentia for eight Chinese government officials charged with directing an employee of a U.S. telecommunications company to prevent Chinese dissidents from using the online meeting platform Zoom to commemorate the anniversary of the 1989 Tiananmen crackdown.

The arrests vindicated the Chinese American activist community. "Chinese surveillance is not getting enough attention," said Zhou Fengsuo, the activist Li Jiabao had sought out for advice and among those affected in the Zoom case. "Just imagine the efforts the CCP puts into sabotage," he mused. After years of lobbying for protection against Chinese state surveillance, Zhou and others felt they were finally being heard. "America is the only place we have left in the world where we are safe from the Chinese Communist Party," said Guppy Dong, a Chinese dissident who moved to California in 2018.

The arrests are part of a more aggressive American law enforcement approach toward Chinese state influence in the U.S. The diaspora also worry that these efforts are stoking even more anti-Asian racism. Chinese students and academics now face stricter visa requirements in the U.S. if they want to study or conduct research in certain science and engineering areas and can be stopped and searched at the U.S. border.[11] In Texas and Florida, lawmakers proposed bills banning Chinese nationals from buying land in those respective states on national security grounds. (Florida's was signed into law; Texas' did not pass.) In the most egregious cases, U.S. law enforcement agencies have gone after academic researchers, predominantly of Chinese-origin, after misinterpreting open scientific collaboration and using arcane financial reporting rules.

In 2021, New York City police notched what they believed to be a victory against Chinese long-arm surveillance: the arrest of one of their own, an ethnically Tibetan officer named Baimadajie Angwang, charged with spying for China on the Tibetan diaspora in New York.[12] Two years later, however, federal prosecutors abruptly dropped the case for lack of evidence. Angwang has maintained his innocence throughout. Born in Tibet, Angwang was roughed up by Chinese authorities because of his Tibetan ethnicity. At the age of seventeen, he came to the U.S., where he successfully applied for asylum and later went on to serve in the U.S. Marines before joining the NYPD, a job he is lobbying to get back.[13] "The birthplace of your origin and that of your parents, it's not something we can control, and they shouldn't become our crime," he told me.

Similar cases have abounded in the academic world, where dozens of researchers were investigated under a broad U.S. government campaign to root out Chinese influence and intellectual property theft called "the China Initiative." Most academics were dinged for receiving funding from or working with Chinese institutions, though a majority were cleared after career-destroying investigations. Under the Initiative, more than four-fifths of the scientists singled out by the National Institutes of Health (NIH), a major funder of basic research in the U.S., were Asian, while 91 percent of the research collaborations under scrutiny by the institutes were with researchers based in China.[14]

Clay Zhu, the California lawyer, who helped defeat the ban on WeChat, is still fighting discriminatory policing of Asian Americans through Freedom of Information Act requests on federal prosecutions. "You need the entire picture and that means getting the data," he told me—data on how investigations into academics shows the ethnicity of their targets. Peripatetic and brimming with energy and ideas, Clay embraced with gusto the American way of life, its defense of civil liberties, and its robust court system. What he feared was that in containing China, the U.S. would become more like it.

In 2022, Chen completed the *CCP VIRUS 2.0*, his new sculpture. He refashioned the same likeness of Xi Jinping embellished with coronavirus spikes but this time with steel rebar and wiring— more durable and fire-resistant than the original fiberglass. He spent weeks welding the rebar together in the desert, his cheeks reddened by heat and eyes watery from the harsh winds. The occasional car stopped by, intrigued by the unfamiliar sculptures emerging like desert apparitions off the side of Interstate 15. Chen was always happy to take a break from his painting and welding to explain the anti-Communist message behind each of his artworks.

During that year's June 4 commemorations, Chen held a triumphant reopening ceremony for the new sculpture. A motley coalition of about one hundred attendees trekked out to the Mojave to see the unveiling. They included pro-Taiwan independence advocates, Hong Kong exiles, mainland Chinese dissidents, and younger diaspora members. Some of them were second generation, born in the U.S. but curious about the politics of the country their parents had left behind. A woman named Wahata Today kicked off the unveiling ceremony with a Native American peace prayer. Today said she was a direct descendant of Crazy Horse, the Lakota chief Chen Weiming admired and had memorialized in his park with a bronze bust. A licensed real estate agent, she told me she met Chen years before while showing him some houses in the Yermo area and found herself drawn in by his stories of repression in China.

I ran into some familiar faces along the sidelines of the event. Many were people I had interviewed for previous stories about China—a Hong Kong journalist detained under the national security law, Taiwanese American activists, veteran Chinese dissidents from the 1989 Tiananmen protests. Someone waved the baby blue East Turkestan flag to support Uyghur rights. We had taken very different paths to get here, but somehow we all found ourselves gathered together that day in the dusty and windswept Mojave Desert, far from any land China had once claimed. Yet each of us that day was thinking of China, the China they had known and the China about which they still dreamed.

ACKNOWLEDGMENTS

Reporting in China was the dream of a lifetime. The opportunity to do so and, later, to write a book drawing from my nearly seven years there has been the result of dozens of friends, family, and colleagues who offered emotional nourishment, mentored my work, and often inspired my reporting.

I arrived in China with almost no professional reporting experience, but I was kindly taken in by the *New York Times* bureau in Beijing, where Amy Qin and Andrew Jacobs first took a chance on me. Throughout, then–bureau chief Edward Wong offered useful advice to an aspiring foreign correspondent. Javier Hernandez was a joy to work with during my first few months in China. My temporary desk mate, the late editor Carlos Tejada, gave me my first taste of what good news writing could be. My fellow researchers in the bureau—Yufan Huang and Adam Chen in particular—were warm companions from whom I learned much.

I will be forever grateful to Jamil Anderlini, then the Asia editor at the *Financial Times,* and Tom Mitchell, at the paper's

Beijing bureau, for taking a chance on a cub reporter and giving me a real break in the journalism industry. Lucy Hornby, Charles Clover, and Yuan Yang were constant fun to be around in the bureau, from whom I learned tons and got my taste of what great reporting looked like on the daily.

I found my professional home at NPR, where creative storytelling and sharp news reporting are valued in equal measure. A job in journalism is only as good as the people you work with, and I have been immensely lucky with my colleagues. International editors Didi Schanche and Will Dobson were always supportive of my most ambitious ideas. Nishant Dahiya, editor extraordinaire, tolerated my deluge of harebrained ideas and complaints, and during the dark depths of pandemic reporting in China, he was a comforting voice on the other end of the line. Greg Dixon made sure the bureau and all our equipment ran smoothly. Alex Leff and Hannah Bloch, my tireless digital editors, made all our stories better.

I also benefited hugely from the sagacity of fellow China watchers within NPR, who were always available to share tape and their wealth of knowledge. They include John Ruwitch, Vincent Ni, and Frank Langfitt. Anthony Kuhn and Rob Schmitz first encouraged me to apply for NPR's Beijing posting, despite my utter lack of radio experience; thank you for believing in me before I believed in myself.

Most of all, NPR producers Amy Cheng and Aowen Cao, whom I worked with during my time in China, deserve my biggest thanks and heartfelt gratitude. We spent much of our waking hours together, whether on the road, brainstorming our next stories, calming the other's frazzled nerves, or enjoying deliciously odiferous lunches in the bureau office that no one else seemed to appreciate. The reporting in this book could not have happened without them, and they remain two of my closest, lifelong friends. In Beijing, Dana Heide and Tomasz Sajewicz were the ideal office mates and friends, there by my side during my highs and lows. In Taiwan, I was lucky to meet the renaissance man Hugo Peng, who opened my eyes to the island's magic and its complex history as well as its rich bar scene.

Other journalists whose work helped broaden my understanding of some of the themes in this book include, in alphabetical order by surname: Kou Aizhe, Abduweli Ayup, Chris Buckley, Alex Palmer, David Rennie, Christian Shepherd, Alice Su, and Sue-lin Wong. Special thanks to Ian Johnson, whose writing I have always looked up to and who was an early supporter of the book project.

Writing a book is a daunting endeavor, but not when you have great friends who are also great writers. Thank you to Nate Gallant for looking at early drafts of the book proposal; to Zachary Small, Matt DeButts, and Philip Roin for their friendship and for giving insightful feedback on some of the first chapters; my sister Kathleen for reading drafts with precision; my sister Nicole for keeping me real; as well as professor Claire Conceison, who offered support.

My agent, Sylvie Carr, was a patient and incisive editor, instantly grasping what I wanted the book to be while clarifying the book's ideas and sharpening the writing. She continued to look over chapter drafts, and without her editing I would be lost. Madhulika Sikha, at Crown Publishing, was the perfect editor to work with; she gave me room to let the stories shine while gently curbing my writing excesses and providing wonderful company to boot.

My partner, Sjoerd den Daas, was my rock throughout, in China and beyond. It is no coincidence I hit my stride as a

6 ACKNOWLEDGMENTS

reporter after meeting you. Your humor and tenacity have shown me what true companionship and love looks like in action.

Finally, my parents, Lijuan Shi and Xuwu Feng, gave me a life I am grateful for every day. Their unconditional love gave me the courage to try my hand at journalism, and their endless sacrifice led them to support me in ways big and small, even when I chose to move far away from them. This book is dedicated to them.

ENDNOTES

PREFACE

1. Sophie Beach, "Leaked Speech Shows Xi Jinping's Opposition to Reform," *China Digital Times (CDT)*, September 29, 2016, chinadigital times.net/2013/01/leaked-speech-shows-xi-jinpings-opposition-to -reform/.

CHAPTER 1

1. 肖扬：人大法律人的家国情怀, 明德公法, April 20, 2019, mp.weixin .qq.com/s/jv_sJao09EbkLdvlBIvW7Q.
2. Susan Finder, "Farewell to Justice Scalia from the Supreme People's Court," *Supreme People's Court Monitor*, February 14, 2016, supreme peoplescourtmonitor.com/2016/02/15/farewell-to-justice-scalia-from -the-supreme-peoples-court/.
3. Shenghui Qi and Dietrich Overbitter, "On the Road to the Rule of Law: Crime, Crime Control, and Public Opinion in China," *European Journal on Criminal Policy and Research* 15, no. 1–2 (June 2009): 137–57, https://doi.org/10.1007/s10610-008-9094-3.
4. Nicholas D. Kristof, "Beijing Journal; Crime Is Up in China, and so Is the Public's Rage," *New York Times*, January 20, 1992, www.nytimes .com/1992/01/20/world/beijing-journal-crime-is-up-in-china-and-so -is-the-public-s-rage.html.

5. Liang Zai, "The Age of Migration in China," *Population and Development Review* 27, no. 3 (September 2001): 499–524.

6. Amy Qin, "In China, the Formidable Prosecutor Turned Lonely Rights Defender," *New York Times*, October 20, 2020, www.nytimes.com/2020/10/20/world/asia/china-prosecutor-lawyer.html, accessed February 27, 2024.

7. Wu, Xiuyun, "女检察官'解救'女囚," *The People's Procuratorate of Guangdong*, December 27, 2010, www.gd.jcy.gov.cn/xwys/wzxw/201012/t20101227_483573.html.

8. 一个检察官的六年救赎（上，CCTV节目官网，October 26, 2011, tv.cctv.com/2011/10/26/VIDE1355584166518375.shtml?spm=C55924871139.PT8hUEEDkoTi.0.0.

9. "Opinion: Xi's Speech Shows China Is Still Haunted by Soviet Union's Collapse," *South China Morning Post,* April 6, 2019, www.scmp.com/week-asia/opinion/article/3004897/xi-jinpings-speech-shows-chinas-communist-party-still-haunted.

10. "孙大午被捕事件反映的问题．"美国之音，美国之音中文网，August 24, 2003, www.voachinese.com/a/a-21-a-2003-08-24-14-1-63342177/987429.html.

11. Emily Feng, "Rights Activist Xu Zhiyong Arrested in China amid Crackdown on Dissent," NPR, February 17, 2020, www.npr.org/2020/02/17/806584471/rights-activist-xu-zhiyong-arrested-in-china-amid-crackdown-on-dissent.

12. Josh Chin, "Chinese Activists Challenge Beijing by Going to Dinner," *Wall Street Journal*, November 6, 2013, https://www.wsj.com/articles/SB10001424052702304672404579181373425115430, accessed February 27, 2024.

CHAPTER 2

1. Tim Maughan, "The Dystopian Lake Filled by the World's Tech Lust," BBC News, February 24, 2022, www.bbc.com/future/article/20150402-the-worst-place-on-earth.

2. Leslie Hook et al., "Xi Stokes Economic Reform Hopes in China," CNN, December 12, 2012, www.cnn.com/2012/12/12/business/xi-stokes-economic-hope/index.html.

3. "Court Overturns Verdict Against Woman Who Reported Rural Pollution," *Sixth Tone,* August 18, 2020, www.sixthtone.com/news/1006072/court-overturns-verdict-against-woman-who-reported-rural-pollution.

4. 帮家乡村民举报污染获刑，陕西女工程师李思侠被取保候审，澎湃新闻，June 16, 2020, www.thepaper.cn/newsDetail_forward_7869078.

5. Chris Buckley, "'Drive the Blade In': Xi Shakes Up China's Law-and-Order Forces," *New York Times*, October 20, 2020, https://www.nytimes.com/2020/08/20/world/asia/china-xi-jinping-communist-party.html, accessed February 27, 2024.

6. Emily Feng, "Regulators Squash Giant Ant Group IPO," NPR, November 3, 2020, www.npr.org/2020/11/03/930799521/regulators-squash-giant-ant-ipo.

7. Chao Deng and James T. Areddy, "Once-Highflying Anbang Chief Isn't Able to Do His Job." *Wall Street Journal*, June 13, 2017, https://www.wsj.com/articles/anbang-insurance-group-ceo-wu-xiaohui-hands-over-reins-1497395474, accessed February 27, 2024.

CHAPTER 3

1. "China Closes 66,000 Online Accounts for Rumormongering, Imposture," China Daily, May 27, 2023, www.chinadaily.com.cn/a/202305/27/WS6471c54ea310b6054fad5676.html.

2. Eduardo Baptista, "China Deletes 1.4 Million Social Media Posts in Crackdown On . . . ," Reuters, March 27, 2023, www.reuters.com/technology/china-deletes-14-mln-social-media-posts-crack-down-self-media-accounts-2023-05-27/.

3. "Xi Calls for Letting Internet Better Benefit People of All Countries," State Council, November 8, 2023, english.www.gov.cn/news/202311/08/content_WS654af08bc6d0868f4e8e1118.html.

4. Adam Segal, "China's Vision for Cyber Sovereignty and the Global Governance of Cyberspace," National Bureau of Asian Research, August 25, 2020, www.nbr.org/publication/chinas-vision-for-cyber-sovereignty-and-the-global-governance-of-cyberspace/.

5. "Remarks by H.E. Xi Jinping President of the People's Republic of China at the Opening Ceremony of the Second World Internet Conference," Ministry of Foreign Affairs, China, December 16, 2015, www.mfa.gov.cn/eng/wjdt_665385/zyjh_665391/201512/t20151224_678467.html.

6. 中国全网最火，窃格瓦拉，"打工是不可能打工的"周某出狱视频, YouTube, April 21, 2020, www.youtube.com/watch?v=mbAzNTrUcPA&ab_channel=FunnyVito.

7. 郭峰, and 彭亮. 对话"这辈子都不可能打工"周某：不给网红公司打工，出狱后打算种地, 红星新闻, April 20, 2020, static.cdsb.com/micropub/Articles/202004/212bde2c107a7374f5b7772df9dedb31.html.

8. 国家广播电视总局办公厅关于进一步加强文艺节目及其人员管理的通知, 国务院办公厅, September 2, 2021, www.gov.cn/zhengce/zhengceku/2021-09/02/content_5635019.htm.

9. 争夺"不可能打工者"，价值观扭曲才会娱乐化犯罪行为, 新京报, April 20, 2020, www.bjnews.com.cn/opinion/2020/04/20/719053.html.

10. Li Jinzhong et al., "Clinical Features of Familial Clustering in Patients Infected with 2019 Novel Coronavirus in Wuhan, China," *Virus Research* 286 (September 2020): 198043, https://doi.org/10.1016/j.virusres.2020.198043.

11. Zhicong Lu, Yue Jiang, Chenxinran Shen, Margaret Jack, Daniel Wigdor, and Mor Naaman, "Positive Energy: Perceptions and Attitudes Towards COVID-19 Information on Social Media in China," *Proceedings of the ACM on Human-Computer Interaction* 5, CSCW, Article 177 (April 2021), https://doi.org/10.1145/3449251.

12. "'Wuhan Diary' Writer Fang Fang Removed from Latest National Committee of Chinese Writers Association," *Global Times*, December 17, 2021, www.globaltimes.cn/page/202112/1241749.shtml.

13. "China Makes Defaming Revolutionary Heroes Punishable by Law," Reuters, April 27, 2018, www.reuters.com/article/us-china-lawmaking/china-makes-defaming-revolutionary-heroes-punishable-by-law-idUSKBN1HY14N.

14. "Defaming Martyrs, Attacking Police to Be Punished by New Amendments to Criminal Law," *Global Times*, February 28, 2021, www.globaltimes.cn/page/202102/1216750.shtml.

15. Cate Cadell, "China Launches Hotline for Netizens to Report 'Illegal' History Comments," Reuters, April 11, 2021, www.reuters.com/world/china/china-launches-hotline-netizens-report-illegal-history-comments-2021-04-11/.

16. "Govt Staff Rewarded for Tip-off on Anti-China Media Which Sneak into China's Poverty Alleviation Model City Bijie, Spread False Info," *Global Times*, October 10, 2021, www.globaltimes.cn/page/202110/1235914.shtml.

17. "'不可能打工男'致歉：想做普通人照顾父母." "不可能打工男"致歉：想做普通人照顾父母_新浪新闻, June 3, 2020, news.sina.com.cn/s/2020-06-03/doc-iircuyvi6498083.shtml.

18. "永不打工＂周立齐当网红，短视频吸粉百万后入驻B站, 观察者网, August 23, 2020, www.163.com/tech/article/FKNFBISP00097U82.html.

19. 行业发声：网络直播抵制恶意流量炒作, 中国演出行业协会, April 21, 2021, mp.weixin.qq.com/s/RzbKx-EpDzU6QdD_UWMKGg.

20. 中国官方再发限娱令　要求不得播偶像养成节目、封杀"娘炮": 娱乐, 東方網 馬來西亞東方日報, September 2, 2021, www.orientaldaily.com.my/news/entertainment/2021/09/02/435145.

21. Julienna Law, "China Bans Effeminate Men and Abnormal Esthetics from TV," *Jing Daily*, September 2, 2021, jingdaily.com/little-fresh-meat-sissy-men-china/.

22. 国家网信办指导督促网站平台依法处置违法违规"头部账号", 网信中国, December 15, 2021, mp.weixin.qq.com/s/n9A86dWr64XitM4OJ31w1Q.

CHAPTER 4

1. "Population Ageing in China: Crisis or Opportunity?," *The Lancet* 400, no. 10366 (November 2022): 1821, https://doi.org/10.1016/s0140-6736(22)02410-2.

2. 《中国走失人口白皮书》发布，2020年全国走失人次达100万." 中国日报网, tech.chinadaily.com.cn/a/202102/26/WS60386587a3101e7ce9741248.html, accessed April 7, 2024.

3. Susan Greenhalgh, "Science, Modernity, and the Making of China's One-Child Policy," *Population and Development Review* 29, no. 2 (June 2003): 163-96.

CHAPTER 5

1. Abdullah Qazanchi, "The Disappearance of Uyghur Intellectual and Cultural Elites: A New Form of Eliticide," *Uyghur Human Rights Project*, September 25, 2023, uhrp.org/report/the-disappearance-of-uyghur-intellectual-and-cultural-elites-a-new-form-of-eliticide/.

CHAPTER 7

1. Christopher P. Atwood, "Bilingual Education in Inner Mongolia: An Explainer," *Made in China Journal*, August 31, 2020, madeinchinajournal.com/2020/08/30/bilingual-education-in-inner-mongolia-an-explainer/.

CHAPTER 8

1. "HK Bookseller Splashed with Paint in Taipei," *Taipei Times*, 台北時報, April 21, 2020, www.taipeitimes.com/News/front/archives/2020/04/22/2003735067.

CHAPTER 9

1. "Hong Kong Crafting 'Patriotic' Oath for Local Councils, Beijing
    Wants Loyalists in Charge," Reuters, February 23, 2021, www.reuters
    .com/article/us-hongkong-security-idUSKBN2AN087.

CHAPTER 10

1. "The Taiwan Straits Crises: 1954–55 and 1958," *Office of the Historian*,
    U.S. Department of State, history.state.gov/milestones/1953-1960
    /taiwan-strait-crises#:~:text=Tensions%20between%20the%20People's
    %20Republic,islands%20controlled%20by%20the%20ROC, accessed
    April 7, 2024.
2. "Memorandum of Conversation between Mao Zedong and Henry A.
    Kissinger," *Digital Archive*, Wilson Center, October 21, 1975, digital
    archive.wilsoncenter.org/document/memorandum-conversation
    -between-mao-zedong-and-henry-kissinger-0.
3. Matthew Wills, "Hong Kong Was Formed as a City of Refugees," *The
    Daily*, JSTOR, October 1, 2019, daily.jstor.org/hong-kong-was-formed
    -as-a-city-of-refugees/.
4. Ka-sing Lam, "Emigration, Rising Rates Weigh on Hong Kong's
    Lived-in Home Market," *South China Morning Post*, July 22, 2022,
    www.scmp.com/business/article/3186280/loss-making-deals-hong
    -kongs-secondary-home-market-jump-sellers-take-hit.
5. Almond Li, "Over 113,000 Residents Left City in 12 Months, as Hong
    Kong Sees Largest Mid-Year Population Drop on Record," *Hong Kong
    Free Press,* August 15, 2022, hongkongfp.com/2022/08/12/over-113000
    -residents-left-city-in-12-months-as-hong-kong-sees-largest-mid-year
    -population-drop-on-record/.
6. "Student Activist Tony Chung Jailed for 43 Months for Secession and
    Money Laundering," *The Standard,* November 23, 2021, www.the
    standard.com.hk/breaking-news/section/4/183361/Student-activist
    -Tony-Chung-jailed-for-43-months-for-secession-and-money
    -laundering.
7. Emily Feng, "'Where No One Dares Speak Up': China Disbars Law-
    yers on Sensitive Cases," NPR, February 18, 2021, www.npr.org/2021
    /02/18/963217332/where-no-one-dares-speak-up-china-disbars
    -lawyers-on-sensitive-cases.
8. Emily Feng, "Hong Kong Residents Reflect on the Future on Anniver-
    sary of End of British Rule," NPR, July 1, 2020, www.npr.org/2020/07

/01/885878557/hong-kong-residents-reflect-on-the-future-on
-anniversary-of-end-of-british-rule.

9. Karen Gilchrist, "'Hong Kong Is Not Going to Be under the Rule of
   Law': More than 100,000 Apply for New Visa to Britain," CNBC,
   March 3, 2022, www.cnbc.com/2022/03/02/hong-kong-bno-visa
   -100000-apply-to-live-in-united-kingdom.html.

10. "The Chinese Government Resumed Exercise of Sovereignty over
    Hong Kong," *Events and Issues*, Foreign Ministry of the People's Re-
    public of China, November 17, 2000, www.fmprc.gov.cn/mfa_eng/ziliao
    _665539/3602_665543/3604_665547/200011/t20001117_697854
    .html.

11. General Information on Chinese Nationality, Hong Kong Immigration
    Department, www.immd.gov.hk/eng/services/chinese_nationality
    /general_info.html, accessed February 29, 2024.

CHAPTER 11

1. Kristina Kironska, "Discussion Needed on Refugee Law," *Taipei Times*,
   October 13, 2022, https://www.taipeitimes.com/News/editorials
   /archives/2022/10/13/2003786920, accessed February 26, 2024.

2. Twitter, June 30, 2020, twitter.com/iingwen/status/1277889561440337
   923?s=20.

3. John Pomfret and Yimou Lee, "Hong Kong Protesters Fete Landslide
   Election Win for Taiwan's Tsai," January 13, 2020, reuters.com/article
   /uk-taiwan-election-hongkong-idUKKBN1ZB07B, accessed February 26, 2024.

4. Patrick E. Tyler, "Chinese Couple Hijack Plane to Taiwan," *New York
   Times*, December 29, 1993, https://www.nytimes.com/1993/12/29
   /world/chinese-couple-hijack-plane-to-taiwan.html, accessed February 26, 2024.

5. "Chinese Air Force Fighter Pilot Defects to Taiwan," *New York Times*,
   July 8, 1977, www.nytimes.com/1977/07/08/archives/chinese-air-force
   -fighter-pilot-defects-to-taiwan.html.

6. Dominic Meng-Hsuan Yang, "The Exodus," in *The Great Exodus from
   China: Trauma, Memory, and Identity in Modern Taiwan* (New York:
   Cambridge University Press, 2020), 40–85.

7. "Demining Efforts Completed in Kinmen County," *Taiwan Today*,
   Ministry of Foreign Affairs, Republic of China (Taiwan), April 1, 2014,
   taiwantoday.tw/news.php?unit=10&post=20584.

8. Chan Ho-him et al., "Taiwan Blocks Hong Kong Immigrants over KPMG China and Cathay Pacific Links," *Financial Times*, October 6, 2022, https://www.ft.com/content/58ef9713-8b1b-49cd-8491-2f0dd 626f1df, accessed February 28, 2024.

9. Kristina Kironska, "Discussion Needed on Refugee Law," *Taipei Times*, 台北時報, October 12, 2022, www.taipeitimes.com/News/editorials /archives/2022/10/13/2003786920.

10. Rhoda Kwan, "Blaze Forces Taipei Restaurant That Supports Hong Kong Pro-Democracy Protesters to Halt Operations," *Hong Kong Free Press*, August 20, 2021, hongkongfp.com/2021/08/20/blaze-forces -closure-of-taipei-restaurant-that-supports-hong-kong-pro-democracy -protesters/.

11. "Chinese Student Who Criticized President Xi Jinping Applies to Marry in Taiwan," *Radio Free Asia*, October 11, 2020, www.rfa.org /english/news/china/applies-07232020135344.html.

CHAPTER 12

1. Abby Budiman, "Key Facts about Asian Americans, a Diverse and Growing Population," Pew Research Center, April 29, 2021, www.pew research.org/short-reads/2021/04/29/key-facts-about-asian-americans/.

2. Justin T. Huang et al., "The Cost of Anti-Asian Racism during the COVID-19 Pandemic," *Nature News*, Nature Publishing Group, January 19, 2023, www.nature.com/articles/s41562-022-01493-6.

3. Frank Langfitt, "The U.K. Is Welcoming Tens of Thousands from Hong Kong on a New Path to Citizenship," NPR, October 26, 2021, www .npr.org/2021/10/25/1048918729/the-u-k-is-welcoming-tens-of -thousands-from-hong-kong-on-a-new-path-to-citizensh.

4. Kari Soo Lindberg, Kri Soo, "UK BNO Visa: Number of Hong Kong Applicants Plunged in Latest Quarter," Bloomberg, November 25, 2022, www.bloomberg.com/news/articles/2022-11-25/hong-kong -demand-for-british-visas-plunges-in-latest-quarter.

5. Elida Moreno, "Migration Through Panama's Darien Gap Spikes Despite US Plan," Reuters, May 10, 2023, www.reuters.com/world /americas/migration-through-panamas-darien-gap-spikes-despite-us -plan-2023-05-10/.

6. Emily Feng, "A Deadly Church Shooting Exposes the Complexities of Taiwanese and Chinese Identities," NPR, June 8, 2022, www.npr.org

/2022/06/08/1103653026/a-deadly-church-shooting-exposes-the
-complexities-of-taiwanese-and-chinese-ident.

7. Lotus Ruan et al., "One App, Two Systems: How WeChat Uses One
    Censorship Policy in China and Another Internationally," The Citizen
    Lab, Munk School of Global Affairs & Public Policy, University of
    Toronto, August 26, 2020, citizenlab.ca/2016/11/wechat-china-censorship
    -one-app-two-systems/.

8. "Executive Order on Addressing the Threat Posed by WeChat," Na-
    tional Archives and Records Administration, August 6, 2020, trump
    whitehouse.archives.gov/presidential-actions/executive-order-addressing
    -threat-posed-wechat/.

9. "We the People Support the Ban on WeChat and TikTok," National
    Archives and Records Administration, August 9, 2020, petitions.trump
    whitehouse.archives.gov/petition/we-people-support-ban-wechat-and
    -tiktok.

10. "FBI Arrests 2 on Charges Tied to Chinese Outpost in New York
    City," NPR, April 18, 2023, www.npr.org/2023/04/17/1170571626/fbi
    -arrests-2-on-charges-tied-to-chinese-outpost-in-new-york-city.

11. Emily Feng, "As U.S. Revokes Chinese Students' Visas, Concerns Rise
    about Loss of Research Talent," NPR, September 23, 2020, www.npr
    .org/2020/09/23/915939365/critics-question-u-s-decision-to-revoke
    -chinese-students-visas.

12. Nicole Hong, "N.Y.P.D. Officer Is Accused of Spying on Tibetans for
    China," New York Times, September 21, 2020, https://www.nytimes
    .com/2020/09/21/nyregion/nypd-china-tibet-spy.html, accessed Febru-
    ary 26, 2024.

13. Ed Shanahan, "U.S. Asks to Drop Case Accusing N.Y.P.D. Officer of
    Spying for China," New York Times, January 13, 2023, https://www
    .nytimes.com/2023/01/16/nyregion/nypd-officer-china-spy-angwang
    .html, accessed February 26, 2024.

14. Jeffrey Mervis, "Pall of Suspicion," Science 379, no. 6638 (March 23,
    2023), www.science.org/content/article/pall-suspicion-nihs-secretive
    -china-initiative-destroyed-scores-academic-careers.